From Start-Up to Global Success
The Zensar Story

Thank you for choosing a SAGE product!
If you have any comment, observation or feedback,
I would like to personally hear from you.
Please write to me at **contactceo@sagepub.in**

Vivek Mehra, Managing Director and CEO,
SAGE Publications India Pvt Ltd, New Delhi

Bulk Sales

SAGE India offers special discounts
for purchase of books in bulk.
We also make available special imprints
and excerpts from our books on demand.

For orders and enquiries, write to us at

Marketing Department
SAGE Publications India Pvt Ltd
B1/I-1, Mohan Cooperative Industrial Area
Mathura Road, Post Bag 7
New Delhi 110044, India

E-mail us at **marketing@sagepub.in**

Get to know more about SAGE

Be invited to SAGE events, get on our mailing list.
Write today to **marketing@sagepub.in**

This book is also available as an e-book.

Advance Praise

"I have had the pleasure of interacting with Zensar CEO Ganesh during his stint at Harvard and later during the writing and teaching of the case at HBS. Ganesh and his team have built an exemplary company; their Vision Community and HR processes are especially innovative and world class. My MBA students are always thoroughly engaged when we teach the case."

—**David Garvin**
C. Roland Christensen Professor of Business Administration, Harvard Business School

"I have had the pleasure of working with Zensar for more than a decade. I have watched the organization grow from small distributed offices to a large world-class campus location. Through all of this growth, the organization has continued to be humble, modest, and customer focused. Over the years, I have come to value the easy access to great talent and key leaders in the organization. Zensar is truly a relationship-based organization that is flexible, creative, and innovative—and above all, it has a customer-first mindset."

—**Veresh Sita**
CIO, Alaska Airlines

"In a number of ways, the story of Zensar is the story of the Indian IT services industry—from bit players in the global IT value chain to an industry today that is $100 billion in revenue, from body-shopping and Y2K staff augmentation just 15 years ago to complex digital transformation that will define what the world of the future will look like. Ganesh and his team have built a significant and differentiated market position for Zensar in digital, retail, and Oracle; and Apax is delighted to partner with the team on its next journey of success."

—**Shashank Singh**
Partner and Head of India, Apax Partners

"It has been my proud privilege to know Dr Ganesh Natarajan and through him, several members of the Zensar family.

As a proud citizen of the city of Pune, it is extremely heartening to see the leadership role that Zensar is playing in establishing a strong 'connect' between the corporates and the other stakeholders of the city. I am extremely delighted to see the pioneering work being done by Zensar for the city. Zensar has also been a strong catalyst in mobilizing the support and partnership of other IT organizations in the city to make Pune the first city in India for such a public–private partnership.

My association with Zensar is a decade old now and I am delighted to see their sustained social transformation program spanning across multiple dimensions of community development—education, healthcare, socioeconomic development, and environment.

Zensar's commitment and perseverance in its pursuit to bring about social transformation in the society as a whole is extremely encouraging and augurs well for the city and the country. With the strong social energy that emanates from Zensar and Zensar Foundation, I am sure our lives in Pune will continue to be enriched."

—**Vandana Chavan**
Member of Parliament

"Kapela made an investment in Zensar three years ago. We find Zensar to be very professional and honest partners. They have a blue chip client base in South Africa, especially in the financial sector. An indication of their exceptional work ethic and delivery is the fact that they retain their clients for many years; many clients have been with them for longer than 10 years. One could also describe them as very innovative in developing new solutions for leading industry players. They also invest heavily in local skills development and employment generation where South Africans get trained in South Africa and in India, and get absorbed here in their mainstream business."

—**Henri Staal**
Executive Director, Kapela Investments Holdings (Pty) Ltd,
JV Partner of Zensar in South Africa

"Zensar has been a very consistent performer under the leadership of Dr Ganesh Natarajan, creating shareholders' value year after year. Zensar has been one of the top performers in the IT industry and has grown through the core values of customer centricity, continuous innovation, and excellence. Zensar has been highly rated in IT industry by NASSCOM for over ten years.

Zensar leaders have demonstrated their commitment to people and community remarkably through diversity and inclusiveness. Zensar's Vision Community initiative of building strategy through cross-functional teams across levels has been a case study in Harvard Business School and the unique Women for Excellence initiative has taken them to the top of the Diversity and Inclusion lists in the IT industry and beyond. Ganesh's own passion and commitment to build IT industry goes beyond Zensar. His initiative to support the SME sector and innovation in NASSCOM is commendable. His current thrust in bringing digital literacy to society through NASSCOM Foundation is extraordinary."

—**B.V.R. Mohan Reddy**
Chairman, NASSCOM

"Zensar was a fledgling software service company that was transformed into a fast growing mid-size company through relentless pursuit of product process and business model innovation. The company adopted a mature framework for sustaining and accelerating growth by managing business opportunities across horizons of core, emerging services, and future technologies.

CEO Dr Ganesh Natarajan had a transformative vision for Zensar that engaged employees and developed software services and technology–leadership capabilities. He spearheaded a movement within the company to create a shared vision owned by all stakeholders. Zensar has a strong performance-oriented culture where meritocracy and openness are celebrated in an environment with a strong emotional connect, enhancing camaraderie within the teams and building alignment with milestones to be achieved."

—**S. Raghunath**
Professor, Corporate Strategy and Policy, IIM Bangalore

From Start-Up to Global Success

The Zensar Story

Ganesh Natarajan
Prameela Kalive

www.sagepublications.com
Los Angeles • London • New Delhi • Singapore • Washington DC

Copyright © Ganesh Natarajan and Prameela Kalive, 2016

All rights reserved. No part of this book may be reproduced or utilized in any form or by any means, electronic or mechanical, including photocopying, recording, or by any information storage or retrieval system, without permission in writing from the publisher.

All photographs' courtesy: Authors.
First published in 2016 by

SAGE Publications India Pvt Ltd
B1/I-1 Mohan Cooperative Industrial Area
Mathura Road, New Delhi 110 044, India
www.sagepub.in

SAGE Publications Inc
2455 Teller Road
Thousand Oaks, California 91320, USA

SAGE Publications Ltd
1 Oliver's Yard, 55 City Road
London EC1Y 1SP, United Kingdom

SAGE Publications Asia-Pacific Pte Ltd
3 Church Street
#10-04 Samsung Hub
Singapore 049483

Published by Vivek Mehra for SAGE Publications India Pvt Ltd, typeset in 11/13 pts Berkeley by PrePSol Enterprises Pvt Ltd and printed at Chaman Enterprises, New Delhi.

Library of Congress Cataloging-in-Publication Data Available

ISBN: 978-93-515-0863-2 (PB)

The SAGE Team: Sachin Sharma, Sanghamitra Patowary, Anju Saxena, and Rajinder Kaur

It is a privilege for us to write this story of the Zensar success on behalf of over 10,000 associates who have built this company over the last 15 years.

We dedicate this attempt at chronicling the history and tracing the unique Zensar story to all stakeholders of Zensar around the world, whose hearts beat as one to realize the One Zensar dream.

Contents

Foreword *by Kiran Karnik* — ix
Preface — xi
Acknowledgments — xvii

1. A Look at the Indian IT Industry — 1
2. Zensar
   Building Credibility and Stature — 14
3. Building a Credible Full-Services Organization — 32
4. Thinking Vertically — 60
5. Inorganic Growth at Zensar
   The Acquisition Journey — 88
6. Profit Maximization
   New Levers and Ideas — 109
7. Motivating People
   The Secret Sauce — 144
8. The Story of Smiles
   Corporate Social Responsibility at Zensar — 174
9. Vision for a Digital World — 211
10. Toward a Billion Dollar Zensar — 234

The Last Word *by Harsh V. Goenka* — 256

About the Authors — 258

Foreword

During my long association with the information technology (IT) industry, I have seen many companies emerge, rise to stardom, and in many cases fall by the wayside because of some shift in paradigm that made them lose their sheen. There are but a few that have displayed the stellar qualities of vision, resilience, and continuous growth, adjusting to changing market needs and quickly tapping the new opportunities. I would surely rank Zensar among this select group.

I was first introduced to the company when I made a phone call to Ganesh Natarajan soon after he became Zensar CEO and I became NASSCOM President. My request was for him to rejoin the Executive Council and lead the movement to enable small and medium companies to find their place in the sun. Despite his commitment to his own company, Ganesh readily agreed. In working with Ganesh over the years, I have been witness to his innovativeness, sensitivity, and inspirational leadership. Little wonder that these traits have also characterized Zensar and been a hallmark of its success. I have no doubt that their story will inspire many others to start from small beginnings and build institutions of stature and repute.

If there is one aspect of the leadership team in Zensar I would like to call out as a model to emulate, it would be their focus on the triple bottom line. The IT industry is an exemplar in the area of growth and profitability, not only in India but worldwide, and many companies have also shown excellent focus on people, which is a key input in all service organizations today. However, the community development initiatives and focus on protecting the planet, which the new CSR law has brought into focus, have been one of the distinctive features of Zensar since its inception. As the world moves into a period of uncertainty and disruption, it is the companies that combine the elements of profit, people, and planet that will win global respect and create value.

It is in this context that I am particularly happy to see a book that documents the Zensar story. The vision of Ganesh and his team, and their actual implementation of this, will serve as a very useful model for other companies and leaders.

The story of our industry and the success of companies like Zensar give me hope that India has a great future. It is a tale of wealth creation in a people-friendly, caring, and sustainable way. I am confident that many Indian companies will build their future on such a model, helping to change the world for the better.

Kiran Karnik
Former President, NASSCOM

Preface

There are some processes and transformations that are carefully planned and meticulously executed by a team of professionals in an industry or community. There are others that are created by a spirit of collective endeavor and a Vision Community of extraordinary individuals, bound by a spirit of "can do," who dare to dream impossible dreams and go out to make them happen. The Zensar story is worth understanding because it is a unique combination of both.

There is a wonderful story about Edmund Hillary, the first man to step foot on Mount Everest. When asked why he chose to climb the highest mountain in the world, he simply said, "Because it was there!" The few of us who came together in 2001 to pick up the pieces of a fractured organization have not only done that successfully, but also created an edifice that many thousands are proud of. Our journey has seen us climb many a mountain, but it has always been pleasant and full of team work and made us better human beings in the process.

Zensar is an interesting story that has never been written in full. The innovation journey and the "love" culture enshrined in the Vision Communities that form every year in the company have been well captured in two case studies written and taught regularly at Harvard Business School. The approach toward Human Resource Management and the company's conscious focus on community and societal good have been mentioned in many publications and received accolades and awards nationally and internationally. And today, the prowess the company demonstrates in focus areas such as retail, Oracle applications, and digital transformation of businesses has made it one of the leaders in its chosen areas of consulting with industry, leading to an increase in shareholder value.

The full strength of the Zensar story lies not in its innovations and focus on the customer to define and develop end-to-end value propositions. It does not even lie in its remarkable focus on talented people and its ability to report industry, beating retention of critical talent at all levels over a decade, and more. And while its approach to corporate social responsibility (CSR) has been laudable, that is not the only key point either. The success of Zensar is its ability to manage the triple bottom line and the ability to balance its focus on profits, people, and planet through its evolution and growth.

In writing this book, as in everything at Zensar, the whole team has pitched in, with details, anecdotes, and ideas that would have been beyond the reach of just one or two authors. It is intended to educate, entertain, and enlighten, which is the spirit with which the book has been written and the approach we would like readers to take. If we are able to set off a few light bulbs in the heads of some CEOs, many executives, and some researchers of corporate strategy, the book would serve its purpose.

We recommend you browse through this book on an aircraft journey or a couple of hours on a weekend and pick the sections that interest you most for a deeper understanding. To introduce you to the thought process, concept development, and articulation of the book, here is how it is structured.

The first five chapters of the book develop the theme of Zensar and its journey within the industrial context to become a company of substance. We start with a bird's eye view of the IT industry in India, the way it started, its path toward offshore legitimacy, the roller-coaster years of "Y2K" and "Dot Com," and its ability in the last 15 years to build a defensible position of quality, process maturity, and innovation in all service areas. Today, verticalization and specialization in chosen domains are defining the investment areas for most of the medium and large players. Moreover, the imperative of digital transformation is driving change in business models and encouraging incumbents to build collaborative ecosystems with smaller players creating exciting opportunities for market leadership that companies like Zensar are well placed to exploit.

From an analysis of the industry, we move to the Zensar story, its emergence from a history of hardware marketing and maintenance to becoming a software start-up at the dawn of this millennium and its formal christening on Valentine's Day 2000. The first 10 years as a new company going through various stages of growth until it reached credibility are traced through the eyes and words of key role players in the company until it reached a stage in 2010 when it was ready to challenge the early incumbents for its place in the sun as a full-services organization.

The third chapter describes the development of the three pillars whose strength determines the quality of a robust outsourcing organization and Zensar's own process of building them—applications management, package implementation, and support and infrastructure management. For any student or practitioner within the industry, we explore the nuances of success in each of these services areas and end with the implications of "digital" and Zensar's early moves in this space. The fourth chapter explains the rationale and the process of moving toward vertical domains as the way to approach clients, and the fifth chapter articulates the company's track record and philosophy toward new geographies as well as acquisitions.

Chapters 6, 7, and 8 of the book explore the triple bottom line approach that Zensar has taken to differentiate itself from many others in the industry. The sixth chapter focuses on number achievement, revenue and profit growth, and maximization of shareholder value. With the initial focus on organization stability and strengthening of its three pillars, Zensar's extreme focus on customer satisfaction and a judicious mix of organic growth and acquisitions has led it to overcome multiple challenges on its path and demonstrate a solid track record of growth on all numerical parameters. We tell you why and how!

The much-lauded story of Zensar's focus on people is recounted in the seventh chapter, with "love" being the dominant theme driving the attract–enable–retain continuum across the organization, leading to industry-leading retention of critical talent. Unique experiments such as Vision Communities, iZen, and Jugnu and their impact on the morale of associate are the key features of this chapter, where we also explore innovations in talent acquisition and reinforcement of the employee value proposition for prospective hires and existing employees. Zensar's strong focus on diversity and its unprecedented success in developing a cadre of very successful women for senior management roles is an important aspect that is detailed with interviews in this chapter.

The eighth chapter focuses on a theme that has been very dear to many Zensar hearts—the community and planet. Zensar has been one of the early industry movers in CSR, well before the government decided to make CSR spending mandatory for all significant corporations in the country. In this chapter, we develop the vision for CSR at Zensar and present the rationale for many successful initiatives pioneered by the company in the areas of education, employability, and environment. The unique approach to new ideas, which has now been followed by many others in the industry, is presented in this chapter, and the ability to get "everybody into the act" of showing care and responsibility for the community and environment is brought out for the benefit of researchers of sustainability and caring organizations. By the end of Chapter 8, the entire story of Zensar till date would unfold for the reader to absorb and understand.

Chapters 9 and 10 take a peep into the future—the future of the world of information technology, the challenges for the industry and the country, and the approach that Zensar is taking to secure and enhance its own position. At a time of enormous change brought in by the rapid progress of new technologies, such as cloud, mobility, social media, and big data, countries, societies, companies, and individuals are witnessing sweeping changes in the way marketing, supply chains, healthcare, and education are being used and delivered in the new world. The ninth chapter attempts to take stock of the progress of technologies and their impact on individual and corporate behavior, and the resultant changes that are being imposed on the products and services and delivery models of the IT industry. In the final chapter, Zensar's own response to the emergence of new challenges and opportunities and the vision the company has for the industry and its own position in it are elaborated.

By writing this book, we hope to educate and enlighten our readers—fellow professionals in the IT industry, industry watchers and researchers, the student community, and indeed every person who has marveled at the growth of the Indian IT sector and benefited from the rise of innovative companies like Zensar. We always say that Zensar is an idea, not just an IT company. It is an idea that can create organizations and teams in any industry, in any country. In an increasingly divisive world and industry, which is seeing some fissures developing between the various segments—IT services, business process management, product engineering, and Internet and e-commerce—we believe that understanding Zensar will provide an opportunity to every reader to make choices about the type of organization they want to work for and the lens through which to view the IT industry and the organizations that dot its firmament. And for every Zensarian who has been proud to be part of its journey, we believe Zensar is truly an idea whose time has come!

Acknowledgments

An edifice as strong and unique as Zensar is indeed a labor of love—for every stakeholder involved in the process of building and sustaining the edifice. We have had the privilege to be participants in this journey to success for the last 15 years and hope to have contributed in some way at every stage toward the creation of an empowering vision and its realization in some part. However, we must acknowledge the extraordinary contributions of various stakeholder groups who have made this journey possible and contributed to the creation of this book as well.

Our eminent Board of Directors, headed by Chairman Harsh Goenka, have shared their wisdom freely throughout this journey, and we would like to especially call out Ajit Vaswani and Polly Choksey, whose stewardship of the Audit Committee has led to the highest standards of governance in the company's actions and reporting. Also, Pradipto Mohapatra, John Levack, Kas Kasturirangan, and Arvind Agarwal, whose presence on the Board for many years and their availability for counseling and mentoring have facilitated the journey undertaken by the management team. The broader shareholder community, industry analysts, and members of the press have been wonderful critics and supporters, and fellow CEOs from NASSCOM and CII have occasionally chipped in with thoughts and advice that enabled the correct course to be set for the company.

Many local, national, and global personalities have assisted us on this journey, and we would like to call out a few. Arun and Anu Wakhlu of Pragati Leadership, Anand David of Manford, Noshir Kaka and the team at McKinsey, David Garvin and Michael Tushman of the Harvard Business School, and finally Rati Forbes, Anu Aga, and Pervin Varma, who continue to inspire us in our quest for the triple bottom line of profits, people, and planet.

Our biggest hurrah of course goes to every Zensarian, who has been part of the journey since the birth of the new entity on Valentine's Day 2000. They truly strive hard every day to "rediscover the Zen in Zensar" and their active participation in Vision Communities, and the 5F culture that makes us unique makes it possible to refresh the One Zensar agenda every week. And thanks to our colleagues on the Management Council—Ajay Bhandari, Harish Gala, Krishna Ramaswami, Vivek Gupta, Ruchi Mathur, Lavanya Jayaram, Pushpal Kapadia, and Shubha Kumar in particular, who have contributed to the creation of this book. We would also like to extend our heartfelt thanks to our ex-colleagues, Raj Dhillon and Sanjay Marathe, who have been with us for a significant part of the Zensar journey and continue to be great friends of Zensar.

As coauthors and partners in many visioning and transformation initiatives at Zensar, we—Prameela and Ganesh—have given our all to the success of this company and do not have any hesitation in confessing that traditional ideas such as work–life balance have never deterred us from the pursuit of our goals for Zensar. A word of appreciation for our families who have given us unstinting support in making this happen and of course to our friends and colleagues in Zensar who have lit up the path to success with friendship and fun to make it all worthwhile.

One Zensar is truly a journey, not a destination, and we are sure the road ahead will be as challenging and exciting as the last 15 years. To motivate everyone in Zensar for the journey, we would like to repeat what famous Indian sage Swami Vivekananda said, "Arise, Awake, and Stop not till the goal is reached."

CHAPTER 1

A Look at the Indian IT Industry

There was a time—25 to 30 years ago—when the name India, spoken in the Western world, would immediately conjure up images of snake charmers and religious men with matted hair and flowing orange ropes, performing the Indian rope trick. It must go entirely to the credit of the Indian IT industry that today the more dominant image is one of bright young people, armed with the knowledge of science, technology, engineering, and mathematics, competing with all comers to carve themselves a niche in the global phenomenon called offshore outsourcing—of technology, business processes, engineering research and development (R&D), and a host of other adjacent areas. Nowhere in the world has one industry come up from humble beginning and risen to such a position of dominance in barely three decades that India today has a commanding 55 percent market share of the global outsourcing business.

After some attempts were made in documenting the growth of this fabulous industry, Indian chief executive officers (CEOs) showed their creative best when, during the tenure of the author Ganesh Natarajan as Chairman of the industry association, National Association of Software and Services Companies (NASSCOM) in the year 2008–2009, five CEOs with a penchant for singing got together to produce a music CD that chronicled the history of the industry and the reasons why it rose to the position it has attained today. The growth of NASSCOM itself has been well documented by its second President, Kiran Karnik, in his book published a few years ago. This chapter attempts to give the reader a ringside view of significant events, circumstances, and anecdotes that have occurred since the 1980s to this day to create the wonderful world of Indian IT to which Zensar Technologies belongs.

EARLY BEGINNINGS

The credit for sensing an opportunity for India must surely go to industry doyen Fakir Chand Kohli, who was inducted in the 1970s by the Tata group from one of their companies—Tata Electric—and given the charge of exploring the world of IT. Computers had just begun to make their presence felt in Indian corporations, and the industry was dominated by IBM until 1977, when the then Commerce Minister George Fernandes threw out IBM, Coca Cola, and other multinationals to protect the Indian industry. The emergence of ICIM, the manufacturing subsidiary of ICL UK (which later morphed into Zensar), along with firms such as WIPRO, HCL, and DCM Data Products, was probably facilitated by the absence of Big Blue, IBM, during that period. TCS itself was the first pure-play software company to emerge as a division of the Tata holding company Tata Sons and, in the initial years, pursued a simple model of hiring bright young English-speaking engineers with graduate and postgraduate qualifications and putting them on planes to America and England to work for technology firms and large business corporations in these countries.

It is arguable whether it was TCS or Infosys who first decided that "delivered from India" could be a valid model for a nation and an industry that was initially satisfied earning much-needed foreign exchange through a "delivered-by-Indians" model. However, it was certainly a bunch of young engineers, led by Narayana Murthy, who huddled together in 1980 in an apartment owned by Murthy's wife Sudha in Pune and set up, in 1981, a unique company that would create new benchmarks for many things, not only in IT, but in the entire Indian industry. The scale and global quality of their first campus in Pune, the strong focus on values and process excellence, and the keen sense of competition, initially with TCS and later with other Indian majors such as WIPRO and HCL and global players such as EDS and Cap Gemini, as well as American listed firms such as Cognizant, would all be memorable contributions to the making of this industry. Smaller local firms such as Ashank Desai's Mastek and Saurabh Shrivastava's IIS, along with Harish Mehta and Pravin Gandhi's Hinditron, joined the mix, and a bunch of firms slowly began to come out of the shadow of computer manufacturing and catalyzed the emergence of the software sector in the country.

THE EMERGENCE OF NASSCOM

It was sometime in the 1980s when a group of young men, notably Harish Mehta, Saurabh Shrivastava, Ashank Desai, and Nandan Nilekani, sat down over coffee and drinks in the city of Mumbai and decided that the time had come for the software infant to be weaned away from the bigger hardware parent and the idea of NASSCOM was born. Getting the support of industry doyens such as F.C. Kohli, Narayana Murthy, and Prem Shivdasani of ICIM was a matter of time, and with the first secretariat headed by Sharad Shrivastava, NASSCOM was born.

The real momentum came into NASSCOM at the turn of the century when a young chartered accountant–turned graphics specialist, Dewang Mehta, agreed to come in as the first full-time leader of the association. A consummate showman and passionate India believer, Dewang went about creating an association that, until today, 25 years later, has remained the single voice of the industry.

The greatness of Dewang Mehta lay in his innate simplicity, the warmth he exuded with all stakeholders, CEOs, government, the Press and Analyst community, and every country he visited, and his ability to lace every idea with slogans and humor. His most famous story that was repeated in every country in the world was one where he spoke of the early beginnings of the industry when there was just one company, TCS, and the capability of India professionals was hardly known. In this period, the story goes that a rich Arab Sheikh died somewhere in the Middle East and left a strange will that bequeathed half his camels to his first son, a third of his camels to his second son, and one-ninth of his camels to his third son.

When the Bedouins huddled together the Sheikh's camels in the desert, they found there were 17 of them, which made the mathematics of dividing them infeasible. Bemused, they sent off a fax (this was a time before email) to the corporate offices in Mumbai of TCS and requested help. A week later, the worried men of the desert finally spotted a camel approaching them with a young software engineer from TCS astride it. Listening to their problem, the young man said, "Just keep my camel." That took the camel count to 18, and the first son got nine, the second six, and the third two camels. The men said: "we have one camel left," and the software engineer said: "that's mine of course" and rode back over the desert to his home country—India!

This story, which never fails to bring laughter from any audience anywhere in the world, and many more that Dewang Mehta was very fond of telling his audiences, are worth telling because these underline one fact that Dewang always stated, that Indians brought to the table primarily their ingenuity and the ability to solve problems. Even today, in spite of a majority of the world's Fortune 500 firms having large bases in India, this core virtue remains intact, and whether it is Indian companies or Indians working in Indian companies, which constitute a good percentage of the global workforce in IT, we are proud of the brainpower that works in our campuses and client locations in India and dozens of countries abroad.

Until the unfortunate demise of Dewang in Australia in 2000, NASSCOM was very much a one-man chain band supported wholeheartedly by all industry CEOs and the irrepressible IT Secretary of the country in the 1990s, Mr N.

Vittal, whose pathbreaking Software Technology Parks of India (STPI) policy created the basis for a flourishing software industry in the country. After Dewang, the baton has been passed on to other great leaders, Kiran Karnik, Som Mital, and now R. Chandrasekar, who have ensured that the IT industry continues to be the pride and joy of the country and many parts of the world. Many aspiring outsourcing destination countries—the Philippines, Vietnam, Malaysia, Brazil, and others in central and eastern Europe, Africa, and Latin America—have attempted to copy India by having similar associations (BRASSCOM and GHASSCOM are just two names that even sound similar), but none have managed to take the shine away from the Indian industry. China at one time even had three ministries devoted to competing with NASSCOM, but has in recent years given up the exports chase and focused more on building its own domestic software companies. It is truly a story that would warm the heart of every proud Indian.

Y2K: THE LEGITIMIZING EVENT FOR INDIAN IT

The Indian software story may well have remained the story of Indian talent being deployed overseas if it had not been for a great problem for all computer systems that was spotted early by early movers such as TCS, Infosys, Satyam, and Hexaware and used to good effect to build significant offshore capabilities. Until that happened, clients in the United States (US) and Europe would listen politely to the presentations on the wonders of connectivity from global client locations to Indian centers and how that would enable software facilities in Bengaluru, Chennai, and Mumbai to be seamlessly connected to global locations and still ask: "Do you have four engineers with COB and Visual Basic skills to send to our facility in Dallas?" But one frightening realization was to change all that.

The scenario that worried IT managers most in the concluding years of the old millennium was that of banking systems spewing wrong checks and airplanes crashing because of a very simple problem. Data fields coded into structured programming languages in the 1960s and 1970s were restricted to DD-MM-YY, which meant that when the year 1999 changed to 2000, the field would change from 99 to 00, causing unpredictable outcomes in the performance of computer systems. And these could occur in legacy systems written by programmers who could have retired or even died. And no self-respecting American or European programmer would like to take on the arduous task of cleaning up an old program or system.

Enter the ever-willing Indian IT firm. With the large army of lower cost technical manpower available on Indian shores, the time was ripe and Western ears were now willing to listen to an offshore services story—not of new development or innovation, but code remediation to "fix the Y2K bug." However, this was to be just the beginning of a new phase of growth for the Indian IT industry. With millions and millions of code and hence mission-critical systems moving to India for fixing, migration to new technology and sometimes to application packages such as SAP, Oracle, and Microsoft, the work of software development, testing, modernization, and maintenance was irrevocably moving shores.

Over the years, the code that came to India in those sunset years of the 1990s has created the multibillion dollar Applications Management Services (AMS) business for the Indian IT industry. The large volume of work also led to the eager adoption of the process maturity standard of the Software Engineering Institute of Carnegie Mellon, called SEI CMM, and it is no wonder that most significant Indian firms are today at the highest level of this standard, level 5. And it is not just that, the catapulting of work volumes and the billions of dollar that flowed to India for Y2K work saw the building of software campuses in Software Technology Parks and, in later years, Special Economic Zones in the cities of Bengaluru, Hyderabad, Chennai, Mumbai, and Delhi initially and later in Kolkata, Pune, Gurgaon, NOIDA, Jaipur, Chandigarh, Trivandrum, and over 30 more cities that have all grown at a rapid pace and continue to be the pride and joy of India's most successful services exports industry.

THE IMPACT OF THE DOT COM BOOM

The late 1990s may have seen a scare, Y2K, that caused a major shift of work to India, but it also brought an opportunity in the form of the Dot Com boom. The ubiquitous rise of the Internet and the availability of large quantum of venture capital dollars saw the emergence of companies of all shapes and hues, speaking not in terms of dollars of revenues, but the number of eyeballs they managed to capture, albeit briefly, to witness their glories on the Internet. This new phenomenon in business-to-consumer (B2C) and business-to-business (B2B) commerce would create opportunities for the rapid development of Web sites and portals and saw not only the large Indian firms but also a new generation of start-ups in India gearing up to help the Dot Com firms.

The boom itself was not to last, indeed it was soon apparent that the Internet bubble was going to burst, and for many starry-eyed Indian professionals who had flown to the US and Europe to help the burgeoning start-up community, B2B and B2C were to mean Back to Bangalore and Back to Chennai in the Year 2000. But the skills acquired in building rapid Internet applications and systems would stay with the Indian sector and embellish the considerable skills that were already being acquired.

THE BUILDUP OF ADJACENCIES

The Indian software industry in the years leading up to today has seen the birth of many new sunrise subsectors that have added to the revenues and helped discerning global customers to find myriad new opportunities to look at India. It was the IT services firms that firmly established the validity of the global delivery model, and the other segments have taken this core competence and built on it.

The business process outsourcing (BPO) companies, which have now been renamed as business process management (BPM) to reflect the complexity of processes they handle and the value they add to their customers, now dot the landscape of India and have even reached small towns and villages in the country. From humble call centers to managing multiple processes ranging from customer relationships to supply chain management, there are very few processes that have not been optimized and managed offshore by the hundreds of BPM firms today. The voice-based BPO industry has also spread its wings to the Philippines and China and many countries in Central and Eastern Europe and more recently to Latin America. The globalization of the industry, which has now expanded in all directions and in all service areas, owes a lot to the vision of the early pioneers such as Pramod Bhasin and Raman Roy, whose companies GECIS (now Genpact) and Spectramind (now absorbed into WIPRO) started the revolution.

The engineering services segment was the next to take root, quite natural since the development of application software is only a step removed from building system software, doing hardware programming, and creating embedded software and engineering designs for clients. In more recent years, this has led to the development of a somewhat delayed but now very credible software product ecosystem in the country.

A related growth area for the industry, fueled partly by the increasing confidence of global majors in Indian people and processes and partly by a need to retain control on mission control applications and processes, has been the emergence of captive centers now called "global in-house centers" (GICs). Pioneered by GE and later HSBC, this segment is today one of the faster growing employers and has provided many global managers an opportunity to transfer their learnings seamlessly from Indian firms to global multinationals and vice versa.

INDIA TODAY: A VIBRANT HOME FOR A $150 BILLION INDUSTRY

In the last 15 years, the industry has matured in multiple ways and directions. With NASSCOM providing the leadership needed to all segments and firms, the strategic review for 2014–2015 presented by the industry association proudly points out that

India has continued to maintain its first-mover advantage and retained its leadership position in the global sourcing arena. In spite of competition from the Philippines, Malaysia, and Vietnam in Asia, Mexico and Brazil in Latin America, Poland and Hungary in Europe, and repeated attempts by China, the country has a 55 percent market share in global sourcing.

The NASSCOM report points out the key reasons for India's numero uno status as a global sourcing destination. A future-ready workforce remains the dominant source of competitive advantage, with an industry that now employs over three million professionals, nearly 200 thousand of those with skills in the digital domains of cloud, mobility, social media, and big data and a supply source of over two million trained engineering, technology, science, and mathematics graduates every year. The other key strength is the prevalence of a strong innovation-backed ecosystem, with organizations in India consistently innovating around products, processes, and business models and delivering enhanced value propositions to global and domestic clients. A recent poll of global customers revealed that over 85 percent agree that transformative work can be delivered out of India. Indeed, a number of Fortune 500 CEOs and chief information officers (CIOs) have been quoted as saying that they may have come to India because of the cost advantage but stayed because of quality and are now experience the fruits of true transformation partnerships, a theme that has become the vision and mission of many companies in the country, including Zensar.

Innovation in India today pervades the narrative and the focus of the entire industry with the successful NASSCOM 10,000 start-up program creating start-ups with new ideas not just for digital and e-commerce but a host of areas that have the potential to transform the access and success of people everywhere, using technology. Large and medium firms too are investing in research and development, partnering with innovative start-ups and ensuring that they create cutting-edge capabilities for the benefit of the customer.

In the last reporting year ending March 2015, overall industry revenues crossed $145 billion, a growth of 13 percent over the previous year, and an overall year-on-year addition of $17 billion in global and domestic revenues. The export revenues are expected to have crossed $98 billion, up by 11 billion over the previous year.

IT services remains the largest segment of the industry, with a share of 47 percent of the pie, followed by BPM, which has a share of 18 percent. Engineering R&D and product development have a share of 16 percent, followed by e-commerce and hardware with nine percent each. Manufacturing, utilities, and retail have been the key growth verticals for the industry, with clients increasing discretionary spend on analytics, digital technologies, customer experience and enterprise resource planning (ERP) package implementations, and updates on-promise as well as hosted on the cloud. Exports to the US have remained steady, and the US remains the dominant market for the industry. European demand softened during the latter part of the year, and the impact of Greece and other adverse developments in the continent have kept Europe on a watch list for most Indian companies. The industry continues to grow in Africa, Asia, and the Middle East, though Latin America and China continue to prove elusive for most players.

INNOVATIONS IN THE INDIAN IT SECTOR

The innovation agenda for the Indian industry commenced as a serious initiative of NASSCOM in the early years of the new millennium, even as industry CEOs realized that to maintain strong double-digit revenue growth and profitability, standing still was not an option.

In the early days of offshore outsourcing, the standardization of processes and the deployment of technology and metrics to provide the much-needed predictability and optimization in all customer projects and deliveries had already raised India to a reputation of high quality in the eyes of all global clients. However, the Innovation Forum of NASSCOM and, in some ways, the Knowledge Management National Committee of the Confederation of Indian Industry (CII) supplemented the efforts of companies, created forums for sharing of best practices, and continue to inspire companies to do their best to find new things to do as well as new ways of doing things.

The most obvious innovation that was quick to be adopted by industry leaders was the creation of new products and services at a steady clip, both to augment the revenue potential from existing and new clients and to build new sources of competitive differentiation. Cases in point in the period 2001–2005 were the building of offerings for total banking by Infosys and COSL, the latter eventually morphing into iFlex and acquired by Oracle Corporation. While these were full productized solutions, innovation also became the source of competitive advantage for smaller firms. Zensar's Solution BluePrint (SBP), which embodied the company's point of view that high-quality business solutions needed a building architecture approach, rather than focusing on superior quality plumbing or carpentry work, grabbed attention of global customers and eventually featured in a case study written and taught by Professor Michael Tushman at the Harvard Business School.

Innovation also found its way into the nervous system of organizations. New ways of skilling people for the ever-changing demands of the industry came into being at the end of the first decade, with firms such as Global Talent Track offering next practices in fresher identification training and recruiting. Their value proposition has been to help Indian and global IT and BPM firms to do successful off-campus recruiting, identifying talent in second-tier cities and educational institutions, and training them to the levels needed by the corporation. In recent times, this model has received renewed momentum with the availability of large corporate social responsibility (CSR) funds for skills development, which has seen generic skills imparted to youth across the country and the creation of a large pool of talent for the entire industry to use.

Many models of innovation have found their way into the industry. The Tushman model of ambidextrous innovation, where new initiatives are maintained within the larger firm to enjoy the operating leverage available through the large sales force, has been one of the most popular models, although in some cases, as currently seen in companies such as Infosys and Mastek, complete spinouts of the product organization following the Clayton Christiansen model have been attempted.

At an industry level, NASSCOM continues to play a lead role in the creation of innovation clusters, particularly with its enormously successful 10,000 start-ups program, the new product creation warehouses that are coming up in key IT cities, and the successful product conclaves that have shown the spotlight on many of the exciting new firms emerging from Bengaluru, Delhi, Pune, and other cities. Other interesting associations have emerged, including Product Nation and iSpirt, the latter serving as a think tank for the creation of new product ideas and a new ecosystem that would serve the purpose of new-age entrepreneurs who seek to differentiate themselves from the larger mass of traditional services firms.

The industry today is a proud and vibrant one that represents the face of a new India, full of global aspirations and dreams. Over three million young Indians have been able to achieve goals that were beyond the reach of any previous generation. The ability to work globally, interact with multiple nationalities, and bring up their children in any culture and any part of the world has made Indians in IT the cynosure of attention of the country and has enabled this industry to create a vision of the strong and confident India of the future.

FUTURE OUTLOOK

Nearly 70 years ago, India's first Prime Minister, Pandit Jawaharlal Nehru, had proclaimed from the ramparts of the Red Fort that India was ready for her tryst with destiny. This industry in India has certainly played a role, particularly in the last two decades, and more to ensure that this is a truly global destiny.

The economic forces that are buffeting the world will create a period of uncertainty that will create both challenges and opportunities for the industry. Our global customers will feel the intense pressure of competition, the inexorable pull of wallet tightening by their customers, which will necessitate new ways of lowering costs, and the hard push of technology, particularly digital technology, to develop a much sharper focus on their customer and high visibility of their supply chains and all aspects of their operations. The Indian industry, with its ability to listen, adapt, and innovate for the benefit of the customer, will be tested once again to demonstrate its ability to envisage design and deliver outstanding solutions at the lowest cost and highest quality to meet the ever-changing needs of the customer.

The good news is that these acid tests are not new for the industry. We were tested in the 1990s when customers would not believe in the offshore story, we were questioned at the turn of the millennium when a new story had to build post the Y2K and Dotcom, and one of the authors, Ganesh, has seen firsthand the skepticism among global fund managers when he, as Chairman of NASSCOM, had the task to convince them in 2008 that the industry would grow even in the worst year of the economic slowdown. And grow it did! Like the proverbial Phoenix rising from the ashes, the Indian industry has risen time and again, discovered new sigmoids of growth that have kept firms on a rising track for 30 and more years. We will prevail.

CHAPTER 2

Zensar

Building Credibility and Stature

Since its inception in 1922 as a tabulating machine manufacturing company in the western city of Pune in a country still under British rule to its rise to supremacy in the domestic hardware industry and then its various struggles to build a credible software and consulting business, the story of Zensar is one of rises and falls. Through this sinusoidal progress, the company has successfully completed 50 years of listing in 2013 on the Bombay Stock Exchange and carved for itself a distinctive position in the IT sector. We recount here the early trials and tribulations leading to the creation of the new unit and the first 10 years of Zensar Technologies.

THE 1990S: THE RISE AND FALL OF ICIM

In the sleepy town of Pune in 1922, a British firm set up a tabulating machine manufacturing unit. While very little is known about the progress of the unit in the early years, it evolved to become the Indian manufacturing wing of a very successful European computer hardware manufacturing company, International Computers Limited (ICL). Christened International Computers Indian Manufacture (ICIM), the company listed on the Bombay Stock Exchange in 1963 and welcomed RPG Enterprises as one of its shareholders in 1988.

The company capitalized on the exit of global leader IBM from India in 1977 and quickly rose to a position of preeminence in the Indian mid-range computer industry. At the time when one of the book's authors, Ganesh Natarajan, started his career in 1981, ICIM was known as the manufacturer of choice for both public and private sector organizations. Well known for its ICL 1901 and 2904 computers, the company also launched the ICIM personal computer (PC) range, where it ran into competition from early Indian movers such as HCL, WIPRO, DCM, and PSI.

The 1990s saw the slow decline of the hardware business because of both external and internal reasons. The external environment became one of intense competition and price wars, with nimbler firms sniping at the installed base and weaning away companies to their brands. Ganesh was in fact one of the first IT managers in his role of Planning and Systems Head of the Switchgear Division of Crompton Greaves Ltd. to switch from ICIM to a new firm, PSI Data Systems, and by the 1990s, market share erosion had begun to happen fast. The opening up of the economy and the entry of brands such as Dell and IBM also heralded the arrival of global competition, and the writing was on the wall for incumbents like ICIM.

The company was also suffering internally from a combination of hubris from its successful past and leadership troubles at the top. With Fujitsu having bought out ICL, the two joint-venture partners RPG and Fujitsu were in a rather stormy marriage, and the CEOs of the time showed very little inclination to weather the storms and stick on to build a profitable business. The company in 1991 decided to set up a software and services subsidiary, ICIL, in a somewhat late recognition of the fact that the days of local hardware manufacturing were over and it was software that would power India's future. That was when the US office was also set up.

Fujitsu also came in 1994 as an investor. For the first 10 years, however, the management was caught between the conflicting pulls between the decline of the hardware business and the inadequate attention given to growing the software business, with the result that this became the most traumatic decade for the company.

In fact, by 1996, the company was at the brink of going bankrupt and it was when the company was just 15 days away from filing for bankruptcy with the Board for Industrial and Financial Reconstruction, that Mr A.T. Vaswani, who was then the Vice Chairman of ICIM, was given the responsibility for brining things under control. With both the investors, RPG and Fujitsu, making it amply clear to him that they would invest no further in the company until they began to see some returns, he set about looking for new investors and brought in a new investor, Electra Partners, who continues to stay invested in the company till date.

This was then followed by some hard calls and tough decisions being taken, which included selling off the hardware business and shutting down the manufacturing factory in Pune in 1999. Very soon, Fujitsu disinvested in the company in 2000, followed by ICL also disinvesting in 2003.

The turbulent period of the 1990s is best described in the words of Vivek Gupta, Chief Executive of the Infrastructure Management Business Unit of the company, who joined the company from IIT Delhi in 1985 and has stayed on with the company since then:

> From 1995 to 2001 was a period wherein the CEO's Office was a Revolving Door at Zensar. Midway through 1995, the then Managing Director of ICIM, Mr Ashok Jain, resigned to return back to HCL where he had come from. And within months after that, the President of the International Software Division (ISD), Mr Pawan Kumar, also left to join Square-D, an IT venture of Deepak Dalmia. That triggered 6 years of uncertainty for ICIM and its various stakeholders.
>
> Mr A.T. Vaswani, who was the Vice Chairman of ICIM at that time, had to be parachuted into the role of a caretaker CEO. His main focus was to somehow stop the hardware division from

taking the entire company under water, while keeping the fires burning in the promising software exports business of ISD. He admirably held the fort, dealing with numerous government agencies and creditors and preventing talent from leaving the company by the dozens. Among his top challenges was the daunting task of somehow keeping the company running, finding a capable CEO, helping with bringing in a PE investor, and selling off the hardware division—all at the same time.

Almost every day employees heard a fresh rumor about some well-known industry veteran being interviewed by the board to take on the CEO's chair only to hear a completely different name the next day. Months turned into three long years as ICIM continued to operate headless. Predictably, the company lost many top-notch employees from across both the divisions of Zensar. Those who stayed behind would ask themselves every waking hour whether they should be looking for jobs elsewhere. To this day, it is hard to understand why some chose to stay on when the company appeared to be inches away from a total collapse.

Then in November 1998, Mr Vaswani announced to the employees that the board had appointed one of the top two senior executives of TCS, Mr L.C. Singh (LC), to take over the reins of Zensar. There was much jubilation across Zensar, as it was seen as nothing short of a coup for ICIM to have wooed one of the best from the best software exports company at that time. Thus started a period of stability, albeit brief, in the company when LC and his team, comprising the survivors of ICIM and many newly hired ex-TCS managers, started the process of rebuilding ICIM, which by now was a pure-play software exports company, having sold off its hardware division. LC also led a major initiative of rebranding the company and changing its name in order to free it from the baggage of its hardware past. With much fanfare on Valentine's Day 2000, the company was renamed as "Zensar" to the tune of raga Zensar, a North Indian classical piece created solely for Zensar by one of Indian great music maestros. The world was told that Zensar was like a heavenly star that had just arrived on the horizon with a swoosh (which is still present in the logo today) to revolutionize the global IT industry.

Sadly, that period also did not last very long, and within a couple of months after the renaming of the company, LC left with a couple of senior executives to start his own company. Zensar was back in the darkness of despair, and many valiant survivors felt defeated. It seemed that there was going to be no recovery from this final period of rudderlessness. But they inexplicably soldiered on for some more time.

Another veteran, who was part of the management team during and after the Singh and Vaswani era, says he found it interesting that intelligent and otherwise accomplished professionals forget this fundamental principle of good management. In the early 1990s, ICIM was obsessed with revenue growth, all desperate to stay among "big boys." The secret sauce was to get into a slew of partnerships to widen the forays of offerings in the systems business to expand reach in the market and drive up turnover. This led to ICIM stepping out of its core competency, which was systems integration and strategic account management. Further, it expanded its PC business in the commoditized market, a market quite alien to ICIM. That led to the classical cash flow spiral going south; short shipments leading to debtors, leading to exhausting all (expensive) bank borrowings, leading to delayed materials, and leading to canceled orders. This near-death scenario had one panacea: exit the hardware business and focus on its high margin and profitable software business. ICIM sold its systems business in 1996 to Accel.

The focus on the international software business in the US, the UK, and Japan gave the impetus to get back to basics: sanity of profits coming out of insanely high margins and for the first time the reality of cash flow. However, there were two missed opportunities: first, its late entry into the Y2K business, which had been the legitimizing feature for offshore outsourcing for many of the early software players and, second, its over-indexed "time and material" contracts. As the peer companies quickly transitioned to managing to get a strong foothold into large accounts, ICIL (as it was then known) struggled to find a key value proposition that could differentiate from other establishing players. Fortunately, it stayed away from the frenzied "Dot Com" business as much as it had fledgling start-ups offering equity to pay for development services rendered. And it was wisely declined.

The early moves of L.C. Singh definitely gave the software business the much-needed fillip, and the sale of the hardware maintenance business gave it the opportunity to stand up and be counted as a pure-play software and services company, Zensar. But it still needed a differentiation. And the early departure of LC and team had not provided the time and the latitude to create that differentiation. The year 2001 started ominously, with the first quarter seeing the company slide into losses again. The shareholders of the company were still waiting for a maiden dividend, and the relationship between the original joint venture partners, RPG and Fujitsu, remained edgy.

This was the state then in February 2001 when a new development occurred.

In the words of Vivek Gupta

> And then came the fateful day, February 28th, 2001, when Mr Vaswani caught the Management Committee Members (MCM) by complete surprise by announcing that Zensar's newest CEO, Mr Ganesh Natarajan, was about to arrive in 15 minutes to join the MCM meeting that they had gathered to attend. Just like that. No early warning. No prior confidential mail or phone call. No fanfare. There had been too many missteps and back outs at the last minute in the last 6 years.
>
> This was to be the start of a fresh chapter in the history of Zensar.

THE BIRTH OF ZENSAR

By the late 1990s, Zensar was already operating worldwide under a variety of brand names: ICIL-III and Fujitsu-ICIM. A need was felt to establish a single brand. Mr L.C. Singh, then CEO, was himself very passionate about brand building and initiated an exercise to come up with a new brand name for the company.

The exercise threw up three names: BlueChilli.com, Zensar, and Yellow Hat. The Dot Com revolution was in full swing at that time, and while BlueChilli.com was the favorite of many of the seniors, a company-wide survey showed that the Zensar was the chosen brand favored by most employees. So Zensar it was!

The company was renamed Zensar on Valentine's Day, February 14, 2000, when all the entities worldwide went through a name change.

Zensar, the name has often intrigued many of our customers, partners, and even associates. The "Zen" in Zensar finds its roots in oriental philosophy and stands for knowledge, while "Sar" is drawn from Sanskrit, the philosophical language of Buddhism, Hinduism, and Jainism, and means essence.

Zensar stands for the essence of knowledge, a name very apt for what the company grew to become in the years that followed this rebranding exercise.

NEW LEADERSHIP AND A NEW VISION FOR SUCCESS

Ganesh, the new CEO of Zensar, came in with a track record of great success in training company APTECH, having led it with distinction for just under a decade, grown its revenues 50 times, and listed the firm on the London and Bombay Stock Exchanges. He describes the events leading to his appointment and the early days at Zensar in his words.

> It was spring of 2000 and I was getting bored! I had been given the reins of APTECH in August 1991 when I had just turned thirty-four and had a wonderful time giving a group of youngsters the vision and conviction that they could catch up with market leader NIIT. When we did that and crossed some magic milestones like a thousand training centres and over forty countries where the APTECH flag was now fluttering, the inevitable fatigue was beginning to set in. I was in that state of mind when I became part of a CII delegation accompanying then Prime Minister Atal Bihari Vajpayee to Portugal. A chance encounter with CII Vice President Sanjiv Goenka in Lisbon led

me to think that the leadership skills I had acquired could now be tested in a new domain. A few months and many conversations with RPG Group Chairman Harsh Goenka later, I accepted the offer to lead a company which had clearly slipped in recent times and presented the new challenge I was looking for.

I got off the plane at Pune airport and was taken to a conference room at the two building facility of Zensar to be introduced to the management team and almost immediately asked to deliver my first speech at the EBM (Every Body Meeting) that had been called on the lawns of the company. Little did I know in that first speech, where I spoke of the industry, the global opportunity and the role of every young software professional, the extent of the challenge that lay before me in Zensar.

The company in early 2001 had three major problems that needed to be addressed on priority.

1. A flawed business model, dependent heavily on placing professionals in the UK and the US, possibly a legacy of the "recruiting for ICL" model.
2. Fissures within the leadership team, with India managed by a small team of chief operating officer (COO), chief financial officer (CFO), and Head of Human Resources, UK, the only rock of stability and profitability, and the US operation focused on on-site Oracle services on the West Coast with a new CEO having been appointed for the US, but unable to make connections with the West Coast leadership.
3. Sliding profitability with nearly 200 of the 800-odd employees on the bench and a very weak order pipeline and paltry record of selling and delivering offshore services.

The first few steps taken by the new CEO were a repetition of his tried and tested formula. He built a quick connection with the entire employee base, encouraged ideation at all levels through a Vision Community that transcended levels and encouraged all members to speak up, and traveled extensively to meet every consultant overseas and take their views on what could be done to revive the organization. Some surgery was needed and was quickly done with over a hundred "bench" staff let go. The immediate cost reduction coupled with a reassured customer base meant that the company came back into the black within six months and was even able to declare a small first dividend at the end of the first financial year 2001–2002.

The separation of over a 100 people may be commonplace in many IT firms but for Zensar and its majority shareholder RPG, this was the first time that such an action had ever been contemplated or put into action. The reluctance on the part of line leadership was palpable, but the CEO found a loyal ally in the HR Chief Bala Narayanan, a Cooke and RJR Nabisco veteran, who enabled the operation to be done with dignity and a true spirit for partnering for the larger good of the organization. However, the real malaise lay not within the new hires but with some of the senior leadership who had become set in their ways and in some cases extremely cynical after weathering the many storms and leadership changes they had witnessed. As one General Manager was heard to remark, "This too shall pass and the CEO will get fed up and find another job and leave us in peace."

However, the change process was continued inexorably. Having plucked low-hanging fruit and returned the company to profitability, the next challenge was to get industry understanding, ambition, and candor into the management of Zensar. This was achieved through some induction of new blood and a couple of aggressive "breakthrough thinking" workshops, which saw the departure of some of the old guard. The benefit for many of the management team members, who had genuinely wanted some robust action and the ability to compete with industry leaders, was the openness and candor that was the new style in the organization. The once-divisive forces in the US quickly returned to the fold, and the departure of the US Head and later the HR Head brought the sales leadership of Vivek Gupta in the UK and Nitin Parab in the US closer to the CEO. The signals were clear—sales aggression and customer centricity would be the new mantra of Zensar, and this value coupled with the willingness to include all associates (the new term for employees) in the thinking and execution process brought new winds of change into the organization by early 2002.

During this period, some bold decisions were also taken—to stop all pure staff augmentation business and ensure that a genuine offshore model was created and marketed by the organization, to set up a string marketing group headed by an industry-savvy veteran, Subu, and focus on innovation to develop a "different point of view" for existing customers and prospects. A new chief technology officer (CTO), Dilip, was hired to provide this breakthrough thinking.

By the end of the financial year 2001–2002, the first formal top management structure had begun to emerge, which included five of the older hands and some of the newer elements. Vivek Gupta had moved from the UK to the US to set up the Applications Management Services business, Nitin Parab continued to head the Enterprise Applications business, and Sanjay Marathe headed India delivery, while Ajit Dubhashi was the Chief Financial Officer. With four key positions locked in for the veterans, a new Vice President, Aamod Wagh, was given charge of the rest of the world (ROW) territories that included Japan, Australia, Singapore, India, and the Middle East. Subu headed Marketing, and Dilip, while reporting to Sanjay, was tasked with the innovation agenda for the company. After some time, an old APTECH colleague of Ganesh, V. Bala, joined the company to take over ROW from Aamod who moved to Europe.

BUILDING A CREDIBLE OFFSHORE STORY

The early wins with multinationals, Fortune 500, and FTSE 100 firms—the world's leading manufacturer of networking equipment, one of Europe's foremost utility firms, a diversified multiplatform global manufacturer, and one of the biggest names in retail worldwide—all these and more gave the Zensar teams the confidence that it was building a world-class delivery organization that could compete with the best when it came to providing value to its customers.

The investments of the organization in the middle years up to 2008 were primarily in reinforcing the strengths in multi-technology delivery capability and building the "land-and-expand" strategy—the ability to enter the customer through one well-defined service and then expand into multiple areas within the customer footprint by sheer hard work and demonstrating the value Zensar teams always brought to the customer. During this period, friendly and not-so-friendly commentators on the organization would question the wisdom of this approach, pointing out comparable-size firms that had chosen to sharply focus their energies on just a few capability areas, such as engineering or Oracle, but the Zensar team held true to its value statements.

The primary value that motivated all members of the Zensar leadership team and became a key facet of the sessions conducted frequently with various management layers and the "pizza-and-coke" sessions across the organization was to explore this value thoroughly. How should a young manager approach this total commitment to the customer and what would be the trade-offs with personal time during an all-out effort to make customer delight happen? How should a sales person reach to a new request that might well take the delivery teams far away from its chosen areas of capability? At what point should Zensar push back and say no?

The growth and success of the company have largely been attributable to the culture created in the mid-2000s. The fact that most of the managers who were given their spurs and trained in that time remain with the company or even if they left, have returned to the company demonstrates the success of this approach to building a cohesive, committed customer-centric offshore services organization, rather than have a few superstars and narrowly focused approach that could fall apart because it was not bound in a culture and process that led to the customer. Many cases spring up to demonstrate the track record of Zensar in this area.

The capabilities with Oracle Applications have always defined Zensar and continue to be a key differentiator, as the company today proudly works with Oracle directly and with Oracle clients in a range of areas from the traditional to the very latest e-commerce applications and plans to move from Oracle Platinum to Diamond status worldwide. In the early days, the implementations would tend to be substantially on-site, and led by the US, Zensar had successful implementations and a few challenges in all major geographies—the US, the UK, South Africa, the Middle East, Australia, and India. One of the defining projects for the company was the request from one of the world's largest game development companies to implement an Oracle Order Management system worldwide. The successful handling of this project not only gave the confidence to the team, that a multilocation project of this magnitude could be successfully handled, but it also led to support from offshore and set in motion a large movement toward offshore-centric support and also implementations that would see Oracle projects with half or more value delivered from India in later years.

Zensar also acquired the capability in those early years to spread its wings, when required, to adjacent areas and in cases where the competency could not be built deep enough or fast enough, to partner with other firms, which is rare in the fiercely competitive medium and large tiers of the industry. The Business Process Management unit of the company was set up because of the request from some customers for whom Oracle Financials or Supply Chain or Order Management systems had been implemented. For the customer it made eminent sense that the company, which knew its systems intimately, would now further take on the management of the process. Zensar teams have been successfully handling the Accounts Payable function from offshore for key customers and, in more than one case, have also managed customer helpdesks for key customers and, for a large retailer, have been successfully managing the merchandise allocation process. Investments in adjacencies such as knowledge management platforms, new web technologies, and e-learning have all been made because of an interest of one or more clients. It is only in the area of Geographical Information Systems, which a large utilities client wanted to implement, that Zensar chose to partner with a successful Indian provider and managed the program implementation with full transparency to the client. The transformation of a humble "two-trick pony," which was how Zensar first started out with its credentials in Oracle and applications maintenance, into a full-blown comprehensive services organization, successfully competing with the best of incumbents, has been one of continuous investments in a series of areas and in some cases acquisitions that enabled the company to emerge as the partner of choice for many large and even a few medium and small customers worldwide. No territory is most representative of the success of this strategy than South Africa, where 80 percent of the top banks and insurance firms work with the company, and Zensar has grown from its early beginnings of a two-staff office in Sandton near Johannesburg to being one of the top three service providers with over 600 people employed on projects, a full-fledged resource training center for young local aspirants, and a "proudly South African" heritage. Retail in the UK, a multiagency partnership with the United Nations in Europe, and coast-to-coast success in the US all bear testimony to the successful migration of the Customer Centricity value to the successful dual-shore status that Zensar had achieved by 2010.

TARGETING THE TOP TIER

It is difficult to pinpoint exactly when and where the Zensar management council decided that it would compete to enter the top echelons of the Indian IT industry. The ambition was there since early 2005, when the first divisionalization exercise was initiated and the independent profit centers were created. It would have been logical in the early days for Zensar, with zero track record and the Y2K opportunity, given a historic miss to settle for one of three ways to build a profitable business and all three had been advised to the company. It could have provided a cheaper, "no frills" service to large customers or just offered a very niche set of solutions in which it could build distinctive competencies or focused on smaller clients with smaller budgets who were below the radar of the larger global and Indian top-tier service providers.

It would have sounded foolhardy to some in those years, but the decision to focus on winning through innovation and customer centricity without compromise on client size or pricing has been fully endorsed by Zensar's success and gives wings to Zensar's ambition today to cross the half billion revenue mark soon and fly toward the one-billion-dollar club by the year 2020. The move to providing offshore and dual-shore services has already been described, and commencing with the later part of the last decade and continuing until today, a series of well-planned moves have been initiated that have the full weight and commitment of the leadership sales and delivery teams at all locations around the world.

The creation of the Infrastructure Management Business Unit in the year 2010 was probably one of the first significant moves by Zensar in a completely new direction. Recognizing that the management of infrastructure would be a critical complement to the company's proven capabilities in package applications and the more generic applications development and maintenance services, the hiring of one young professional, Ankit Ghosh, and the support given to him to build a team and an organization was one significant move in the right direction. Within a couple of years, a team numbering over a 100 and key clients in the US and Africa gave Zensar the confidence to acquire the $100 million American Data Centre Services firm Akibia, which after a somewhat slow start has given Zensar the right to play in dual-shore data center and remote infrastructure management services in the US and Europe and also provide a host of new services, from private and hybrid cloud transitions to storage to end-user experience management and security products and services.

Another move made with a clear focus on entering the big league of providers has been the creation of a "big-deals" team focused on moving the sweet spot for Zensar contracts from a couple of million dollars to the 10–20 million dollar league. Planning and executing big deals need the ability to think of long-term contract with price and scope escalations built in, multi-tower integration, including applications and infrastructure and business process management, and creative deal pricing, including taking over client infrastructure and sometimes people. After some initial false starts, the big-deal teams of Zensar are today in a position not only to chase large-defined opportunities, but also to create opportunities within existing clients by developing unsolicited value propositions that integrate service areas that have been developed over time or make a bold thrust into a new opportunity like modernization or even digital.

By the year 2012, Zensar had all the arsenal it needed to compete and succeed in deal sizes of 10 to 50 million, and the real challenge was to get invited to the big parties with so many larger competitors willing to compete on price or commitments to either protect or win deals of that size. Zensar had balanced services across package application areas in the entire range of the Oracle and SAP product lines, a comprehensive suite of solutions and services in applications development testing modernization, and support and capabilities in chosen areas of BPO and BPM. The thrust toward verticalization had begun as well, with manufacturing, retail, banking, and insurance identified as key thrust verticals for the company, and investments made in domain specialists as well as point solutions in areas where a product approach, rather than a "we-will-build-the-solution-for-you" approach, would hasten time to market and improve the nonlinearity of revenues, which is the holy grail for all companies in the industry. And investments in heavy hitters in sales, pre-sales, and solution architecting in the key markets of the US, Europe, and Africa had positioned it well to have consultative discussions with clients in all these markets. New collaborative models with existing and new clients have also been developed and tested, including joint investments, joint ventures, and even the setting up and managing of captive centers for supporting mission-critical products and processes for global clients.

Digital and e-commerce are the big new gorillas that all companies in the sector are chasing, and Zensar has been an early mover in this space, having partnerships with global consulting firms and world-renowned academic institutions and research centers giving it the intellectual bandwidth to stand up and be counted among the ranks of thought leaders in digital transformation solutions in chosen verticals. The recent formation of the 3 × 3 × 3 cube focuses the company on the core verticals and territories and also clearly articulates that Applications Management Services, including Custom and Packages, Infrastructure Management, and digital and e-commerce, will be the focus areas of the future for the company.

The "Big Boys' Club" is a moving target, very similar to the market capitalization levels at which companies obtain research coverage by market and industry analysts or the revenue level at which a service area makes it to the famous Gartner magic quadrant. What is important for Zensar today is the confidence level in the management team that there is no summit too high to be climbed and no challenge within our chosen 3 × 3 × 3 cube of focus that we do not have the ability to take on and win. For a company that emerged from the ashes of a hardware business at a time when the industry was hardly in a growth phase and chose to compete and succeed with the best, the story has been one where the entire team can look back with pride, pause for a moment of reflection, and then move on to an even harder climb to success. Truly, it has been said that excellence is journey and not a destination, and Zensar is one company that truly enjoys the ride!

Pradipto Mohapatra was reminiscing and reflecting upon the Zensar story as he saw it in all the years that he has been associated with the company, first as the Head of the Technology Sector of the RPG group and now as a Director on the board:

> What stands out in my mind when I think of Zensar is a story of sustained "frugal innovation." Innovations need investments. That is truism you might say. This is however not seen with such clarity by the investors. After all, trying innovations is fraught with risks. Appetite to take risks is always proportional to investor's memories of risk–reward experience in the past. This is a true challenge to leaders who manage enterprises. Namely, where lies the boundary to the amount of investments to be made in innovations and the risk profile attached. Few leaders

manage to make innovations "frugal." Zensar is one such story. Let me start with a brief historical perspective.

By the time we entered the new millennium, Zensar was already 75 years old with a very chequered history. As part of International Computers, UK, the company came to India to first manufacture calculating machines and subsequently to become the pioneer in mainframe computer manufacture in India. As mainframe computing began to make way to Unix and Desktops, the company's trouble times began. Inability to move into new technologies brought the company to near financial ruins. Infusion of three new investors, namely RPG Group, Fujitsu, and Electra Partners, brought some new energy and initiatives to resolve a rather difficult past. By the year 2000, the company had grown to some Rs 200 crore revenue, changed its name from Fujitsu ICIM to Zensar, but the ghosts of the past were still lurking! So what did the leaders of the company do to grow the company fifteen times over the next fifteen years and grow the profit before tax thirty times during the same period? It started off by declaring a dividend to the shareholders after a gap of fifteen years. That was only the beginning!

The key task for the leaders in consultation with the shareholders was to lay down clear boundaries to embark on innovations, admittedly frugal. Broadly, they were as follows:

1. Revenue had to grow in high teens and profitability to grow from 5 to 15 percent. Therefore, profit before tax (PBT) should be growing at least between 1 and 2 percent every year.
2. All investments and innovations needed to be internally generated, therefore limiting the scope for big-bang investments. No innovation was to bring down short-term profitability.
3. Adoption of new technology spaces and acquiring new range of customers to reduce overdependence on very limited number of clients.
4. All geographical diversifications to yield both short-term and medium-term profitability.

5. To innovatively fund acquiring clients and competencies through inorganic acquisitions.
6. Providing motivation and stickiness to younger employees by offering them sustainable careers in competition to tier-I companies.

It may seemingly look very contradictory that these boundaries are inhibitors to innovation. The Zensar story is one of intense innovation by using these boundaries as positive guarders to provide a path to the future rather than look at them as inhibitors. Zensar managed to achieve these. It is surely possible if the leaders are committed.

CHAPTER 3

Building a Credible Full-Services Organization

One of the key priorities that the new CEO, Ganesh, set for the organization when he took over the reins was to move away from the flawed business model of being a glorified body-shopping company for clients in the US and the UK and instead focus on building a credible offshore services organization.

Therefore, one of the first things that the new leadership team did was to take the bold decision of systematically moving away from all staff augmentation businesses, while trying to salvage all client relationships that we could. So the team set about figuring out the key growth engines for building the new-order organization that can deliver offshore services to global customers.

The choice of the growth pillars had to be based on both the external market opportunity and trends of the outsourcing industry that was just about beginning to recover from the big Dot Com bust.

The three growth pillars identified for the new business model were as follows:

1. Application services business, which included design, development, maintenance, and support of customer applications across technologies.
2. ERP or package implementation business, which by then was gaining rapid market share among the outsourced services markets and also an increasing share of the client organizations' IT budgets.
3. Infrastructure services, which was a very nascent service in the early 2000s, but did show the promise of becoming one of the core outsourced services in the years to come.

The evolution cycles that each of these three services went through in the next decade have been very distinct and interesting, as we kept tweaking and refining our strategies for each of these based on the dynamic market forces and our own customer needs and wants.

FOCUS ON PACKAGE IMPLEMENTATION PAYS OFF

The Premise of Growth

"Everywhere is walking distance if you have the time," so spoke Steven Alexander Wright, an American comedian, actor, writer, and an Oscar-winning film producer. This, in many significant ways, epitomizes the Oracle growth story at Zensar. Oracle was a clear chosen growth option by Zensar, among others, since its inception in 2000. The growth story for Oracle at Zensar has been that of goals and dreams, which the senior management and several committed associates within Zensar's Oracle practiced, nurtured, believed in passionately, and successfully accomplished, walking on the defined path every day, regardless of challenges, with a unified goal to succeed without distracted by anything else.

The belief that Oracle's growth goals were within walking distance backed by the undeterred focus and time to realize them has resulted in Zensar's Oracle practice today being the fastest-growing, innovative, full-service capabilities across Oracle's breadth of products and a leader among the global tier-II IT service organizations.

In reality, the Oracle growth story success within Zensar was operated like many start-ups within a larger integrated practice. The start-up culture was an integral part of our growth journey, which fueled several successes within the larger integrated Oracle practice. More importantly, it has helped us nurture a futuristic work culture and fostered a solution to attract, retain, and grow non-traditional workforce that thinks differently.

Nitin Parab, chief executive and head of our largest business unit of enterprise solutions, is a career Zensarian and also a boomerang hire. He had started his career with ICIM and rejoined us after a short stint in the industry. Nitin's passion for the Oracle business and his unshakeable and steadfast faith in the potential for Oracle to become Zensar's path to market leadership are folklore in Zensar. He is the man behind the extraordinary Oracle story that we have built in the last one decade.

In his own words, he shares this story:

> I still remember my first day in Zensar. I knew it would be a steep uphill climb to galvanize support for a big-bang approach to building Oracle business. Till then, the management team had decided to keep away from the biggest IT services opportunity of the century (Y2K), was still largely body shopping through third parties, and the notion of Oracle was still alien to most at offshore. Oracle services contributed $2M to Zensar's revenue, and all of it was professional services business through KPMG.
>
> There was no doubt in my mind that the *only* way to fulfill our aspiration of building a scalable direct client relationship-based business was to put to end our relationship with KPMG and shut down the existing $2M revenue stream.
>
> Fast forward, Oracle services is the largest revenue service line in Zensar today and more importantly a service which has opened doors for us in 8 of our top 10 accounts. If I have to look back and point out what worked well, here is how I would summarize it:
>
> Practice leadership proximity to the customer.

Building a Credible Full-Services Organization   35

Offshore leadership's deep involvement in direct customer communication.

Extremely close-knit organization. Founding members of the practice are still in Zensar and share deep bonds with people managing the practice today.

Continued innovation and change in solutions and delivery processes.

Strong customer partnerships.

One of the finest team in the industry.

Big break from Cisco to leverage offshore for the first time.

Organization's willingness to put a structure, comp plan, and other policies in place to incubate a new business which was very different from other service lines in the company.

Last but not the least, management team's bold move to shut down low-margin, nonscalable, third-party professional services business and take the risk of making fresh investments in setting up a direct channel business.

Truly, this growth story has the potential nuances of being a strong empirical case study at management schools for aspiring management graduates and research associates.

TOTAL INTEGRATION WITH ORACLE

Around 2000, most IT services organizations, including valued added resellers, were focused on riding the growth of Oracle Corporation's range of enterprise class products, which presented a viable and real growth opportunity. Oracle, in addition to being the first company to build and sell the relational database management systems (RDBMS) software, also had a strong ERP product and several contextual tools, required for a global enterprise client. Oracle's strategy of plowing back significant part of revenue into research and development, driving close connect with industry leaders and experts for feedback and disruptive ideas, and working closely with its global partners enabled it attain a leadership position across a diverse range of enterprise software products. This further strengthened Zensar's resolve and commitment to be a global leader for Oracle-enabled services to its clients. Oracle's success and focus truly led Zensar's transformation focus to be a leader in Enterprise applications space.

A LITTLE INTRODUCTION TO ORACLE FOR OUR NON-IT READERS

Oracle Corporation is a US-based integrated business software and hardware systems provider, specializing in developing and marketing of enterprise software products. Oracle basically started its business with the database product, popularly known as RDBMS—its flagship product that is today the most sought-after database for enterprise software systems. It is the foundation for all enterprise software systems and supports almost all operating systems and platforms prevailing today.

> Further growth for Oracle came from the realization that companies grow their businesses, crucial needs of managing and monitoring a lot of data emerges beyond the boundary of simple storage. These include managing data for various business functions such as finance, employee records, sales, payroll, manufacturing, supply chain, and logistics, etc. Oracle has since started developing software solutions for an enterprise, popularly known as ERP (enterprise resource planning) including customer relationship management (CRM) software and supply chain management (SCM) software etc. The third category of Oracle's enterprise products includes various tools that support development, integration, reporting, access, security, etc. and several other automation tasks. Considering that various industry/sectors have their own specific requirements, Oracle has developed several products leveraging its RDBMS, ERP products and tools to build vertical configured solutions. Oracle today is one of the leading integrated software and hardware solutions organization for an enterprise.

Zensar's Oracle growth story is one of the key outcomes of its ambition to transform itself into an enterprise solutions organization. The enterprise solutions growth, specifically for packaged ERP and associated contextual tools, has gone through several changes in the past 15 years. Influenced by technology and architecture changes—contemporary as well as disruptive. The movement from client server architecture to the networking computing architecture to the disruptive internet computing architecture and the cloud-based architecture in recent times has been a single important phenomenon shaping the enterprise solutions services growth.

ORACLE'S GROWTH STORY IS ZENSAR'S GROWTH STORY

Oracle as an organization also kept innovating and launched new products, which created new markets for it over a period of time. Oracle also introduced the latest technologies regularly to integrate industry requirements and clearly emerge as a dominant player in IT enterprise solutions industry. Experience assimilated by Zensar from this phenomenon was crucial for its Oracle practice growth. It helped deploy pragmatic and enduring strategies to help Zensar stay relevant and on growth path. Zensar's Oracle growth grew significantly from a value accretion perspective, increase in global markets, consolidate its position, rework its growth strategies, and successfully counter its competition to be a full-services organization.

Zensar, since its inception in 2000, was also subject to various stages of growth influenced by the above emerging technology disruptions that defined its global geographic and competitive status. Oracle's story has been that of aggressive growth, which it achieved by taking risks and investing in the future. The experience assimilated by its Oracle practice by tracking Oracle corporations' growth strategy closely and leveraging it for Zensar as a whole has been instrumental in making Zensar emerge as a competent tier-II IT services organization. Some key benefit accruals, as a result of this across-the-overall Zensar operating ecosystem—internal and external—have notably been:

Oracle Services Growth

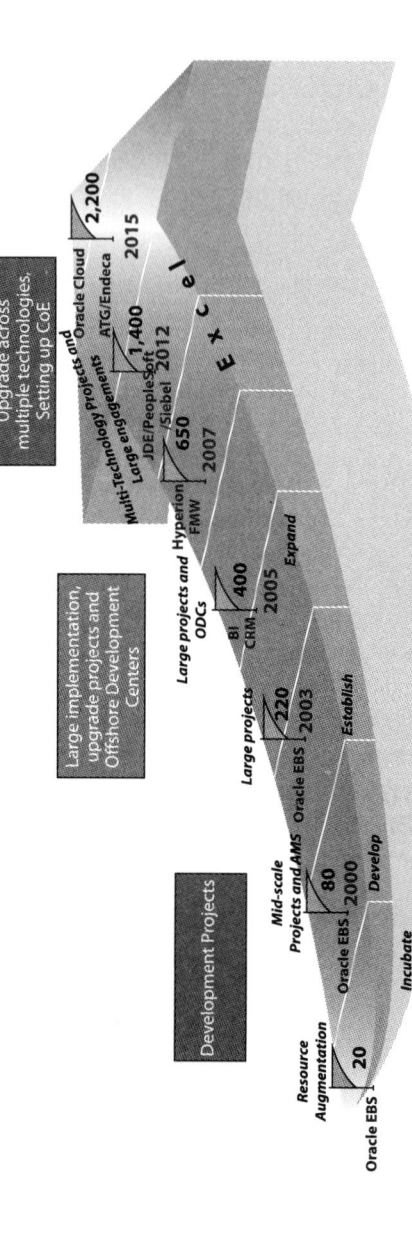

Building a Credible Full-Services Organization   39

1. process optimization.
2. fostering deep quality focus.
3. mindful and tight integration of Zensar's and vendor's process, standards, and best work practices.
4. quest for service delivery innovation.
5. an approach of cautious experimentation.
6. mastering the global distributed delivery model in line with the requirements of a global ERP system.
7. empowerment as a necessity and path to growth and talent retention.
8. eye on future and actions grounded on reality.
9. develop and nurture key visionaries with a concoction of various roles—advisor, strategist, consultant, user, facilitator, and skeptic among the many few.

CONTINUOUS GROWTH AND STAYING RELEVANT

Oracle Corporation's strategy for growth supported by its strategies for products, markets, clients' involvement, and notably involving partner organizations in its growth process, was a key influence shaping Zensar's Oracle growth story. Oracle pursued an acquisition strategy consciously and aggressively over the past decade to exponentially expand its presence in enterprise solutions space. With more than 125+ acquisitions fueling Oracle's core enterprise solutions, for Zensar, the dependence on Oracle as a significant growth driver was natural and crucial. Zensar clearly stayed aligned with Oracle vehicle as the growth for the future—unified vision, strength, and enterprise solutions focus. Zensar's community of visionaries within Oracle practice further reinforced the growth. Some notable actions by Zensar were as follows:

1. Competency of the breadth and depth of core technology and products—database, ERP applications, and functional

and domain-packaged solutions, such as product lifecycle management (PLM), Primavera, human capital management (HCM), etc., was sized up significantly to address the requirements of its global clients.
2. Zensar planned to build a new Oracle competency every year, in addition to strengthening the existing ones further. Significant among these were Fusion Middle Ware given the impending opportunities in areas such as service-oriented architecture, integration, security, etc., and HCM, which covered the conventional and recently acquired products such as Taleo, and business intelligence (BI) and enterprise performance management (EPM).
3. BI and EPM have been significant drivers for Oracle's growth. The product and functional offerings in this space had grown substantially over the years, leveraging technology as well as business functionality options. Zensar today has undeniably the significant BI and Hyperion (EPM) practice among the tier-II global IT organizations. This had been crucial to Oracle practice growth in several ways—expanding its services, opening up new accounts, and leveraging this technology to replace conventional solutions.
4. Partnering with partner organizations in innovative manner much ahead of the product conceptualization as well as across the entire product life-cycle process and subsequently. Zensar leveraged the option to be a beta partner to Oracle to test its future ERP applications ahead of their commercial launch.
5. Codevelopment as an option became increasingly partner focused, and Zensar saw this as an opportunity to leverage further.

GROWTH HAS HELPED LEARN THE ART OF MAKING ACQUISITIONS

Zensar's competency-building initiatives as well as partnership with global Oracle offices, including its global IDC for co-development, were significant for its global clients. Zensar believed that nothing is simple, but the journey it undertook to ascertain Oracle's rationale for its expansion through new products acquisition and new technology initiatives was interesting, as they provided real and plausible growth options. Further, Zensar's partnership with larger Oracle leadership globally across the US, Indian global delivery center, Europe, Middle East, and Africa (EMEA), and South Africa expanded phenomenally.

Zensar learnt the art of making acquisitions as part of the Oracle growth journey. Starting with Thought Digital to acquire focused application tools to promote accuracy and reusability, Zensar has today made a major acquisition in Oracle ecommerce service space by acquiring Professional Access—an acknowledged global leader in dedicated ecommerce space. This helped Zensar learning the overall nuances of acquisitions and firmly realizing that integrating the cultures of Zensar and acquired firm's culture is the final destination for this journey. Thanks to Oracle's focus, today Zensar has come a long way with acquisitions come to be an integral part of its growth and expansion strategy.

ACQUIRING, RETAINING, AND GROWING GLOBAL CLIENTS

Acquiring and retaining clients and their growth is the single most focus for any competency growth and firm acquisition strategy. Zensar's competency-building initiatives, acquisition of firms involved in niche technology and services, such as ecommerce, accelerator solutions, and so on, and partnership with global Oracle offices, including its global IDC for codevelopment, have been a significant advantage for its global clients. This has led to new and enhanced services across Oracle product and technology breadth, acquisition of experienced resources with niche skills that optimize risks, and more important it has helped clients optimize the vendor ecosystem. The presence of several clients with Zensar for over a decade and with expanding business scope over the years is a testimony to this fact.

A significant advantage for Zensar as a result of this Oracle growth story is leveraging other services outside the Oracle stack, including infrastructure management (IM), application support, and emerging skills around digital technologies. Zensar believes that nothing is simple, but the journey it undertook to ascertain Oracle's rationale for its expansion through new products acquisition and new technology initiatives was interesting as they provided real and plausible growth options.

THE EMERGING DIGITAL CHALLENGE AND TEST OF SIGNIFICANCE FOR ORACLE'S FUTURE: WHAT NEXT?

Oracle practice within Zensar over the years has become a global competent professional group. Armed with necessary depth of skills and experience, it is capable to provide complete services across the Oracle enterprise solution stack. What is significant is the ability to nurture new competency and skills quickly and deploy them successfully. This is the result of the continuous focus and resilience built over the years at Zensar. This has also helped Zensar to focus on becoming the world's first enterprise-wide SEI Capability Maturity Model (CMM) level 5 company with industry expertise that spans retail, manufacturing, banking, insurance, and utilities. Zensar also expanded its sales and operations presence across new markets in the US, EMEA, Asia, and South Africa regions using Oracle competency as a focus.

The emerging dynamic cloud market is clearly and rapidly becoming the new model for enterprise computing. Oracle is clearly taking note of this and initiated several strategic and operational initiatives to address this and retain its leadership position in the enterprise applications space. Some key questions that we are addressing proactively within Zensar to address this potentially disruptive opportunity are as follows:

1. Do we need to redesign ERP growth story? This is possibly a question for technocrats, designers, users, industry experts, and the technology graduates who plan to seek an enterprise applications career in future.
2. We need to feel personal about the digital opportunity and the potential impact it has on the ERP-led enterprise applications growth.
3. Continue to ask good questions about growth—what next?

Zensar's Oracle growth journey through the years was marked by exciting happening, including disruptive changes in technology, such as the Internet, cloud, increased commitment by Zensar leadership from a willingness to be a leader and take risks, backed by an outright and selfless commitment at the top and committed Oracle visionary leaders, reinforced by similar passion at the larger execution level among a majority of associates.

Undoubtedly, this journey with Oracle has helped Zensar in emerging as a complete enterprise solutions organization. Truly, these are partners in progress today in every sense.

Srinivas Polsani leads our global Oracle practice organization. He has built this practice over the last six years to become one of the three growth engines for Zensar's future strategy. Srini, as we fondly call him, is superexcited about the opportunity he sees for Zensar to become a market leader in Oracle. In his words:

> Over the last couple of years, we increased our efforts and investments in improving our Oracle capabilities. This has helped us tremendously in strengthening our engagements with existing customers and acquiring new logos. Today, we are able to demonstrate and quantify business value that we deliver to our customers. Going forward Oracle will continue to be a growth

driver for the organization with credible customer references and strong delivery excellence. Our goal of tripling Oracle revenues by 2020 is easily achievable with the comprehensive portfolio of services that we have and the ability to quickly adapt to fast changing technologies. It is definitely exiting times for the Oracle team at Zensar.

THE STRENGTHENING OF APPLICATIONS AND PROCESS MANAGEMENT

The stupendous growth of the Indian IT industry in mid-to-late 1990s, fueled by the Y2K and Dot Com boom, saw the birth, growth, and maturing of what continues to be the core of the Indian IT industry—the AMS business.

Zensar, then ICIM, was largely a staff augmentation company that provided trained software professionals to US and UK clients. For some reason, the company decided not to ride on the Y2K boom and stuck to its model of providing professionals rather than pitching for services to be delivered offshore from India. So in that sense, Zensar missed the Y2K bus that saw the birth of many of today's IT giants in India.

It was only during the short but visionary leadership stint of Mr L.C. Singh, who took over the reins of ICIL, that the company went through a period of transformation, including being rebranded as "Zensar"—the essence of knowledge.

During this period, the company grappled with continuous and rapid changes in technology, which warranted bringing in new skills into the workforce as well as reskilling and retraining of our engineers. Two distinct technology trends that impacted us were as follows:

1. IBM's leadership in mainframes: By this time, ICL's fortunes were on the wane, and IBM mainframes with CICS/Cobol/JCL were filling the mainframe landscape. While we did a few projects in CICS–Cobol, our

mainframe business gradually faded away in the absence of a mainframe development platform.
2. Databases: For some time, it seemed that Informix would emerge as the database of the future, but we saw Oracle fast emerging as the database choice of the future.

These technology shifts meant we had to build a whole new technical organization and a new set of capabilities to service customers in these technologies.

It is to the credit of Mr L.C. Singh that the organization went through a quick restructuring that saw the birth of new lines of business in line with the industry trends and market opportunities.

MISSION PLUS: EMERGENCE OF OFFSHORE DEVELOPMENT CENTERS

In 1996, we carried out a small offshore project (half a million USD) for the IT department of a US technology company. It was a first for them and went largely unnoticed by their IT community until someone in their commercial department realized a year later in 1997 that they had saved a million US dollars for the company on the project that was executed offshore by Zensar. This was followed by a visit by their senior managers to our company in Pune to understand how all this had happened and also validate that they had indeed saved money on the project. The rest is history as the Cisco Offshore Development Center (ODC) was set up at that time and has grown several times in scale and scope to become our largest and longest-standing customer and continues to be so.

What followed quickly was the setting of such dedicated ODCs for other global clients. In 1997, Transco (name adopted by British Gas post legislation to open the industry to competition) sent out a request for pricing for setting up an ODC in India. After a very successful engagement on the 19 Million Sites and Meters scalability project and with a large on-site presence, we were their chosen vendor. Unfortunately, the ODC contract was granted to one of the then big three players of Indian IT. Mr Les Dawson,

CEO of British Gas, told us that we were naturally their first choice, but they could not give us the ODC as we were too small. Undeterred, we continued to delight the customer in the professional manner in which we performed a knowledge transfer to our competitor. This did not go unnoticed, and in 1998, when Transco decided to set up a second ODC in India for their IT function, it came to us.

Like Cisco and Transco, this period saw a number of successful ODC engagements, such as PONL, Sprint, Marks & Spencer, and Fujitsu, to name a few.

By 1998, it was clear that our customers were in need of varied services from offshore. These included the full spectrum of AMS ranging from development and enhancements to support and maintenance. ODCs were the best way to bundle these services for a customer, and the company rose to the occasion by branding these services under a service line called Mission Plus.

FIRST WAVE OF DOT COM: BLUECHILLI.COM

This period was also marked by the first wave of the Dot Com boom that took the industry by a storm. At that time, it seemed that the dot coms were poised to replace brick-and-mortar businesses and would redefine the shape and contours of the IT industry. We too bet heavily on the Internet industry having missed the Y2K bus and set up our own "skunk works." We introduced BlueChilli. Com, our answer to the Dot Com challenge.

Technology investments were made so that our offerings could be hosted on our own servers. Our first offering, "ThreeMumkeys. com," a lifestyle site, was launched in 1998, and we were well poised to take a leadership position in the Dot Com space. Unfortunately, the first wave was not able to sustain the rapid growth and the bubble burst in 2000.

However, BlueChilli.com continued as a subbrand under Zensar for some time for a bundle of services addressing the Dot Com industry.

PROCESS EXCELLENCE DRIVING BUSINESS VALUE: PROCESS PLUS

Even as we consistently evolved in our own process maturity levels, embracing the ISO or CMM quality frameworks, we began to pass on the benefits of our high process maturity to our customers in the form of continuous improvements and innovations in our software deliveries. Soon, many of our customers began to reach out to us for help in their own internal process improvement initiatives. This in fact encouraged us to set up. As we began to pass on the benefits of our high process maturity to our customers in the form of continuous improvements and innovations in our software deliveries, many of our customers began to reach out to us for help in their own internal process improvement initiatives. This in fact encouraged us to set up Process Plus, an IT process consulting practice where we began to work with the internal IT teams of our client organizations to help them in setting up best-in-class software practices and processes as well as readying them for external ISO and CMM certifications.

We also started setting up vendor management office and program management office functions for the clients and advising them on process excellence tools such as Six Sigma and Lean.

We performed our first process consulting assignment way back in 1996—a process definition exercise for British Gas Service in the UK. By then, UK legislation has opened up gas distribution requiring British Gas to scale up their "Sites and Meters" database to 19 million entities from a quarter million. Through a scalability study carried out by us, followed by a series of consulting engagements, we helped British Gas choose and implement a solution. This was followed by a series of process consulting assignments for other global clients.

Today, our IT process consulting practice is a very strong practice that is driven by practitioners who come with extensive experience in software delivery as well as process excellence initiatives.

COMING OF AGE: THE APPLICATION SERVICES BUSINESS

AMS continues to be our dominant service line, driving 60 percent of our business even today. The AMS practice is the largest practice with over 2,000 practitioners and drives a full-services portfolio cutting across technologies, platforms, and industry verticals.

This business has been the dominant growth engine for the organization for the first decade in the new century and continues to be the dominant service in all our strategic client accounts and a critical component today in all our large deal propositions.

This business went through a transformation in the last 10 years, as we mastered the art of supporting our customers' IT platforms and application suites faster, cheaper, and better. While efficiencies, productivity, and quality were the drivers for the growth of our AMS business in the early years, the business has gone through a transformation in the last five years in terms of the delivery platforms, engagement models, and commercial model.

PURSUING AN AMBIDEXTROUS STRATEGY: THE THREE-HORIZON FRAMEWORK

It was around 2006, when the author and CEO came back from his AMP stint at the Harvard Business School, equipped with new tools and frameworks for effective strategy management, that we adopted the Ambidextrous strategy model of "exploit and explore" for rehashing our services portfolio as well as redefining our market segmentation and revising our investment plans in building new capabilities for growth.

We borrowed IBM's three-horizon framework to map and segment our services portfolio and create specific strategies for each of them in terms of market segmentation, go-to-market plans, investment strategies, and demand generation strategies.

BUILDING EXCELLENCE: CENTERS OF EXCELLENCE FOR HORIZON 1 SERVICES

We mapped our most mature services to Horizon 1, where we had reached high maturity levels in terms of capability, competency, and customer credibility. These were services where we were exploiting the high maturity levels to drive efficiencies through automation, reuse, and standardization. Our AMS services were clearly Horizon 1 services along with our Oracle ERP services.

Services in this horizon were dominant drivers of our growth in terms of both scale and profit margins. Therefore, our strategy for these services was to aim for a well-differentiated leadership position in these services where we become the vendor of choice for our customers. Thus, we invested in setting up several centers of excellence (CoEs) for these services with the charter to

1. build world-class services and solutions capability
2. train and groom a set of subject matter experts
3. build a strong partner ecosystem to provide complete solutions to customers
4. develop thought leadership points of view
5. build prototypes for white labeling of new solutions

We set up technology CoEs for Java, Microsoft, and IBM, which have today matured into very strong technology practices driving both growth and differentiation.

NEW CYCLES OF GROWTH: HORIZON 2 SERVICES

Services in this horizon were those that we had been investing in for the past three to four years and had now reached a state of stability and critical mass where they were helping us in acquiring new clients as well as expanding our footprint in existing client accounts. Services in this horizon became our key wedges for exploring new business through new customer acquisition. Our strategy for these services was to continue to invest in scaling the capability and in driving market penetration and demand creation. Testing, infrastructure, and SAP ERP services were the dominant services in this horizon.

Today, all of these Horizon 2 services have moved into Horizon 1, having reached high levels of maturity, and become significant growth drivers for business and customer acquisition.

FUTURE PROOFING: HORIZON 3 SERVICES

Even as we were exploiting the maturity of the Horizon 1 services and exploring new markets with the Horizon 2 services, we were equally focused on the need to build for the future to not only stay relevant in the Industry but to also continue to meet and exceed our customer needs.

So we continued to keep investing in new and nascent technologies and capabilities. Some of the services that we had nurtured in this Horizon are today strong wedges and are driving new market penetration. Our investments in mobility, BI, customer relationship management (CRM), and cloud as part of the Horizon 3 strategy have paid off very well, and today all these are very mature practices with full-services portfolios and strong alignment to our verticalization strategy and plans. They have all moved to Horizon 1 or 2 services now.

However, not all of our Horizon 3 investments reached maturity and they were not expected to either. Some of them were scuttled, as we did not see the business viability for them at that point in time. These included our foray into embedded systems, product engineering services, and Microsoft Dynamics ERP, among other smaller investments.

We continue to rehash our three-horizon services framework every two years, and our current Horizon 3 services include the new generation of digital, platform solutions, robotics and autonomics, Internet of Things (IoT), smart support, and DevOps, among others. We are making significant investments in building solutions and services in all of these areas, as we see that these will drive the future of the IT industry.

Apart from these technology-led services, our Horizon 3 focus is also on industry-specific business solutions driving business outcomes for our customers. More details about our industry-led domain solutions are covered in Chapter 6 on our vertical story.

Prasad Deshpande, a long-term Zensarian for almost two decades, heads our global Applications Practice organization. The practice under his able leadership has been pursuing a bimodal approach to the Applications Business, exploiting the maturity of our Horizon 1 services for bringing in large and strategic deals, while exploring the Horizon 2 services to mine our strategic client accounts. He and his team are making significant investments in building new capabilities in areas such as automation and robotics and are very excited about the opportunity to drive transformation of the Applications Business for our customers. In his words:

> I have been in Zensar little over 19 years and have played various roles across delivery, practice, regions, and services. I have seen and experienced Zensar responding dynamically to the changing business scenarios under the able leadership of Ganesh. In my current role as the Global Practice Head of AMS and Mobility, we have clear focus on innovation and automation in the services bringing in meaningful benefits to our customers. We are constantly building technology solution accelerators to help our customers gain benefits like faster time to market and reduced cost of delivery. We are also transforming our practice and people capabilities to build business solutions for our customers that can drive tangible business outcomes for them.
>
> Our goal is to scale the AMS business of Zensar to half a billion by the year 2020 and become the most respected and recommended services organization for our customers for AMS services and solutions.

DISCOVERING IM: TRIALS AND TRIBULATIONS

Back to the Future

IM is not new to Zensar. As already mentioned elsewhere in this book, Zensar's earlier avatar, "ICIM," started its life as an Indian subsidiary of a British OEM. Not only was it selling ICL-branded hardware in India, it also boasted of having the only manufacturing facility of ICL outside of Great Britain. Warranty and post-warranty maintenance support of the ICL hardware was an integral part of ICIM's offerings and continued to be its main profit engine for decades—right up to the 1980s. Only the hardware support services in those days were not yet called "IM services," as they are known in the IT industry today.

Thereafter, in the 1990s, ICIM's hardware portfolio expanded beyond ICL products to include hardware from Fujitsu, Centronics, Sun, and numerous "IBM compatible" technologies. As a result, the customer services arm of ICIM also had to morph itself to provide hardware break-fix support for the myriad of hardware assets—an offering that is nowadays known as multivendor support (MVS) services. Unfortunately, when ICIM exited from the hardware business before the turn of the century, it also exited the world of MVS and IM services.

With the reintroduction of IM services into Zensar's portfolio of offerings in the last 10 years, and the addition of MVS capability through Akibia even more recently, it was back to the future for Zensar.

Hiring of Employee Number One

During the first five years of Zensar's existence as a software services company, that is, from 2000 to 2005, the focus of the company was solely on servicing the application management requirements of its global customers. However, as Zensar's customer relationships started becoming deeper and the competition in its accounts started becoming more intense, it became evident that by providing AMS alone, Zensar was not addressing all the needs of the customer CIO. Not having IM services as part of Zensar's offerings was giving competition an open invitation to walk into Zensar's key accounts and thereafter attempt, sometimes successfully, to get into Zensar's application management space.

The management team then took a call in 2006 to set up a new IM services practice in Pune. It was to be a classic startup operation, as the practice had to be built virtually from scratch. A Bengali gentleman, Mr Ankit Ghosh, was hired as the IM practice—quite literally employee number one of the IM practice. His task was to put together a small team of IM practitioners, who in turn were to build and launch Remote Infrastructure Management Services (RIMS).

The initial reaction from sales was lukewarm, as not everyone who had been selling AMS for most of their careers was comfortable selling the newly launched IM services. The response from the customers, however, was more positive. Many congratulated Zensar for having filled the void in its offerings, and some were even willing to give IM a try.

Over the next three years, Zensar's RIMS business grew by leaps and bounds from zero to almost $12 million in revenue.

Need for Scale

While the progress made was quite satisfying, it became evident that with sole reliance on organic growth it will be a long time before the IM services business would attain critical mass. And critical mass was needed to demonstrate scale without which Zensar was not getting invited to the larger parties.

If you survey CIOs and ask them what keeps them up at night, they will tell you that one-third of their headaches relate to IT infrastructure, while the rest relate to management of applications. By simple extrapolation, Zensar needed one-third of its capability to be in the IM space. Translating in business terms, one-third of Zensar's revenues or resources should be IM related.

Using this argument, the management team made a business case to its board in 2009 to seek approval for a sizable acquisition that would bring an additional $100 million plus to Zensar's global revenues. The board was appreciative of the progress made to date organically by the IM practice and supported the need to acquire a credible player in the IM space.

The management team then white boarded essential and desirable specifications for an ideal IM acquisition target. Among the identified capabilities were MVS or hardware break-fix services for assets from multiple OEMs and a strong security and compliance practice. The management team was also clear about what they did not want in the target company. They did not want the company to have data centers or other hosting capabilities of its own. Zensar's trusted bankers Chesapeake were commissioned once again to look for candidate companies that met as many of the listed specifications as possible.

Finding Nemo

Then started a long period of search—almost nine months of evaluation, conference calls, face-to-face meetings, due-diligence reviews, and reference checks—before the deal was concluded with Akibia. Zensar's management team were delighted with the selection, as it seemed to be a match made in heaven. Not only did Akibia have a complimentary set of IM offerings, it was also one of the most credible global players in the MVS space. Akibia had also followed a policy of remaining "asset light" and stayed away from the hosting/cloud provision space, and that strategy resonated with Zensar management's own thinking.

The marriage was consummated on January 1, 2011, with much fanfare. Akibia was to be run by the existing leadership team, under the stewardship of the then President and CEO, Tom Tucker, as an independent entity under Zensar for the first nine quarters. Its board was reconstituted, and Zensar veteran of 27 years, Vivek Gupta, was appointed as Executive Chairman of Akibia. Simultaneously, Ankit Ghosh was airdropped into Akibia as head of Global IM Practice, soon to be followed by the US Head of Finance, Anand Mitkari, and later US Head of HR, Shahina Islam.

An elaborate integration plan was crafted and put into play right from day one. While the easy, low-hanging fruits were picked within the first 12 months, the more complex integration initiatives were started only after the next 6 months. By April 1, 2013, when Akibia was renamed as Zensar Technologies IM, most HR, finance, and marketing functions had been fully integrated.

Anyone who has been closely involved with integrating an acquisition would know that the most difficult part of the integration is managing cultural differences. And here we are talking about a New England–based conservative American company merging into an India-headquartered essentially Indian company. We are talking about an owner-run privately held firm blending into a company listed on the Bombay Stock Exchange for over 50 years. And we are talking about a small company with discretionary rewards and remuneration for its employees merging into a larger company that was a part of an even larger business conglomerate with structured and well-defined processes.

The integration team did an excellent job of managing change gently yet firmly across all areas of operation. And Zensar IM, although still a legal entity and a subsidiary of Zensar Technologies, became a fully integrated strategic business unit called the "IM Business Unit (IBU)" of Zensar.

The company now had one of the most comprehensive portfolios of IM services in the industry—even more than some of the global tier-I IT companies of Indian heritage. In Vivek's words:

> No other global IT services company of Indian heritage had, or even today has, its own MVS engine. That gave Zensar a leg up on competition. And the icing on the cake was that the consolidated IM services portfolio, after bringing together the home-grown capabilities of Zensar and the acquired offerings from Akibia, was as complete as one could have asked for.

The sales teams across the newly enlarged Zensar family had to be trained to sell the expanded portfolio through multiple rounds of rollouts. For some reason, it was easier to sell IM services to existing application management customers than to sell AMS to existing IM customers—at least in the first few quarters.

Did the combined business start growing at the pace and in size that was anticipated? Not quite. As everyone knows, no two mergers and acquisitions (M&As) are alike, and most rarely deliver the results in exactly the same shape and form as their original business case. Here, the business got into the hockey stick of growth that we are all too familiar with. Both the revenue and profits shrank initially, as the business model was radically changed, before recovering and picking up pace. In the words of Ankit Ghosh, "we took longer than anticipated but we got it right. Zensar's IM practice today has all the ingredients needed to be the growth and the profit engine of Zensar."

ZENSAR IM TODAY

The Global Infrastructure Management services business today is a seamlessly integrated strategic business unit of Zensar, being managed as a profit and loss (P&L)—complete with its own sales, delivery, and practice teams. Within that, the MVS business is a sub-P&L ably led by Senior Vice President, Scott Fiore, who is the only remaining executive from the Akibia days.

The IM practice has also been tightly integrated with the application management practices, both package solutions based and custom/bespoke applications based, so as to give the customers an integrated IT experience and expertise that is second to none.

Zensar's IM services portfolio is unquestionably the widest among all tier-I and tier-II IT companies of Indian heritage. Even the multinational IT companies such as Accenture, Cap Gemini, and the like do not have as wide a portfolio. What sets Zensar's portfolio apart from these competitors is the presence of in-house global MVS (or hardware break-fix) capability that today services more than half a million assets spread across 140 countries around the world. A little trivia for you: do you know how many countries are there on our planet? Before you Google the answer, let me tell you that there are between 189 and 196 countries in the world, depending on which document Google throws up. You will agree that 140 countries are possibly as far as one would want to extend oneself before running into "problem countries." So for all practical purposes, Zensar IM is providing post-warranty hardware support, including the provision of technical support, spare parts, and field support, to every relevant country on mother Earth. While some of Zensar's larger (read tier-I) competitors do pick up MVS orders from time to time, they are usually a part of larger IT deals. And to service these MVS deals, these companies then look for credible third-party maintenance companies like Zensar to service their MVS contracts.

The second aspect of Zensar IM that sets it apart from most tier-I IT companies of Indian heritage is being "global" in every sense. Not only does Zensar operate in 140 countries, it has a workforce that is almost all-American in the US, almost all European in Europe, and of course almost all Indian at Indian offshore facilities. It services global customers who have assets spread across dozens of countries but managed through a single contract. Without mentioning names, we are talking about companies like the top retailers, high-tech manufacturers, and cloud providers of the world.

As everyone knows, you can only be as successful as the team that you put together. The current management team is a healthy mix of mainly American, Dutch, and Indian nationalities. They have blended with each other so well that they can finish each other's sentences without the usual cross-cultural hurdles and mind blocks coming in the way. But collaboration between the globally distributed IM team was not this smooth initially. A lot of effort was put in by Vivek, who is a student of Professor Geert Hofstede's theories on cultures, to make the key IM members aware of the cultural differences between associates coming from different nationalities. Until the associates were shown the mirror, the geographically spread teams were frequently intolerant of each other's behavior. The Dutch were often stereotyped by the Americans as blunt, aggressive, and insensitive, while the Americans were seen by the Dutch as political, sometimes noncommittal, and often too "indirect." Integration with Indians added another level of complexity on which enough books have been written already. The cultural integration that has been achieved can easily serve as a role model for global organizations.

EARLY MOVERS IN DIGITAL

The word "digital" is all pervasive today and has taken the industry by storm in the last few years. Today, there is no strategy of any customer, vendor, OEM, or even the government of states and countries that is not centered around a digital theme, and digital is now seen as the new mantra for all transformation plans.

Zensar's own tryst with digital began very early even when digital was not talked about in its current form. We were early enough to notice the blurring lines between business innovation and technology innovation and the changing role of the CIO function in exploiting new technology innovation to drive business growth and organizational agility.

Therefore, we felt the need to transform our CIO function to make it more market and industry facing. And since it is important to have the right leadership to drive this transformation, we moved one of our brightest delivery leaders, Ajit Pethkar, from our largest global client account into the CIO role and also entrusted him with the CTO function as well. His extensive exposure to a global client like Cisco, a technology leader by itself, has brought a new perspective, ambition, and energy to the CIO function.

It is under his stewardship that we laid the early foundation of our digital story. We set up centers of excellence for cloud, mobility, and analytics that focused on building business solutions fueled by the digital technologies for our customer to help them with their business challenges.

We also set up the IP Council under the new CIO's leadership. This council carried the charter of working with all the industry vertical experts and the digital CoEs to identify and build solution accelerators and IP solutions to create new business opportunities for Zensar through differentiation as well as drive automation and efficiencies. The CIO team has had a key role to play in our IP-led growth story, which is detailed in a later section in the book.

Under the new leadership, we transformed our CIO/CTO function from an inward-looking support function to an outward-looking business-enabler function. Today, our CIO function runs with all our innovation initiatives.

So, while a dedicated Digital Enterprise Practice was set up in 2013, the capability building had begun much earlier, and this has helped us in adopting a very holistic approach toward a Digital Vision and charter and prepared us well for the Digital Enterprise Journey.

CHAPTER 4

Thinking Vertically

THE SHIFT FROM COMMODITIZATION TO SPECIALIZATION

The move to verticalization of the Indian IT industry is a reflection of a maturing services industry and secular pressures on the provider community. The Indian outsourcing industry, which included IT and business process vendors, began to experience slower growth rates in the last five to six years due to global financial crisis and European sovereign debt crisis. Outsourcing clients began to expect and even demand rationalization of prices to deliver more for the same IT budgets. Many of them went through vendor rationalization exercises to identify vendors who can deliver greater business value by providing them technology solutions and services that can drive significant business value for them. So it was imperative for IT vendors to make the shift from service providers to solution creators and contribute to business outcomes of the client's businesses and thereby help them in their business transformation journeys.

Another trend that drove the industry toward vertical alignment was the explosive growth seen by the industry in the first decade of the new century that saw vendors expanding rapidly into new geographies and extending their services portfolio to service a wide range of customers. This explosive growth and expansion, coupled with accelerated client acquisitions and pressure from competition, had forced IT organizations to implement complex organizational structures that were not only causing internal conflicts but also affecting the organization's growth. This also led to the creation of very complex incentivization and revenue credit-sharing models that were not only too complicated to implement but further led to internal conflicts.

Therefore, it became important to simplifying the organizational structures to ensure alignment of goals, so that the energies of the organization could be focused on external market penetration, client acquisition, and business growth, instead of internal battles for revenue credit. Verticalization helped in addressing this challenge to a large extent, so this was another driver for IT firms to adopt the verticalization strategy.

It is in this context that the Indian IT players began to critically evaluate and explore ways to move up on the value chain of their client organization by aligning their services and solutions to the business needs of their clients. This saw the emergence of verticalization as a business strategy of IT players to create more value to their clients. Many Indian IT vendors, including Zensar, TCS, Cognizant Technologies, Infosys, WIPRO, and HCL Technologies, were early adopters of the verticalization strategy and over the past five years have reaped significant benefits from this strategy.

PUTTING THE PUZZLE TOGETHER: TRUE VERTICALIZATION

For a start, verticalization for most players started with simply regrouping their customers as per industry verticals, instead of services or geographies, and converting these groups into profit centers for the purpose of tracking and reporting business performance. This meant a mere realignment of business that allowed the tracking and reporting of growth differently, but did nothing much to improve customer centricity or drive business strategy of specialization and differentiation.

As the industry evolved in the last 10 years, verticalization has taken on a new dimension, and in today's context, verticalization means much more than how firms organize their business entities and report their performance. The key tenets of a truly vertically organized organization are as follows:

1. Business strategy built around vertical markets of focus
2. Sales and marketing organizations aligned to chosen verticals
3. Sales supported by strong domain subject-matter experts (SMEs) in the field
4. P&L ownership being entrusted with the vertical business leaders
5. Alignment of Sales and Marketing function to the verticals
6. HR alignment in terms of training, competency building, and career progression
7. Specialization and innovation performance (IP) to build vertical business process-centric solutions and platforms
8. Partnerships to augment domain expertise and capabilities
9. Customer value addition measured by contribution to business outcomes for customers.

THE EARLY BIRDS WON THE PLOT: EARLY ADOPTERS OF VERTICALIZATION

Cognizant Technology Solutions was one of the first IT players to have adopted the verticalization strategy in early 2000, initially focusing on the verticals of financial services, information services, and healthcare. Cognizant had not only achieved significant revenues from these verticals but also dominated these verticals for a long time. Strong client relationships, domain knowledge gained through successful execution of projects in verticals, and building strong practice leadership in these verticals are what helped them in driving their verticalized strategy. Further, some strategic acquisitions in these key focus verticals helped it in gaining a leadership position in healthcare, while moving into the top 5 in other verticals of focus.

Some players such as TCS set up industry solutions groups with multiple units, each focusing on a industry-specific vertical and independently developing resources, technical expertise, financial support, and responsible for P&L. This structure has helped in driving good revenue growth. TCS has also performed well in its strong verticals, such as banking, financial services, and insurance (BFSI), and has also entered into new verticals and seen good growth all around.

Infosys also adopted the verticalized strategy quite early in 2007 and restructured itself into six vertical industry business units and five horizontal business units, cutting across all the verticals. The strategy seemed right, but it did not deliver the expected results. So in 2011, the six verticals were collapsed into four, with the vertical heads becoming P&L heads and independently driving their merger and acquisition (M&A) strategies, managing talent and operations. The heads of geographies and service lines supported the vertical heads in the execution of their vertical strategies.

WIPRO, on the other hand, started with a more geographically aligned structure but later reorganized itself into six vertical business entities, each led by a P&L leader with client ownership and dedicated sales and delivery teams.

Therefore, there was no perfect success formula for the industry for making the verticalization strategy work. Each key player slowly evolved its own strategy over time and went through many revisions and revamps before building a vertical structure that worked best for it.

SERVICE VERTICALIZATION: BPM PLAYERS FOLLOWING SUIT

By the end of the first decade, the BPO industry had reached an inflection point in its evolution. BPO customer needs and demands had changed drastically, and for them, it was becoming increasingly important that the outsourcing partner has a comprehensive understanding of their business processes. They were no longer satisfied with vendors providing lift-and-shift BPM services or just running some of their processes in a cheaper way. They began to expect their outsourcing partners to be more strategic in their outlook and help them with BPM and optimization. Customization and specialization began to take center stage in an industry that owes its foundation to commoditization.

Industry-specific customer preferences and goals became drivers for the new era of "verticalized BPM services." For BPO companies, this meant a new orientation in the way they offered their services. To adopt a vertical focus, the BPO providers need to invest significantly in talent and technology, and this strategic shift has to be reflected as much in the way as the services are offered and billed for. Buyers want to see a high level of domain knowledge and expertise in the provider team in order to gain the confidence to go into partnership. For example, clients in the research industry wanted to see statisticians and analysts on the provider's end to be assured of industry-specific delivery. Clients in the healthcare industry wanted to see doctors or medical professionals on the provider's end to understand payer/payee issues.

There are several successful examples of M&A-led verticalization strategies in the Indian IT industry. TCS's acquisition of Citi Bank back office in India and Diligenta, an insurance outsourcing specialist, drove significant insurance business growth. Infosys's acquisition of Lodestone Consulting and sourcing and procurement vendor Portland Group along with its Infosys 3.0 strategy emphasizes its verticalization focus. HCL Technologies acquired Axon, while WIPRO has also been looking at M&A for driving its vertical strategy. The verticalization strategy is being pursued for driving nonlinear revenue growth.

CHOOSING OUR PLOT: THE FOUR VERTICALS

By 2010, we were fairly well spread in terms of both our geographical footprint and our industry verticals with the United

States continuing to be our dominant market, closely followed by the UK and South Africa. Europe, Asia-Pacific (APAC), the Middle East, and India were relatively smaller markets for us, where we were in a wait-and-watch mode.

On the alignment to industry verticals, our dominant vertical was the manufacturing vertical, given that our largest customer was a global leader in networking equipment, and this vertical was contributing to over 40 percent of our global business.

The next dominant vertical was insurance, where we were already servicing all the top insurance providers of South Africa, apart from some of the top insurance firms in the United States and the UK. Closely trailing behind the insurance vertical was retail, where we were servicing top retail players in UK and Middle East territories. Banking was the fourth largest vertical with a good footprint again in South Africa and, to a lesser extent, in Singapore in the APAC region.

We were also servicing smaller industry segments of energy and utilities, aviation, gaming, public sector, dairy, and independent software vendors, although the business from these verticals was relatively much smaller and our services were largely confined to professional services.

Therefore, the choice of verticals for us was quite straightforward when we were ready for transforming ourselves from a horizontally aligned services organization into a vertically aligned solutions organization. The drivers were the same that were driving the rest of the industry toward verticalization—specialization, nonlinear growth, and market leadership. We decided to build our vertical strategy on four key verticals: manufacturing, retail, banking, and insurance. We chose these as the four pillars of our verticalization strategy for the following reasons:

1. These were our dominant verticals of business even if it was more by accident rather than by design or as a result of any strategic market trust.
2. We had strong customer relationships in all these four verticals, many of whom were Fortune 500 and Fortune 1,000 companies and among the market leaders in their own chosen markets.

3. We had strong project execution experience in these verticals, which meant that our technical workforce, especially our project management teams and business analysts, had a fair understanding of the key business functions and processes of these client organizations. This was a good starting point for us to build a vertically aligned and domain-oriented technical workforce.
4. Lastly, the extensive experience of having serviced these clients for several years gave us good insights into their business challenges that could be leveraged to build specialized business solutions, IP, and platforms to service their stated and unstated needs.

Thus, we began our verticalization journey in 2011, but formally restructured ourselves in 2012 into a vertical organization that, we believed, would enable maximizing customer alignment, market penetration, nonlinear business growth, and business transformation.

The Four Verticals

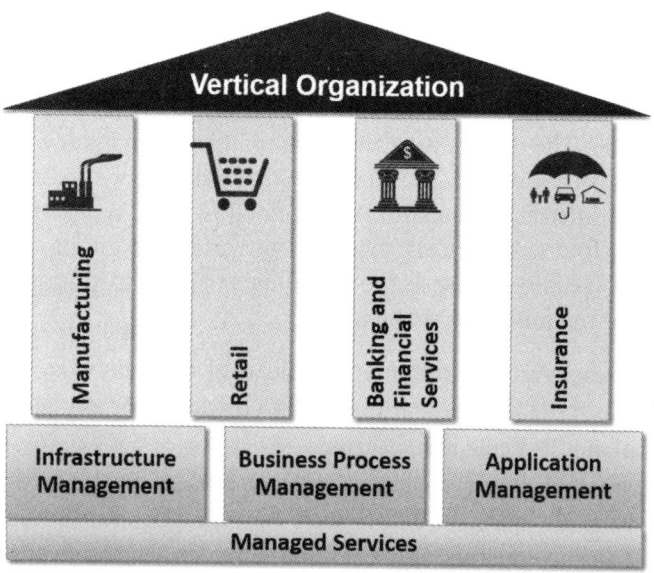

GOING BEYOND VERTICAL GROUPING OF CUSTOMERS: THE ROAD TO TRUE VERTICALIZATION

True verticalization calls for many intrinsic and extrinsic changes to the way businesses are organized, the way we segment and choose our markets to play in as well as alignment of supporting functions and operating entities from sales and marketing, business development, human resource management and IP agenda to knowledge management, and of course capability building and creation of resource pools trained in domain skills.

Embarking on the verticalization journey meant all of the above for us. We decided to go through this transformation in a phased manner, to ensure that we got it right and also had the opportunity and latitude to refine our strategy as we went along.

MOVING TO A VERTICAL STRUCTURE: BIRTH OF THE TRINITY

For the first wave of the transformation, we decided to start with laying down the foundation for creating a sustainable vertical organization. This meant restructuring our businesses and putting together a strong vertical leadership team.

By the end of the start of 2012, we had rolled out the new structure that was built on three pillars:

1. Vertical business units (VBUs), which were fully integrated profit centers with dedicated and independent delivery organizations, domain SME teams, and HR functions. The VBU heads have the ownership of the client accounts and are responsible for delivering services and solutions to meet the clients' commitments. They are also responsible for conceiving and conceptualizing domain solutions to meet their customer needs. As P&L owners, they carry the

business goals for the VBU, which include both topline growth and bottom line maximization, in addition to customer satisfaction and people management key result areas (KRAs).

The VBU heads own and drive the vertical strategy globally and have the end-to-end ownership for the growth of the vertical across all territories, service lines, and technologies. We identified three strong leaders to lead the three verticals. Deepanjan Banerjee for manufacturing, Krishna Kumar for retail, and Mohan Hastak for BFSI. While Deepanjan and Krishna Kumar were home-grown leaders having successfully led and scaled our Cisco and retail businesses, we brought in Mohan, who came with very strong BFSI domain experience as well as IT industry experience.

2. Regional business units (RBUs) are the territory units that own and drive the business strategy for each region and are headed by senior sales leaders who, as business unit heads, carry the business goals for the region. The RBUs are responsible for driving territory growth across VBUs, service lines, and technologies and carry business goals for revenue growth through both mining and hunting and also territory margins. We created four RBUs—the United States, UK and Europe, Africa and Middle East, and India—that were entrusted to four of very successful sales leaders as the RBU heads. Chakrivardhan Reddy for our US RBU, Gurdeep Grewal for the UK/Europe RBU, Harish Lala for Africa and Middle East, and Krishna Ramaswamy for India.

3. Strategic services units (SSUs) are the practice organizations that are responsible for capability building and capacity management, in addition to demand generation and fulfillment as well as sales support, which includes solutioning, presales, and IP development.

The SSU practices are organized service line wise and the practice heads carry business goals for growth of the business from the service lines from across the VBUs and RBUs. We identified practice heads from both within and outside, to lead these practices, which were logically grouped as Enterprise Solutions that were predominantly package solutions and custom solutions under two SSU heads. Prameela, one of the authors of the book, took the charge of the custom solutions practice organization, and Harish Gala was hired from Deloitte to lead the Enterprise Solutions practice organization.

In the first wave of transformation, sales continued to be aligned to the RBU organization and did not have any alignment with the verticals. And so did all the other business support functions of HR, marketing, and sales enablement.

TAKING THE BIG LEAP: DRIVING ALIGNMENT

In the second wave of the verticalization in 2013, we worked on the vertical alignment of the sales organization in our mature territories of the United States and the UK, with the sales teams getting reorganized vertical wise. This meant that we needed to equip our sales teams with solution-selling skills. Therefore, we invested in intense sales training in the vertical domain solutions and also augmented our sales organization by bringing onboard sales leaders with strong vertical alignment and solution-selling experience. In the growing territories of Europe, Africa, and India, we did not attempt this alignment yet, so they continued to sell our entire portfolio of services to their customers.

Another huge task ahead of us was the urgent need for domain orientation of our vertical delivery organization and the presales organization, which were both predominantly technically aligned. This not only meant imparting domain skills on a massive scale but also meant equipping them, especially those in customer-facing roles, to have a different kind of conversations with their client teams. It also meant understanding how our technical solutions and services were impacting the customer's business outcomes.

It was in this second wave that we took up alignment of the business support functions of sales enablement and marketing to the verticals. This meant dedicated sales support teams and marketing functions for each vertical, so that they could work closely with the vertical sales teams in driving their sales and marketing strategies. Our lead generation engine, called inside sales, also got aligned to the verticals. So, now we had telemarketing teams dedicated for each vertical that were trained by the vertical on their domain solutions and value propositions. This significantly strengthened our sales pitches and saw a huge upside in our lead generation efficiency as well as effectiveness.

In this phase, the verticals also made significant investments in the development of point solutions and domain-centric IP. They worked very closely with the SSU practice teams to create technology-enabled business solution prototypes that they began to white label for some of their customers. Thus, by the end of this second wave, the SSU practices were working on a clear charter for developing capability to design and deliver domain-centric solutions commissioned by the VBU teams.

FROM SERVICES TO BUSINESS OUTCOMES: DOMAIN-LED SOLUTIONS

Our vertical strategy focused on delivering business and technology solutions and services to our customers by developing a deep understanding of their industry, business challenges, and needs as well critical business processes. The combination of this business process understanding and domain expertise has been helping us in enabling our clients to meet their global market demands through rapidly deployable solutions. We took an integrated approach of combining processes, technology, and innovation with the help of a strong team of domain experts and backed this up with robust execution and operations rigor. This technology agnostic consulting-led system integration approach has helped us to quickly become the partner of choice for many global companies.

MANUFACTURING SOLUTIONS

In manufacturing, we began to focus on changing the way the customer produces, sources, and distributes products as well as supports the products post sale throughout the product life cycle. From digital manufacturing to promoting collaboration with the supplier ecosystem, we began to work with manufacturing customers to help them work effectively.

Whether it is increasing sales effectiveness or enabling supply-chain tracking, we are working to redefine the way manufacturing companies operate and manage their critical business processes.

We are also closely tracking the trend uptake in the world of manufacturing. While the key challenges in manufacturing have always been reducing costs and improving productivity, we see that the next big shift in the industry is not going to be about numbers, but about aligning with the digital age of technology and information. Modernization of legacy systems, reducing time to market through the use of agile practices, and automation are all opportunities for vendors such as Zensar to leverage their technology expertise and understanding of the business domain, to provide business solutions to our clients.

The IoT promises to have a major impact on manufacturing, by making the best use of production with the application of preemptive analytics. Interestingly enough, IoT is also being interpreted as integration of everything and that is a sweet spot for system integrators such as Zensar.

It is very evident that through the continuous use of digital technology, we can ensure tremendous business benefits and, combined with new business models, we can help clients grow in today's competitive marketplace.

DRIVING BUSINESS OUTCOMES FOR MANUFACTURERS

Our new-age solutions support connected products, factory floor, supply chain, and services. Here is a preview of such solution areas:

Digital Factory/Connected Shop Floor Solution

Our digital factory/connected shop floor solution offers a comprehensive portfolio of seamlessly integrated hardware, software, and technology-based services in order to support clients in enhancing the flexibility and efficiency of manufacturing processes and reducing the time to market of products. The suite comprises a large and unique portfolio of IoT, manufacturing engineering services, analytics, shop floor, and industrial automation.

Our connected shop floor solution connects shop floor to top floor for strategic decisions and policies impacting the topline.

Some key features are advanced analytics, real-time monitoring, proprietary algorithms and filters, and solid dashboards, which help strategy and policy decisions and real-time control charts to transition from a reactive to proactive approach for resolving root causes to avoid defects/breakdown, reducing cost of quality, customer satisfaction, and profitability. The smart analytics also enable the manufacturer to measure the capability of each process and ensure that they are meeting targeted performance.

Connected Shop Floor Components

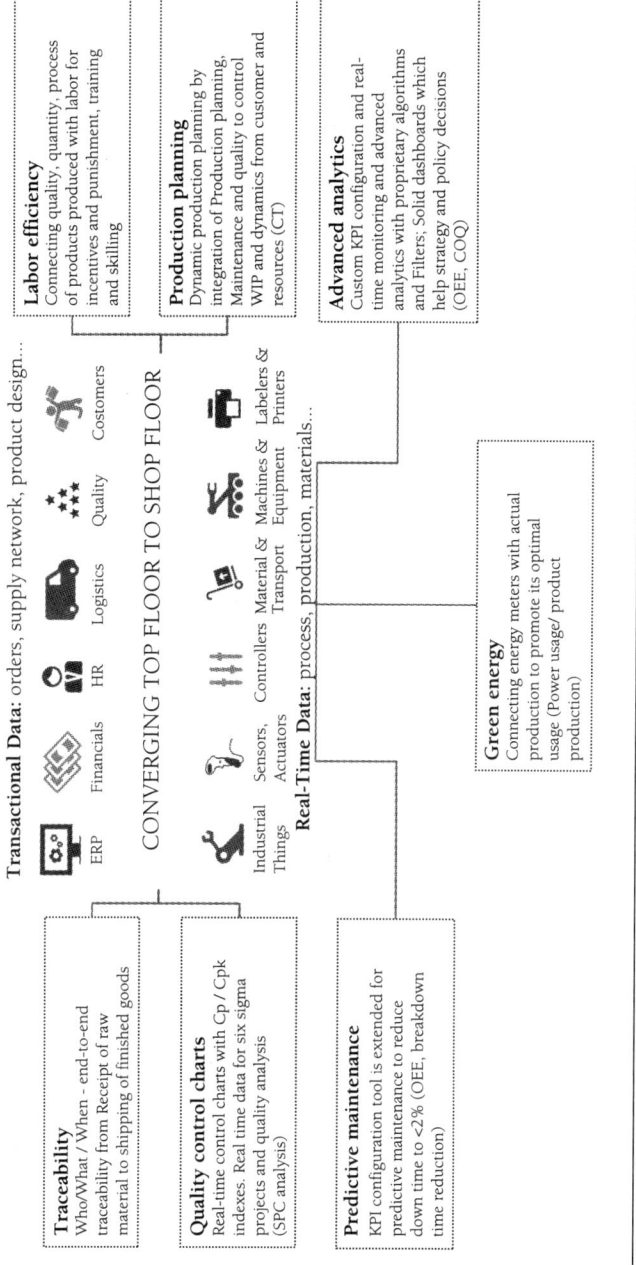

Advanced Analytics

Networked Manufacturing

An end-to-end" solution with a catalog of services including remote monitoring, predictive maintenance, global visibility dashboards and security

Remote Monitoring

Technology agnostic solution that integrates with a range of plant controllers and MES applications to provide information near real time

Good Data

Consulting team helps figure out the relevant performance indices for a plant and filters the data collection process to get to the "good data".

Social Command Centre

Scalable Cloud based Infrastructure, Framework and Model for Social Analytics behind and after new product launch

Traceability

Instant information on traceability attributes of components, products during a certain time period for the purpose of detailed analysis

Advanced Analytics Solution

Our advanced analytics solution is helping manufacturers to handle the complexity of huge data sources by providing business-relevant key performance indicators (KPIs) and detailed analytics to quickly identify potential root causes impacting process and product quality. The solution empowers manufacturing managers/engineers to make effective and accurate decisions related to opportunities for saving cost, improving product quality and overall productivity, and reducing wastages. With our solution, manufacturers can now predict future scenarios much better, proactively anticipate problems, and improve processes effectively. The solution is backed up by our industry experience, analytics expertise, as well as innovative tools.

Lean Warehousing Solution

Lean warehousing refers to designing a distribution system to create efficiencies and eliminate waste in the area of "lead time," "storage space," "warehouse head count," and "inventory" [raw, work-in-progress (WIP), and finished goods]. Lean is a continuous process where Kaizen projects help to eliminate waste in all the above areas.The waste can be identified easily by Zensar's preconfigured lean warehousing solution, which provides KPIs along with the interdependencies between multiple KPI parameters. It also helps in understanding and identifying wastes easily, along with providing industry best-in-class indexes to benchmark against and work toward.

The Traceability Solution

The traceability solution from Zensar provides the ability to trace products and parts to their origin and usage, thereby helping in the identification and isolation of defective products at any point in the value chain. Our traceability solutions help in accurately enhancing day-to-day operational visibility across the value chain—from the supplier to the end customer—thus aiding in quick and accurate decision making and hence reduction in cost of recalls and repair.

Supply Chain Risk Management Solution

Our supply chain risk management solution provides a framework to

1. identify, assess, and measure risk profiles across end-to-end supply chains
2. develop capabilities to proactively detect risks and put in place mitigation plans to minimize disruption
3. implement controls to continuously reduce risk exposure
4. improve supply chain resiliency, that is, to recover from disruption as quickly as possible in case of risk occurrence
5. develop and implement strong analytics to provide visibility to monitor and control critical risks proactively

Our solutions are helping us in driving business outcomes for our customers and some key business outcomes being powered by our solutions are as follows:

1. Increased asset/equipment utilization and availability
2. Increase in the percentage of productive time of equipment/machines
3. Decrease in breakdown time
4. Increased productivity of resources
5. Reduced wastage and non–value-added activities
6. Increased yield, process capability, and compliance
7. Reduced cost of quality
8. Improved profitability
9. Enhanced customer satisfaction
10. Improved supply chain resiliency
11. Improved inventory turnover
12. Improved order fulfillment capabilities

Catalog and Grades of Service

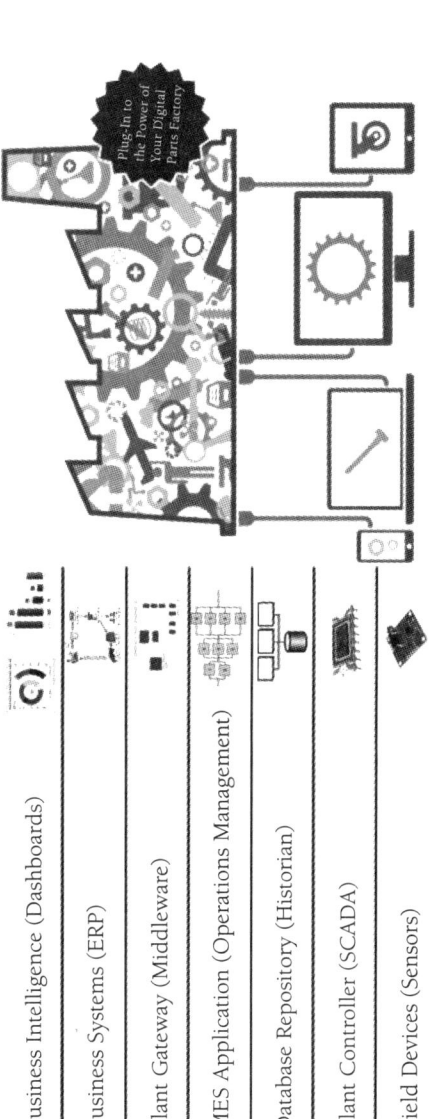

- Business Intelligence (Dashboards)
- Business Systems (ERP)
- Plant Gateway (Middleware)
- MES Application (Operations Management)
- Database Repository (Historian)
- Plant Controller (SCADA)
- Field Devices (Sensors)

Managing the velocity of business change today requires new levels of access to real-time manufacturing information, the ability to enable rapid, decentralized decision making, and an unprecedented degree of collaboration. *This is where workflows that connect the shop floor and the top floor become critical.*

Digital Technology Trends

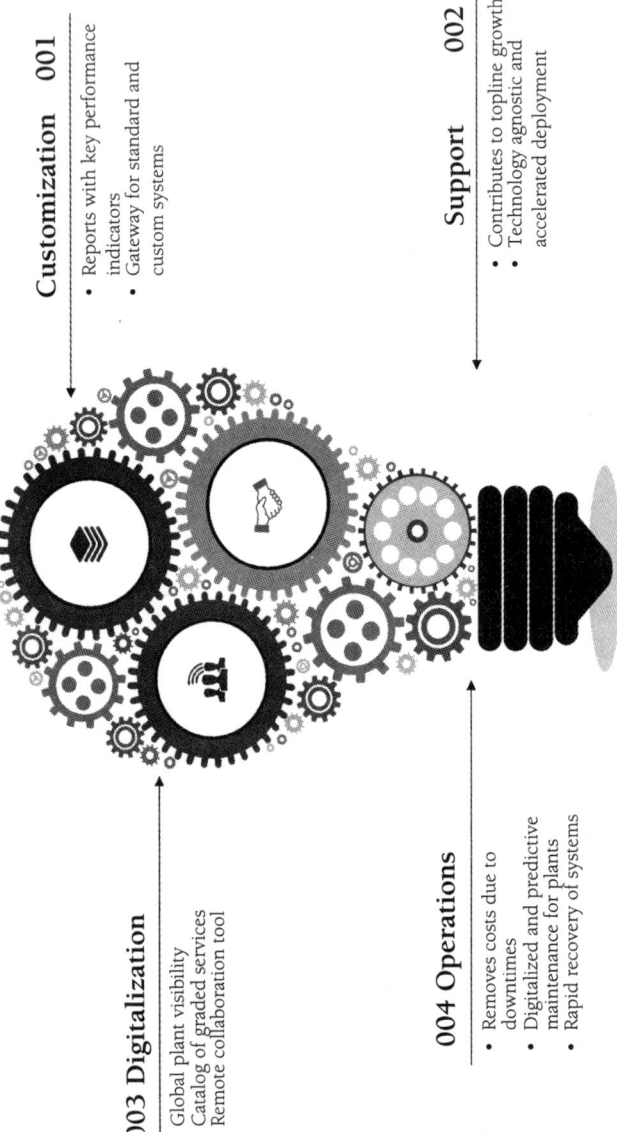

Customization 001
- Reports with key performance indicators
- Gateway for standard and custom systems

Support 002
- Contributes to topline growth
- Technology agnostic and accelerated deployment

003 Digitalization
- Global plant visibility
- Catalog of graded services
- Remote collaboration tool

004 Operations
- Removes costs due to downtimes
- Digitalized and predictive maintenance for plants
- Rapid recovery of systems

We see the new digital technology trends and a "networked economy" transforming the future of manufacturing.

SUPPORTING INSURANCE CLIENTS IN THEIR TRANSFORMATION

Our team of insurance domain SMEs is supporting our clients in driving OmniChannel customer experience and operational efficiencies by building technology-enabled solutions for policy administration, risk management, claims management, underwriting, and product development.

We have built a solution for re-insurance that is offered in a platform-as-a-service model, thereby doing away with capex investments. This integrates easily with the core administration systems and helps clients in driving efficient cash management, better decision making, and financial control.

The solution also helps in operational cost reduction by controlling financial leakages, enhancing operational efficiencies, account reconciliation, and performance visibility. This drives capital optimization and increased focus on core portfolio for our clients.

ENRICHED CUSTOMER EXPERIENCE: OMNICHANNEL CUSTOMER EXPERIENCE

Our solution framework looks at customer experience holistically by focusing on all the customer touch points across the various channels (for example, portals, call centers, mobile, and social) and integrating with the backend enterprise IT systems and the business domain systems to provide a unified and enhanced customer experience across all the channels.

Solution for Re-insurance

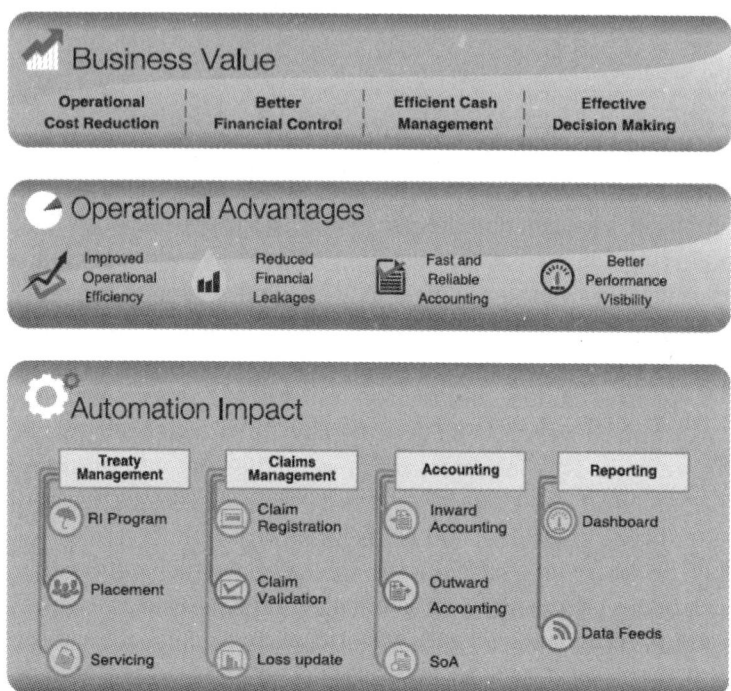

This is helping our clients in
1. increasing revenues by turning around potentially lost customers
2. reducing the time and costs involved in new customer acquisition
3. increasing effectiveness of marketing, sales, and operations by providing deep insights into customer behavior and preferences
4. enhanced customer experience by standardizing experience across all channels
5. active engagement with existing customers to retain them and cross selling of other products

6. proactive post sales customer engagement to drive customer mining

In addition to these, we have built an SME-led policy administration transformation framework based on the ACORD information model, which helps customers in reengineering their end-to-end policy administration, underwriting, and claims management processes.

We have also set up a state-of-the-art social command center for insurers taking customer engagement to the next level by leveraging real-time alerts and insights to reduce turnaround time for service requests and enhance customer satisfaction. This also helps clients with valuable insights and inputs for product development and also helps them in maintaining competitive positioning by leveraging insights into the competitor's strategies.

Mohan Hastak, who heads our insurance business unit, has exciting plans for scaling the insurance business, which he shares here: "Going forward, we will continue to build solutions that address current and emerging business needs, such that we continue to be seen by our customers as a partner they can depend on."

For our banking customers, we have built integrated lending solutions to handle the entire business process of the ending life cycle starting from lead generation to loan closure, which are helping our clients in driving both topline and bottom line growth through reduction in non-performing assets using predictive analytics and enhanced operational efficiencies from IT consolidation.

Our central payment hub enables our banking customers to handle domestic and international payments from multiple channels through a single integrated platform while complying with local and global regulations. This is driving better margins for our clients through process automation and also topline growth from handling higher transactional volumes.

We have taken the power of OmniChannel to our banking clients through our OmniChannel banking solution that is helping them with increased cross-sell opportunities and higher customer self-service capability by leveraging consistent customer experience across all banking channels.

FROM ENTERPRISE TO CONSUMER CENTRICITY: RIDING THE RETAIL WAVE

Retail has been a dominant vertical for Zensar for the past decade and more, and we had bet big on Oracle as the technology partner for our retail strategy. Today, our retail vertical strategy continues to be one of Oracle dominance riding on the digital wave.

With the Professional Access (PA) acquisition, our retail story just got further strengthened and we are now among the global top 3 players in the Oracle ATG and Endeca with over 800 e-commerce specialists added to our workforce.

We are working with some of the global retailers on their digital transformation programs. Social listening, connected beacons and other chief marketing officer (CMO)-directed solutions have been launched for retailers and insurers.

Solutions for optimized Omnilocation supply chain that chain enable flexibility to deliver anytime, from anywhere to anywhere, using built-in intelligence to choose the optimal source and ensure on-time and quality delivery to the end customer. This is driving topline growth for our global retailers through enhanced delivery efficiency and consistency. Our solutions for OmniChannel customer experience, powered by real-time insights and smart analytics, are helping in increased footfall, high conversion, and increased transaction size. All these enhanced KPIs are driving topline for our clients.

The retail industry is going through a transformation from an enterprise-centric business model to a consumer-centric business model. Zensar is ready with solutions to drive this consumer-centric retail strategy of retailers. These solutions are powered by Oracle's technology suite and are driving business solutions for connected enterprises, flexible retail operations, and omnipresent consumer engagement across the dimensions of time, space, and channel.

All of these leverage the digital technologies of mobile, cloud, analytics, big data, and IoT.

Omni Channel Retail Powered by Oracle

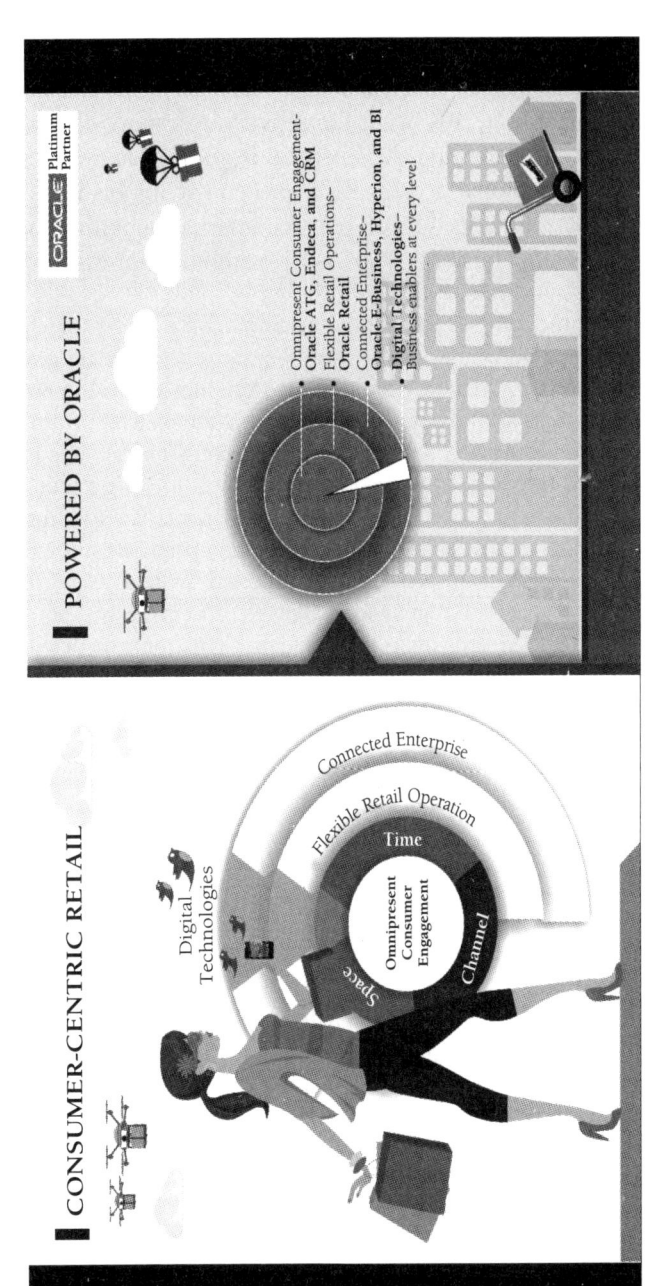

Krishna Kumar, fondly called KK by all of us, has been the man behind Zensar's retail story, having built it from scratch over the past 15 years. Today, KK heads the delivery operations of our global retail business, including the business from our latest acquisition in retail, professional access. KK's excitement for his business is evident in the ambitious three-year roadmap he is putting together for Zensar's retail business. Here is KK's ambition for his business:

> As Mckinsey advises that we should zero in on granular strategy, I am excited to see that today within Zensar in retail we are geared up to do that. Today we have all the right ingredients to partner with Oracle and transform the business for retailers "from an enterprise-centric model to a consumer-centric model." We have the right mix of ecommerce and digital tools to delight retailers' end consumers across time, space, and channel. This is further backed up with flexible and dynamic retail operations and finally we have the tools to provide the connected, wired-up enterprise which gives required agility to retailers to proactively work toward exceeding their consumers' expectations. What puts the icing on the cake is our ability to leverage all these services over the internet i.e., provide them in a boundaryless flat world. With all these ingredients in place, I am looking forward to position Zensar as an end-to-end leader in retail solutions and as a default partner for all retail solutions and services offered on Oracle platform.

VERTICALIZATION DRIVING GROWTH: WIRING THE $1 BILLION ORGANIZATION

By the end of 2013, we were a fully verticalized organization, with our VBU driving double-digit business growth in our chosen verticals, supported by strong domain teams that were continuing to create next-generation business solutions for our customers and actively engaging many of our key clients in supporting their business transformation programs. The verticalization of the sales organization is now complete in all our territories.

The sustained focus on business outcomes has helped us to drive home a mindset shift among our technical teams in the vertical and practice organizations, to constantly look at opportunities to leverage technology to drive business benefits for our clients. Over the last two years, we have made significant investments in strengthening our domain leadership team by onboarding SMEs from the industry.

We have also built strong domain partnerships with partners whose products complement and augment our solutions. The practices are actively collaborating with the domain teams to continue to build business solutions for our clients. The Domain Academy that we set up last year is helping in cross skilling our technical teams through a combination of internal and external domain certifications so that program managers, client partners, relationship managers, delivery managers, business analysts, and the technical professionals are fully conversant with the domain and be able to understand the business needs of customers.

Today, four years into the verticalization journey, we have built a very strong organization where the manufacturing vertical continues to blaze and dominate our vertical growth story. Our retail and insurance verticals have also emerged as very strong verticals driving double-digit growth in all our chosen markets today. All of them are driving our business transformation story, supported by a strong team of domain experts and practice leaders.

Nitin Kasbekar, who heads our manufacturing vertical practice out of San Jose, California, comes with extensive industry experience and is leading the development of IP and business solutions for manufacturers. Umesh Chandolikar leads our insurance domain practice and brings with him extensive experience of having conceived, developed, and deployed business solutions for global insurance firms. Krishna Kumar, fondly called KK, has built Zensar's retail story from scratch over the past 10 years and now heads our retail deliveries globally, including the delivery organization of the recently acquired PA business.

DRIVING BUSINESS TRANSFORMATION FOR CUSTOMERS

Verticalization is helping us not only in strong differentiation of solutions but also in partnering our customers in driving their business transformation roadmaps. Our team is working very closely with the CIO of one of our largest insurance clients in implementing the global rollout roadmap for their premier insurance product.

Mohan, our BFSI vertical head and a very experienced industry veteran, sees the domain focus, driving nonlinear growth for us.

> The insurance vertical in Zensar today is one of the fastest growing verticals. Over the last few years, the focus has been to develop a unit that not only addresses business problems of our insurance customers but also partners with customers as they leverage technology to enable new business models. This focus has resulted in building deep knowledge of the insurance industry, insurance processes and the ability to craft technology solutions for emerging business needs. This has resulted in Zensar successfully delivering solutions that have enabled customers achieve business transformation goals. Going forward, we will continue to build solutions that address current and emerging business needs, such that we continue to be seen by our customers as a partner they can depend on, to meet their business transformation objectives.

TRANSFORMING MARKET POSITIONING

Verticalization is also helping us in better management of the pricing pressures. While horizontal services are subject to commoditization and pricing pressures, since verticalized solutions address core needs of the customer businesses, are better shielded from such pricing pressures. Since the customer's success and growth are closely tied to the benefits derived from our vertical solutions, quite often, our customers are willing to pay a premium for our solutions.

SITTING AT THE TABLE: ENABLING CLIENT STRATEGIES

Strong verticalization has also significantly changed the nature of our conversations with our customer teams, which are no longer about how much cost can we save for them. Instead, we now engage with our customers to understand the business KPIs that drive their own business and market strategies and work with them to build solutions that drive business outcomes and help in driving the business KPIs for the clients.

NAKUMATT, the leading retailer in Eastern Africa, has been our customer for the past four years and its Managing Director, Atul Shah, shares their experience of working with Zensar for all their technology needs:

> NAKUMATT has grown from the humble beginning to become the leading retail chain in East Africa, competing with the local-grown competition and the global ones as well.
>
> The brand is built on core values of win–win partnership, differentiation, unmatched service levels, making sense, and offering the best possible value proposition. We have expanded our footprints in Uganda, Tanzania, Rwanda, besides Kenya, which is the backbone of our business establishment.
>
> In the light of efficient and informed decision making and offering the best experience for our customers and all the stakeholders, we embarked on establishing the IT platform with oracle as the base, and we engaged Zensar as our IT partner. We are proud and pleased with their professional excellence and commitment to deploy the best resources to ensure implementation in time and train our staff to manage the system efficiently and independently. Zensar's involvement has gone beyond IT to align with our corporate vision to engage additional partners to do gap analysis and offer management restructuring program and CRM etc. Their business intelligence software development is very handy and user friendly across the region. We are happy and pleased that our region is fully connected on one platform and we have visibility of our operations on one screen.
>
> We wish Zensar to go places and expand their network to benefit various businesses, and excel in their IT sphere.

CHAPTER 5

Inorganic Growth at Zensar

The Acquisition Journey

THE ACQUISITION PHILOSOPHY AT ZENSAR

Zensar has always had a unique advantage compared with many others in the entrepreneurial IT industry. The company has been run not by owners but by professionals from the very beginning. The advantage of this has been that strategy formation and execution have always been done professionally, and the strategies and tactics toward acquisition have been very much driven by the growth opportunities in the industry and the company. The strategy formation process therefore clearly identified gaps and markets where we had to be present. An acquisition idea therefore was only entertained when Zensar could not afford the time it took to build a new product or service line or market organically. This was and continues to be the process and philosophy that Zensar adopted and also explains the reason for the success of its acquisitions, although some may have taken longer than others to deliver results, for reasons we shall see later in the text.

The company has a rolling three-year strategy planning process where the company listens to four voices—customers, shareholders, analysts, and associates. This process throws up areas of focus for the future as well as areas where the company has to invest afresh. There are cases in which organic investments are adequate to develop the capability or markets, as the company did in the case of growing Africa as a market or in the case of capabilities with Oracle Customer Relationship Management, Oracle Supply and Demand Chain Management solutions, Microsoft Sharepoint, or more recently with the SMAC stack of social, mobility, analytics and cloud to enable digital transformation for its key clients. The story that follows narrates the methodology of acquisition opportunity identification post sifting through opportunities and candidates and the anatomy of the deal, its execution, and eventual integration.

GETTING STARTED WITH SAP: OBT

Around the time when we concluded this acquisition, our first, the India sales team of the company had been asking for an SAP story from the management for quite some time. The need for an SAP acquisition, however, was acutely felt when one of Zensar's large American clients that operated multiple platforms, and multiple companies within each platform, decided to acquire a company that was a user of SAP. At this time, while the company was toying with the idea of investing in a team to cater to the urgent requirements, came the opportunity to acquire OBT.

OBT, originally called Oakbrook Technologies, had been set up by a team of four Indians with the purpose of developing solutions and marketing them with complementary services in India and the US. Starting in India with a strong focus on the small-to-midsize enterprise segment and a partnership with SAP, which enabled them to develop solution templates for the manufacturing, textile, life sciences, dairy, and retail industry and get them certified by SAP, the company, when it first came into Zensar's radar, had established a reputation in India and was now preparing to launch in the US. This stage of the company and the plan for the future seemed to align with Zensar's needs at the time.

Since this was the first significant, albeit small acquisition the company would make, the management committed itself to the task, with a team dispatched to the company's premises in Hyderabad and significant efforts to bring global customers to the city to understand the nuances of the SAP story. Of particular interest was the way in which OBT had developed industry vertical solutions as this verticalization was the direction in which Zensar was headed as a company and also the templatization element looked like a replicable model for the Oracle practice. Conversely, the SAP practice could learn from the Oracle practice in winning large global opportunities and delivering them successfully. Being a predominantly Indian company, the culture fit was not too much of an issue and the founding team of OBT were willing to collaborate and participate in all integration activities.

The OBT story would play out over the next 10 years through various phases of success, disappointment, and finally stability for the SAP business of Zensar. In the initial years, there were some disappointments, which were only to be expected, given the background and geographic focus of the company. One of these was the inability to match the capability of the Zensar team when it came to bidding for global projects and meeting the expectations of partners and customers. And the New Jersey office of the company, which had been set up with much expectation of making a significant dent in the US market, never really found the skills to take off and bag the kind of projects the Zensar Oracle team on the other coast were pulling off at regular intervals. While the Oracle team too never mastered the art of templatizing solutions on vertical lines, this did not seem to deter it from growing at a rapid pace.

Over a period of time, a degree of maturity came into both teams. The OBT team genuinely tried, with the exception of some of the founders, to scale their own capabilities to match the enterprise applications folks in Zensar. At the same time, once the OBT brand was dissolved and it became the Zensar SAP practice, a sense of being one team began to spread through the organization.

Today, SAP is one of the pillars on which the success of Zensar in India continues to ride with significant projects won and executed in both private and public sector organizations. The learning processes of acquisition management and integration have been valuable from OBT but quite well learnt and assimilated in Zensar.

EXPANDING THE ORACLE FOOTPRINT: THOUGHT DIGITAL

As has been mentioned in the previous chapters, competency in Oracle and the ability to compete with the big boys on their own terms had been one of the core pillars for Zensar's growth. Through the first five years of Zensar's existence, the first bastion of the Oracle business in San Jose, California, got strengthened with the core Oracle applications implementation capabilities. Many present-day leaders of the company, Nitin Parab, Head of the Enterprise business worldwide, Ajay Bhandari, Chief Corporate Development Officer, Chakri Reddy, Head of the US Sales operation, and Srini Polsani, Global Head of the Oracle practice, have won their spurs in the organization through their innovative leadership of the Oracle practice.

However, in the year 2007, after identifying global dominance in Oracle as a key pillar for future growth of the enterprise, Zensar realized that moving toward a Platinum and eventually a Diamond partnership with Oracle would call for spreading the capabilities from its then-dominant presence in the electronics manufacturing industry on the West Coast of the US to a Pan-American and global presence. Chesapeake, an investment banker out of New York, was appointed and, after an initial search period, Thought Digital, a 20 million dollar company based out of New York, was identified as a possible candidate.

Those were the days when Zensar was still, like most Indian IT firms of its ilk, more of an Indian multinational and not a truly global company, and the opportunity to acquire a firm that had been built and run by five Americans was not one that the team would want to spurn. The fact that this would turn out to be the most disappointing acquisition for Zensar was hardly an outcome that the company or its management team could have anticipated.

During the dating period, the company and its founding team seemed almost too good to be true and, as the old saying goes, if something is too good to be true, it probably isn't true! The sell side bankers of the company presented the fine founders of the company as a united team, passionately committed to the business and willing to work with the Zensar management to build the company to further levels of success.

Alas, this was not to be. While the initial marketing was well handled by a joint team from Zensar and TD, it was not long before the wheels began to come off the TD sales and execution wagon. With relationships between the founders quite poor and the ability and willingness to retail critical team members suspect in the face of vicious local competition, the revenue of the firm never grew and eventually declined. The only silver lining in this cloud was perhaps the establishment of the Zensar presence on the East Coast of the US, one of the key original drivers of the acquisition and a few senior people who could be assimilated into the Zensar culture. Here again, there were many lessons to be learnt and Team Zensar learnt them well, albeit with a fair degree of disappointment and pain along the way.

TAKING THE BIG IM PLUNGE: AKIBIA

The growth story of Zensar through the first decade of the new millennium had been given a new impetus toward the end of the period through a vision community suggestion and management and board thought process that infrastructure management (IM) was one missing piece in its overall value proposition. Other firms, particularly HCL and WIPRO, had demonstrated the capability to chase and win large deals in the area of remote infrastructure management, a capability that Zensar had been missing. The first step in this direction was the appointment of Ankit Ghosh, a one-man army with both the confidence and the skills to make new breakthroughs in this new area for the company.

Inorganic Growth at Zensar: The Acquisition Journey 93

Extensive evangelism and selling support from Ankit took Zensar to a position that was small but still respectable—70 crores or so of business in IM by 2010, and then the opportunity came about that would change the fortunes of Zensar in many ways in the next four years—Akibia.

The company had been set up by a New England entrepreneur in the suburbs of Boston, Massachusetts, and at the time of acquisition employed close to 300 Americans in Boston, Dallas (Texas), and New York with a small 30 people presence in Veenendaal near Amsterdam in Europe. The focus of the company was maintenance of data centers as a managed service comprising help desk, technical and field support, fixing and replacing spare parts and logistics, and a sizable security products businesses, consisting largely of third-party software products largely deployed in client data centers and networks. The company managed its own supply chain with spare parts warehouses in Northborough, near its main facility in Westborough, and in Veenendaal and also had around 150 third-party—managed stocking locations in various parts of the world that gave it a global presence.

Ajay Bhandari, our head of Strategy and Corporate Development, played a key role in the acquisition and integration of Akibia with the Zensar business. He saw this acquisition as both strategic and complementary to Zensar's existing IT capabilities.

> By the year 2010 Remote Infrastructure Management had started becoming popular and Cloud computing had muscled its way into CIO conversations. Zensar too by then had established itself as a strong player in the Applications Management space but lacked a strong Infrastructure Management capability. The Akibia deal happened by the third quarter of 2010 and fundamentally impacted Zensar. Not only did it substantially add to Zensar's size, it gave our now impatient sales force the confidence and ability to have a more composite outsourcing discussion with their customers. Our Revenue per customer started improving but the Akibia deal also delivered one material differentiation— Our ability to take our customers to the cloud.

Having suffered through the Thought Digital issue of an evaporating management steam, Zensar decided to lock in the core members of the Akibia team for three years to ensure continuity, and this seemed to work well in the first year when most of the targeted numbers were met. However, the business model of the company, designed for a 100 million dollar American firm predominantly focused on proximate customers with a limited range of maintenance services and products, was never going to be optimal in the longer term for an offshore company committed to double-digit profitability after tax.

A number of decisions were taken in the second year, some supported and some rather reluctantly accepted by the local management team. The decision to focus more on IM services and the immediate movement of the Zensar IM pioneer Ankit Ghosh to Westborough got some initial momentum, although more with the non-Akibia Enterprise sales team than with the Akibia groups. The decision to downplay both the data center staffing business and the products business and replace this revenue by dual-shore services business was a good one, but the decline because of the deliberate shutting of low-margin business was too quick to be compensated by the services deals that were slow to come and even slower to translate into revenue dollars. Some other decisions, for instance the plan to focus only on profitable and manageable maintenance partnerships with OEMs, were accepted but not fully implemented, with the results that the revenues and profits both started to decline and the business, like the Titanic, slowly started sinking into the red.

Guido Timmerman, who is a re-hire after having worked with Akibia in the past and come back to join us post the acquisition, now heads the US sales of our integrated IM business. He now works with sales, practice, and delivery teams across shores and shares his perspective on why organizations succeed:

> I started with Zensar originally in the Netherlands working throughout Europe for an American Company called Akibia. With the merger that took place in 2010, the organization all of a sudden got a true global character. The combination of the Indian culture,

the American roots and my own Dutch background has had a profound impact on the overall mix of both cultural and professional way of looking at business and especially on how to communicate effectively within the organization. Now after a number of years I can only conclude that the true growth and success both internally and with our global customers comes from understanding the common ground and celebrating our differences!

During all this, however, Zensar had learnt from its earlier problems of retaining acquired personnel and did all the right things to motivate and retain the fine folk of Akibia. A key HR initiative, the Vision Communities, well described in a frequently taught Harvard Business School case study by Professor David Garvin was transported successfully from Zensar to Akibia, and the presence of Vivek Gupta and Ankit Ghosh and later the US Financial Controller and Human Resource Head of Zensar in the Akibia premises did much to keep morale high even during critical times and in spite of the loss of a few stalwarts, the retention track record remained fairly stable in the US as well as in Europe.

Julie Lightbody, one of our key sales managers in Akibia, has been a part of this transformation journey from being a part of an organization headquartered in the suburbs of Boston to becoming a part of a global organization. Here is her experience in her own words:

> Over the last almost five years of being an employee with Akibia now Zensar, the experience of working for a true global organization has been amazing. I have had the opportunity to be part of an organization through a merger where I was and continue to provide inputs into Zensar's future growth and direction. I have had the opportunity to visit our Pune, India, location several times. This is a company where I feel I can stay and grow for the rest of my career and continue to scale. Thank you to the Zensar leadership and teams that support me day in and day out and equip me with proper tools and infrastructure to contribute to the growth and success of the organization.

It was in the third year that Zensar could contractually and practically take over the management of the business, and it took another two quarters to get the business back to profits. A journey that was intended to be completed in six quarters had taken 12, but, nevertheless, Zensar was now firmly in the infrastructure management business with light at the end of the long tunnel.

Pinaki Kar, the new business leader for the infrastructure management business, is the newest addition to our executive leadership team and brings with him great industry experience, global IM experience, and above all great optimism, ambition, and passion to steer the business through its next growth phase:

> At Zensar, we understand that Infrastructure Management is the foundation for achieving business outcomes in today's pervasive digital world, with convergence of applications and hardware enabled by mobility and innovative consumption platforms like Cloud computing. In this ubiquitously connected and hybrid IT world, we help our clients in maximizing the value from their IT investments through 2 differentiated tracks: (a) as a trusted advisor and system integrator for their digital transformation journey, and (b) as a best-in-class Managed Services provider assuring hyper efficiency of the IT operations in the run state. Leveraging on our strong customer franchise, agility and innovative service offerings, we have aspirations of being the key growth driver for Zensar as it approaches the billion dollar mark.

CLIMBING THE COMMERCE MOUNTAIN: PA

Some acquisitions happen through great strategic planning, opportunity identification, a formal search process, and then due diligence and candidate finalization, while others just happen. The successful acquisition of Professional Access, a New York- and Bengaluru-based company, was one that happened almost by accident but has turned out to be one of the most interesting additions to the corporate capabilities of Zensar.

This was in 2014 when Zensar had successfully transformed itself from a purely horizontal IT services company to a company that specialized in few verticals and provided business-impacting solutions to its customers. The company was shifting gears in the digital space and was already doing close to 5 percent of its revenues from digital. Online was a big area of investment for Zensar, and the process of capability building had just started when Professional Access, or PA as it is called, happened.

For a company with revenues just exceeding $40 million, to be a partner of choice to software behemoth Oracle Corporation in the exciting e-commerce space would be like a dream come true, and all credit must go to the founders and team of PA that they had made this happen. The quality of the sales management, the unwillingness to compromise on quality of deliveries, and the commitment to look for new opportunities for growth are all great qualities that characterize the approach to customers and business growth at PA.

The transaction too was concluded in record quick time thanks to the alacrity demonstrated by both parties and the advantage of having cash in the balance sheet.

For Zensar, the integration with PA, which is currently in its final stages, has been an excellent demonstration of the lessons it has learnt through its previous acquisition forays and its commitment to be a leader in the exciting digital and e-commerce space.

Ajay Bhandari has been leading the PA integration efforts and is very excited about the opportunity for Zensar to create a unique position for itself in the OmniChannel e-commerce space, as he says here:

> PA was added in August 2014 as one of the significant investments we will make in Digital. With all businesses thinking Omni-Channel and disintermediation through online sales, presence in the Online Commerce was a

necessity. With PA's strength in that area Zensar was uniquely positioned to exploit the emerging spin-off opportunities from Omni-Channel.

LESSONS LEARNT FROM M&A

As you would have read through the narrative, each acquisition presented learning opportunities to Zensar in the way it identified and integrated acquisitions. It can be said with reasonable confidence that mistakes have not been repeated and processes have been reinforced. To narrow down the key lessons learnt from the M&A experiences at Zensar, it would come down to the few lessons given below:

Clarity of Purpose

Be very clear on why you would like to acquire a company. Zensar's philosophy was to acquire for capability or acquire for market share. Of the four acquisitions made by Zensar, three were for capability and one was for market penetration. Irrespective of the integration outcome of the four acquisitions, we believe the decision to acquire at that time was the right one as all the acquisitions made a positive impact on business. Acquisitions done primarily for "bulking-up" have rarely delivered any value and the company has stayed clear of those.

Don't Venture into Unchartered Territory

Zensar has always been wary of acquiring capabilities where the company has no existing capability, however meager our prior knowledge of what it takes to build that capability. In case of all four acquisitions, Zensar had begun the process of growing capability or markets and used the acquisition only to accelerate the process. New and unknown capability with new management was not regarded by Zensar as good acquisition candidates due to the risk it posed in integration.

Create a Yin and Yang Team

As mentioned in the very beginning of this chapter, the strategy process should be a robust one if one has to acquire in the right areas. For every M&A transaction, Zensar created two teams with a "Contrarian" team always challenging the M&A team to come up with better answers. This process was refined with every successive acquisition to ensure that mistakes made in earlier transactions were not repeated.

Be Prepared to Walk Away

Do not get so invested in the process that you cannot or do not walk away. After Akibia Zensar came very close to acquiring a few companies, but maintained a discipline that if at any time the synergy benefits were compromised in relation to the cost we pay, we will walk away. Zensar ended up walking away from quite a few deals that later on turned out to be the right decision.

If It's Too Good to Be True, then Look Closer

Typically in an M&A process, the financial, accounting, and customer diligence processes are quite well covered, as these are normally done by specialists and there are prevalent governance standards that are well accepted, which both parties cannot challenge and have to accept. It is the softer aspects of relationships of owners/promoters, organizational culture, and management processes that are often either ignored or the time estimated for amending/changing these processes is often underestimated. Zensar learned the hard way that these processes needed the same attention as the financial diligence during the due diligence phase.

Intervene Sooner if Necessary

Zensar has always believed in working with the current owners and management and making them a part of Zensar's overall growth plans. However, if the owners do have different plans and begin to be a bottleneck to Zensar realizing its overall vision for the acquisition, then intervening sooner and parting ways may be the only solution. This is especially true when it comes to integrating solutions and management processes and culture. Zensar has had mixed experiences with all the owners of the four acquired entities, but in hindsight there are cases in which had we intervened sooner and taken over the reins of the entity, the acquisition would have been a bigger success.

Get More Information on Promoters

The promoters of any company define the cultural fabric of the company. Feuding promoters can ruin organizations, especially when the conflict at the top leaves the rest of the organization confused. This is especially true where organizations are small and driven top down and management processes are underdeveloped. In the modern connected world, it is not too difficult to get disconfirming evidence if the relationship between promoters is not as hunky-dory as they project it to be. This is an important lesson learnt by Zensar and which is now followed as a rule as part of our due diligence process.

PA is certainly not the last company Zensar will acquire, and there will be many more to come. Zensar will continue to look for opportunities to accelerate its pace toward the $1 billion dollar mark, especially in the exciting digital space. However, what can be said with a reasonable degree of confidence is that old mistakes would not be made, and we will continue to strengthen the acquisition process to ensure we do not make new ones.

NEW GEOGRAPHIES, NEW CULTURES

Growth through acquisitions is a valid agenda when it is tightly linked to the strategy of the firm, but there is always a need to look for new horizons for organic growth. In other chapters, we have discussed the expansion of services and the move to verticalization, and it may be appropriate to call out the history of expansion into new geographies and cultures as well. There are two critical success factors in the growth processes of any successful multinational firm and both are true for the IT sector in India and for Zensar: The first is the assessment of new geographies to expand into, and the second is the ability to assimilate new cultures and build an environment of true diversity and inclusion in the organization. During the 15 years of its existence, Zensar has demonstrated this ability in full measure, and the 2014–2015 annual report to shareholders, titled "Diversity Driving Sustainability," celebrates the financial outcomes of this core competence that the organization has developed over the years.

In the beginning, thanks to its British pedigree, Zensar management and consultants were very comfortable with the English culture, and the frequent interaction with British directors also enabled Zensarians to deal with them with considerable comfort. The early foray of the software business into the US and the leadership of people experienced in the US, such as Nitin Parab, also facilitated the understanding of the US culture, particularly the relaxed style prevalent on the West Coast, since high-tech manufacturing clients interested in Zensar's Oracle capabilities were the first target segment chased by the company. Similarly, the early foray into Australia did not create any new stress, given the cultural affinity toward the UK in that part of the world.

Chakravardhan Vaddi, who joined us in our US team even before we became Zensar, now heads our US sales organization for our enterprise solutions business, leading the company's largest and most successful sales team. His is a story of personal transformation from a young technical professional into a star sales leader. Here, he shares his journey:

Seventeen years and counting—I have had the pleasure of being part of this amazing growth story and it feels great. Interestingly, looking back, the journey seems short! I look forward to more goals that we are all set to accomplish and the several years ahead. It feels like only yesterday we met for focused strategy discussions, and the smallest ideas from them have had some big impact. I also clearly recollect goals and expectations when I started my career here, am happy to have found more than expected—strangely I am still looking and have the drive to achieve further. To me and am sure many more Zensarians, this Organization provides a canvas to paint freely; a tremendous platform to grow and a culture that we belong to, one that we can never leave.

The first real challenge for Zensar occurred when it made its foray into Japan with a view to working with Fujitsu in their headquarters. Zensar appointed industry veteran Masato Nozaki to set up the office, and his seniority and access to Fujitsu senior management made it easy for visiting managers and consultants to get familiarized with a very different culture. For Ganesh, when he came I as CEO in 2001, it was a first-time experience to be introduced by the then COO Sunil Kunte into the finer nuances of the Japanese culture—The leader must always speak the most and formally ask colleagues to speak if they were to add something, direct disagreements were to be avoided at all costs, and even negotiations would have to be conducted in a spirit of total subservience to the hosts; moreover, while the number of "Hais" uttered by Nozaki-san even in telephonic interactions with Fujitsu was a source of some amusement to the other members of the Zensar leadership, they took his cue and ensured that the norms and culture of the great country of Japan were always followed to the last detail. Other Japanese employees followed and a large number of Indian consultants in Pune were also inducted with Japanese language training from the city's Ranade Institute and through the first seven years or so, the Japanese business grew slowly but was always a source of pride for the company.

Questions about the validity of the Japan business for a fast growing organization started to be asked after the Legacy

Modernization services group of the company made its forays into the country with the specific charter of changing the pace of growth of business in the country, which had largely been focused on hardware programming and testing services for some of Fujitsu's divisions. The group first found great excitement from Fujitsu as well as other large Japanese systems integrators to help them with their strategy to move IBM Legacy systems to modern software. However, a couple of false starts with automation tools, which the Japanese partners could not ever fully understand as a valid method of migrating software, led to this opportunity being nipped in the bud. A new country manager tried for some time to take the business to the next level, but new business deals were small and few, and the interest of Fujitsu had waned after RPG took over their shareholding in Zensar. The company withdrew from the Japanese business, with more than a twinge of sadness in 2014.

The Chinese odyssey of Zensar has also been a mixed bag. After an initial false start with a collaboration with a Hong Kong–based firm, the company decided to take the plunge toward the end of 2010 with the establishment of a wholly owned foreign enterprise in the Shanghai suburb of Baoshan. Within an additional center coming up in Pudong for the benefit of an Australian client, the company's operations, under the watch of a Chinese IT professional with excellent English, Charles Song, turned profitable after two years. However, like most other Indian firms, growth of the China business, with the private sector as well as the State-owned enterprises, was stubbornly slow, and the company has decided to just retain the Shanghai center as part of its "India-plus-one" strategy available to global clients seeking to mitigate the India risk. One could also argue that the Chinese mind has remained more inscrutable to most Indian firms and to Zensar as well, as compared with other non-English-speaking countries, including Japan, Mexico, and Germany, and while the comfort of living and working in China has been established and the Zensar leadership have all had excellent experiences with their travels to China, the future business prospects in that country remain uncertain at best.

The most successful foray for Zensar outside the traditional strongholds of the UK and the US has undoubtedly been South Africa. In 2001, two young MBAs recruited from the SP Jain Institute of Management were put on a plane and sent off to open an office in Johannesburg. The initial entry was predictably rocky, with Harish Lala, one of the two, reporting that the car in which he was traveling was once chased by a bullet. However, Harish Lala stayed and built a truly successful operation that is today "proudly South African" and has also elevated Harish himself to be one of the youngest Senior Vice Presidents of the company.

Harish Lala continues to be a role model for many young Zensarians, and here is what he has to say about his Zensar journey:

> When an organisation puts trust in young talent and give them responsibility along with authority, and support them, things do happen. Same was our South Africa story, when in 2001, I was asked to start and build this region. Starting as a one man office, in this unknown territory what was once called "A Dark Continent," to today more than 750 people operation, it's indeed been a journey. Starting challenges, ups and downs of growth, people centric challenges brought huge learning and development for me and the team involved while the entrepreneurial spirit, collaborative approach, can do attitude of the team with a clear focus of giving back to society, made it happen. Today Zensar is recognised among the top Indian IT firms in South Africa and is growing further into rest of Africa.

The success of the South African operation is a case study of successful expansion, and much of the credit must go to the leaders and the team Harish Lala has assembled over the years in Sandton, Joburg, Durban, Cape Town, and recently Kenya. Some of the best-known clients in banking, insurance, financial services, manufacturing, mining, and retail work with Zensar both on-site and offshore, and the territory has many firsts to its credit in terms of the new projects signed and successfully delivered. Zensar is a regular speaker at Gartner summits and has successfully completed Digital Transformation workshops in partnership with BCG, as well as more recently with the Gordon

Institute of Business Sciences. All this has happened through assiduous efforts on brand building, personal mentoring of the territory by the senior leadership, ensuring that the best resources were made available to travel and work in the territory, and attracting and retaining the best talent to work in the territory. The focus on creating an environment that would also attract local talent is visible in the 130 plus young South Africans who have been identified and trained at the Talent Development Centre in Sandton as well as in India to become part of the local workforce.

The company gets high scores in the Broad-Based Black Economic Empowerment tables, which is a critical component of a multinational firm's ability to succeed and grow in the country. In the last couple of years, the joint venture with the Kapela group led by Israel Oskana has further strengthened the company's roots in the continent and given it the right to bid for government projects as well. Zensar's move into Kenya has been the next step in the company's planned foray into East Africa, and there are already visible signs that both the private sector and the local government welcome the company's moves to build world-class software and skills development practices to Nairobi and beyond.

While Africa is a true exemplar, Zensar's moves to expand in Europe and Latin America are also worth mentioning. The European presence had started with collaboration with Fujitsu for projects with the Hungarian Railways and Nokia in Finland, but these were more client specific and episodal. The company made its first serious foray with the opening of an office in Amsterdam, the Netherlands, which was further strengthened by the acquisition of Akibia with its fulfillment and marketing center for the continent based in Veenendal just outside Amsterdam. Led by territory head Anurag Nautiyal, the company has since made planned forays into Vienna and Geneva and does work with four prestigious United Nations agencies.

Anurag shares his thoughts about the success we have seen in Continental Europe:

In 2008 when we started our Continental Europe operations, our challenge was to identify a focus sector with appropriate service lines to land and over time expand.

The Continental Europe IT services market has unique psychographics and the prevailing attitudes, opinions and beliefs create a complex operating environment which is not kind to new entrants.

After the initial years of struggle, we got our first large deal to roll out Oracle ERP for a specialised agency of the United Nations in Austria. While at first it appeared as serendipity, we realised very quickly that we had hit a niche in the market which was very suited for us. Leveraging our significant Oracle technology competency, we went about systematically pursuing other specialised agencies of the United Nations in Austria, Switzerland, and Italy which too were Oracle install bases. We are now working with 5 significant UN agencies and are a recognised partner of choice for managing large transformation programs in this sector.

Establishing anything successful from scratch takes an enormous amount of effort and team work. I was the first employee of Zensar in Continental Europe in 2008 but it never felt like I was the only one. While the work culture in Zensar is clearly performance driven and everyone strives to be the best at what they do, yet it is not a detached mechanical set up which only cares about numbers. In essence, Zensar is one big family, where each individual is recognised, has a place and is given the freedom and desired support to reach for the stars. It is such unique nuances which interestingly attract not just the employees but also draws customer organisations to Zensar.

Planned expansion into Germany and the Nordics is on the cards as well. And in Latin America, the acquisition of PA has given it access to a functioning office in Mexico City, and with projects started in Mexico, El Salvador, and prospects in other countries, the Latin America footprint is likely to see expansion as well.

Chaitanya Rajebahadur, who recently took our territory leadership for the UK and Europe, is very upbeat about the opportunities he sees in the region:

Zensar in Europe today has enviable logo in UK and Europe—I have had the privilege to head the region for the last 6 months and I am extremely impressed with the culture of the organisation, its people-centric policies, ethics and strong corporate social responsibility. Most importantly the clients of Zensar are extremely pleased with the quality of services provided by Zensar. This provides me with a strong platform to deliver phenomenal growth in the region and be recognised as a dominant player in the markets and verticals that Zensar operates in. Watch out for Zensar in Europe!

What truly differentiates Zensar today from many other firms that decide to foray into a territory with scant regard for cultural sensitivities and local context is the willingness to embrace the "think-global, act-local" mantra for success.

Deb Baroni, who was responsible for the HR function in Akibia, now handles the HR portfolio of talent development and engagement across all our US businesses. She is driving the integration of our HR practices across our US organization, and here is how she experiences the cultural integration:

> After the Akibia acquisition, I became part of Zensar's global HR organization that offered me the opportunity to learn from Zensar's global best practices in employee engagement, talent management as well as learning and development. It has been an exciting opportunity for me to collaborate with teams from across the globe with diverse approaches to enable and support the various business units. As Zensar continues to invest in its associates I look forward to being a part of the team that drives growth and results through its people programs.

The addition of Katri Stein in Europe, Tixo Augustus in Africa, and Anabel in Latin America may seem just a few more foreign names like Masato Nozaki and Charles Song, but these frontline managers are supported by a fully sensitized team that goes the extra mile to make successful projects and programs happen on a planned basis.

TAKING STOCK

New markets, new geographies, new services, and new companies to collaborate and acquire—all these have been integral to the growth strategy of Zensar from its inception. During the journey, some mistakes have been made and many new lessons learned, but the excitement, confidence, and new knowledge that the team has gained has been invaluable. The Zensar team is confident that this experience will stand us in good times as we renew our mission every year to succeed and grow.

Vivek Gupta, a career Zensarian, who, after leading several business portfolios in Zensar, has led the infrastructure management business for the past three years and has played a leadership role in the integration of two diverse cultures, shares his experience with the cultural integration process:

> Perhaps the most enriching experience during my long tenure with Zensar has been that of leading Akibia's integration with Zensar. Anyone who has been closely involved with integrating an acquisition would agree that the most difficult part of the integration is managing cultural differences. Here we were merging a New England based conservative American company into an India headquartered essentially Indian company. We were blending an owner-run privately held firm into a company listed on the Bombay Stock Exchange for over 50 years. And we were merging a small company with discretionary rewards and remuneration philosophy for its employees into a larger company with structured and well defined processes. It was no doubt stressful yet at the same time a highly satisfying experience.

CHAPTER 6

Profit Maximization

New Levers and Ideas

As the Indian IT industry matured, we saw rapid commoditization of the core IT services where quality of deliverables was now table stakes and no longer a differentiator that customers looked for when selecting their IT vendors. This was coupled with the increasing cost of offshore resources as the demand for skilled IT workforce began to fast outweigh the supply. These two trends began to quickly erode the cost arbitrage of the offshore outsourcing model, which was once the single business driver for the aggressive growth of the Indian IT industry.

This period also saw the emergence of alternate outsourcing destinations outside of India, predominantly in China, Latin America, and the Philippines. What all these countries had in common was a large English-speaking talent pool and aggressive and ambitious governments that were willing to do what it takes to go after the IT outsourcing markets of the West. While Latin America and the Philippines had a natural language advantage, we have seen the aggressive charter of China to create an English-speaking workforce to grab a share of this market.

We soon saw clients seriously evaluating these alternate destinations for outsourcing their work, as they matched the cost arbitrage and English advantage that India had to offer, not to mention the time zone advantage that some of these destinations had.

Therefore, by the mid-2000s, two emerging trends were pushing the Indian IT industry toward an inflection point. Market conditions were increasing the risks for clients in relying on a single IT vendor: so many larger clients were adopting a strategy of having a combination of tier I and tier II providers. At the same time, many customers wanted their IT vendors to be close to them, to be able to handle on-site emergencies and ensure accessibility. So soon near-shore outsourcing models began to come into existence and this encouraged the industry participants to establish resourcing engines and networks outside of India.

We were very clear that we did not want to be a poor man's tier I IT vendor. Our goal was to become the referred tier II IT supplier, and hence our strategy was built around this objective. The bigger IT services companies had three clear advantages—they were commanding a price premium because of their brand, they were benefitting from their economies of scale and thus had lower unit costs, and they were able to attract better talent.

The Indian industry was faced with the challenge and urgent business need of creating new differentiators and value propositions beyond cost and quality. It was time to reinvent, renovate, and innovate to sustain the high growth rates and the client relationships.

There were three dominant models that Indian IT players pursued for market leadership positions:

1. Customer advocacy. Building and leveraging outstanding trust relationships with clients that ensured that clients stayed with their vendors for reasons beyond cost and quality. They perceived them to be true partners adding value to their businesses and believed in building win–win partnerships with such vendors.
2. Operational excellence. Building best-in-class delivery organizations that delivered gold-standard services

and solutions to the clients and set the bar for the industry on operational efficiencies. This required constant improvement in operation efficiency, and cost leadership was the dominant theme in this approach. TCS was a leader that pursued this option and continues to be the industry leader when it comes to operational excellence.
3. Innovation. This was the third model that emphasized on building and leveraging an innovation culture in organizations—driving both incremental and disruptive innovations. It meant innovation in every dimension of an organization—choice of market segments, engagement and delivery models, technology tools, disruptive business models, and even people practices. This requires a strong culture of innovation and a supportive ecosystem to succeed.

We were sure that we did not want to be a cheap alternative for a tier I vendor. Our goal was clearly to become the preferred tier II supplier and hence we decided to build our strategy entirely on strong customer advocacy and innovation to give us a strong differentiation and market positioning. We knew that the bigger IT services firms had three advantages—they got a price premium because of their brand, they benefited from scale economies, and could attract better talent. Our strategy was to play to our strengths, and those were our nimbleness and very strong customer connects, which helped in building trust relationships with our customers coupled by our ongoing quest for innovation and doing things differently. And by this time, we had also achieved a fairly mature state of process maturity in our deliveries thanks to our focus on the quality frameworks.

Therefore, we pursued a differentiation strategy that included all the three models of customer advocacy, innovation, and cost leadership:

1. Process excellence through a robust quality management framework to drive the culture of quality in letter and

spirit, going beyond compliance and instead driving adoption and assimilation.
2. Innovation led by IP and accelerators to give us a different point of view and drive nonlinear growth and margins.
3. Culture of operational excellence in operations to constantly drive us to raise the bar for excellence to stay ahead of the game.

MAKING QUALITY A WAY OF LIFE: OUR QUALITY JOURNEY

Zensar's strong belief in process maturity and respect for quality processes goes way back to the 1990s, and our strong Japanese and UK lineage have got a lot to do with the strong quality culture in the organization.

Our quality journey started in the early 1990s, by when we were executing fairly large (almost 100 person years) projects out of Pune, India. Some of these were for prestigious clients, such as the British Gas (100+ person years), Open Patient Administration System (30+ person years), and HOSPRO (Hospital Administration for New Zealand; 30+ person years).

These large project teams were led by very experienced project managers, and projects were executed very successfully. However, with rapid growth the need was felt to bring in this wealth of knowledge into the organizational domain.

As the major chunk of our business at that time came from Europe and other English-speaking countries that preferred ISO as a quality management system, it was only natural that we decided that "software exports" should also go in for ISO certification. This gave birth to our Operations Manual, and our first ISO certification followed in 1994.

To this day, our Operations Manual and ISO are the backbone of our quality management system, which ensures that our software deliveries consistently meet our customers' requirements and expectations. Even as we have transformed, expanded, and extended our services portfolio, ISO continues to be one of our dominant quality frameworks.

Capability Maturity Model (CMM)

By the mid-1990s, there was much better integration of the UK and Europe operations with the operations in the United States. ISO was not very popular in the US software industry. Instead, the SEI, set up under Carnegie Mellon University, developed the capability maturity model (CMM) for organizations to attain higher levels of process maturity. Naturally this put pressure on us to be CMM certified too.

Thus, Zensar also adopted the CMM process maturity framework, given that our own business footprint was fast expanding beyond the UK and Europe to the United States.

We began the CMM journey seriously in 1995 and obtained our first Capability Maturity Model Integration (CMMI) certification in 1996 when we were assessed at level 3 maturity of the CMMI framework. We then set a very ambitious target for ourselves—to move to level maturity in three years. This meant an aggressive and focused roadmap as we set our aim to go for an enterprise-wide process maturity, across all our functions and service lines. This was very ambitious, given that the rest of the Indian IT players were working toward reaching the CMM level 5 maturity in one of more functions and/or service lines.

The three-year journey from level 3 to level 5 was both exciting and challenging, as this meant transforming the quality culture in the organization to go beyond compliance and drive adoption and continuous improvement under the CMMI framework.

In 1999, after a successful three-year internal process transformation journey, we readied ourselves for our second CMM assessment and attained the highest level of process maturity, that is, level 5. This made us the eighth company worldwide to only achieve level 5 of the CMM framework and, more importantly, the first to be assessed "enterprise wide." It was indeed an exhilarating moment for us to stand tall and stand alone as the "world's first enterprise-wide CMM level 5 company." Soon after, many more IT firms scaled their processes to reach the level 5 maturity, and today most of the Indian and global IT players have reached the level 5 maturity, we will always be the first one and no one can take it away from us.

By this time, we had the experience of having adopted and implemented both the ISO and CMM quality frameworks, and we felt that both the frameworks had their own strengths and were relevant to our kind of business. Therefore, rather than choosing one over the other and in the process losing out on some of the benefits that each framework has to offer, we decided to embrace both the frameworks and derive the best from both.

We then moved on from the CMM to the CMMI framework as the SEI came up with the integrated maturity model. Very soon, we were at maturity level 5 for services in all of our delivery centers.

Through these high maturity practices, we are able to understand the past, control the present, and predict the future in a better way. This has helped us in bringing more predictability, consistency, and repeatability in our software deliveries and has greatly helped us institutionalizing pockets of excellence in the organization as best practices.

Some of the key benefits that Zensar has derived from implementing these high maturity practices are the following:

1. Clearly defined business objectives
2. Better visibility of key performance indicators
3. Optimized processes that are aligned to business objectives of the organization and the customer
4. A culture of continuous improvement and innovation
5. Statistical tools and predictive models to measure and minimize variances in performance

Keeping pace with the changing business demands and expectations of our customers, we also adopted the ISO 20000 standard, which is an international standard for service management. We were certified for this standard in 2011, and this alignment to ISO 20000 has helped us greatly in benchmarking our practices of delivering managed services, measuring our service levels, and objectively assessing our performance.

In addition to these international quality frameworks, Zensar has also been leveraging techniques such as Six Sigma (DMAIC: define–measure–analyze–improve–control) and lean for driving continuous improvement in projects. We have trained and skilled our own internal team of Six Sigma professionals to drive these initiatives and today continuous improvement and process excellence has become a strong culture in the organization, and we continue to leverage these tools and techniques for driving productivity enhancement initiatives.

Today, our quality management system (QMS) is very comprehensive and comprises the following standards and frameworks:

QMS

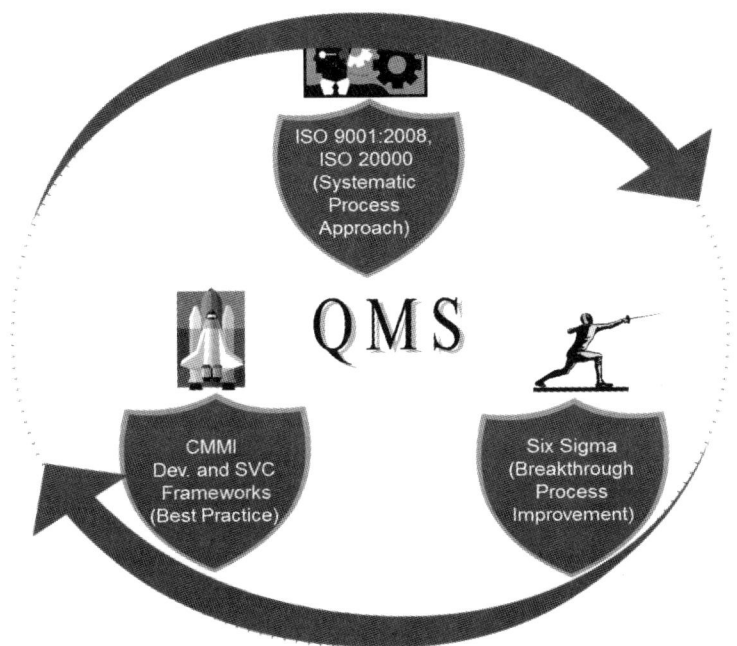

www.zensar.com | © Zensar Technologies 2013

With the emerging concerns of customers on information security, especially in the context of outsourced IT services, and the increasing compliance requirements for information security, we also adopted the BS 7799 standard, which is a British Standard for information security management. In early 2004, the IT division of Zensar Technologies Ltd. (TIMS) started its journey on information security, which resulted in an independent certification against BS 7799.

Later on, Zensar recertified its compliance program to ISO 27001 based on the process approach, thereby replacing its earlier BS 7799 certification. This certification to ISO 27001–based information security brought Zensar huge visibility and confidence among its existing and prospective customers spread across the European Union, the United States, and APAC. This has also made Zensar comply with related information security frameworks, such as PCIDSS and HIPAA.

Currently, Zensar is certified to ISO 27001:2013, in addition to other client-specific compliance programs, such as PCIDSS and HIPAA. The information security management system has benefitted the organization in managing its customer data effectively and efficiently, thereby aligning the information security with business strategy.

Standards and Frameworks at Zensar

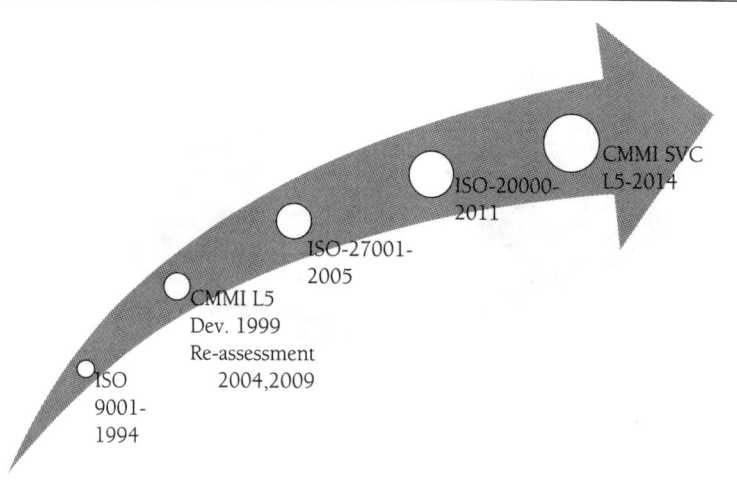

The Lean program, which was initiated in 2012, was targeted at driving Zensar's global delivery, institutionalization of best-practice management systems, and establishing and sustaining a high performing culture. The lean implementation and sustenance program at Zensar has resulted in the streamlining of processes for optimum results, waste reduction, and sharper focus on customer deliverables. The lean framework also focuses on the empowerment of the team to deliver better through better work segmentation and knowledge management. Associates are enabled to practice the lean principles through lean trainings and lean study circles disseminated through formal classroom courses.

From 1996 to 2004, Zensar also implemented total quality management (TQM) through various organizational excellence award schemes, that is, MAIT, RPG, and CII. Key aspects of this implementation are (a) driving TQM down to business unit and department levels within the organization (internal plan) and (b) setting an inspirational goal for the organization (external plan). Many initiatives for bringing a culture of excellence in the organization were born out of this program.

Implementation of the European Foundation for Quality Management (EFQM) framework was initiated in Zensar since January 2010 toward TQM, and Zensar has since then continued to participate in the group-level annual assessment, which has fostered a spirit of organizational excellence within the organization.

The quality mantra at Zensar is to promote adoption, as opposed to compliance, through inclusive and partnership-driven equations with delivery teams. While the achievement of certifications keeps us competitive in the market, the ongoing endeavor is to broaden the scope of quality assurance to provide relevant frameworks to new and emerging services, and hence align quality functions seamlessly with ever-changing business requirements.

Organizational Excellence Framework: EFQM

In the early 1990s, when the CII adopted the EFQM excellence model for the Indian industry and institutionalized CII–Exim awards,

Manufacturers Association for Information Technology (MAIT) followed suit and took an initiative to prepare IT companies for the CII-Exim award. ICL too had adopted EFQM and participated in the CII–Exim awards and won the same in 1993.

This was how the culture of excellence found its roots in the organization. Like everything else, we took this journey of excellence very seriously and invested in training our people to be certified assessors in EFQM under the MAIT program, so that we could drive and institutionalize the culture across the operations of the company. Since then, we have evolved significantly in our excellence journey, and many of our subsequent excellence programs in the organization were born out of this program. The next section talks of one of our most comprehensive and successful excellence programs.

INNOVATION: DRIVING NONLINEAR GROWTH

We brought on board our first CTO, Dilip Ittyera, in 2001 at a time when very few companies in the industry had a formal CTO function. As CTO, Ittyera's clear mandate was to identify new technologies to help the company develop a different point of view in the market and also drive innovation through technology—both continuous and disruptive.

Dilip quickly built a small team under him drawn from existing projects within Zensar and also some good recruits with strong technology and entrepreneurial skills from outside.

The Holy Grail of Software Development: SBP

One of our earliest successes in disruptive innovation was the SBP, a framework for automated software development. Zensar acquired the IP for SBP from a California-based product development company for which our CTO worked with before joining us.

SBP is a software development tool that enables graphically modeling of business processes, designs, and architecture. This was a total disruption from the conventional waterfall method of going from documentation to design to programming. SBP allowed programmers to create a robust diagram of business processes and application designs, much like how an architect creates a blueprint for a house. This was a civil engineering approach to software development and had the power to disrupt the software industry as it reduced delivery cycle times, increased productivity, lowered costs, and improved quality. SBP was clearly ahead of its time because at a time when community development and open source were not even talked about, SBP was a framework that allowed distributed software development.

Each SBP diagram had functional models of the applications, and from these models, a code could be automatically generated on any technology platform. Thus, SBP allowed us to create libraries of use cases, along with corresponding diagrams, that can be automatically generated over and over again on multiple technology platforms. We were grouping these use cases by the industry segments and had soon built a library of solution blueprints for key industry verticals.

SBP clearly had implications for how we would interact with our customers. We began to closely collaborate with the business teams of our customer accounts where we deployed SBP. This was because creating an accurate blueprint of business processes required engagement with the end user. Customer CTOs and CIOs welcomed the involvement of the end user earlier in the software development process as this helped in accurate capture of business requirements. SBP helped in deepening and enhancing our relationship with the customers.

The SBP approach to software development was a paradigm shift from the traditional methods that software engineers in both Zensar and the IT industry were used to. This meant a shift in the kind of skills that our people needed to work on this model as it meant that the programmer's skill set had to be enhanced beyond just programming languages to now understanding of business processes. This implied large-scale training to be able to roll out SBP on a large scale.

In the early days of SBP, Dilip and team faced significant resistance to SBP from all quarters. Our sales executives were reluctant to talk of SBP in their sales calls with current customers, especially with those happy with the service they were receiving from Zensar. They perceived introducing SBP as too much risk into their accounts, as they did not believe the promise that SBP held out in terms of automation, productivity gains, and cost savings. SBP also challenged pricing on projects based on the traditional time and materials contracts because it promised to cut down drastically on the time and effort, and hence it also threatened to reduce revenues from regular Zensar contracts, a possibility that made many sales managers on existing accounts apprehensive about pitching SBP.

While the resistance of sales teams was understandable, our delivery teams too took a very long time to begin to believe in the power of the tool and adopt it in their projects.

Customers also resisted the new technology because industry applications of Unified Modelling Language (UML), which we were using in SBP, had been promised for several years, and had yet to materialize. Thus, they preferred to go the traditional proven route, rather than experiment with an unproven technology. Also, some of our customers perceived that the SBP tool would mean their loss of control over such projects. In addition, deploying SBP required an initial investment in terms of forging new communication mechanisms with the business teams and also additional training of the project teams. Although the projected long-term returns were higher, SBP involved a substantial change of mindset for the customers, and they were not ready for it at that time.

So here we were—we had a tool that our CTO and his team strongly believed to be a disruptive tool that had the power to change the way the industry looked at software development, brought immense value to our customers in terms of quality, time and cost of software development, and had the power to change the lives of software professionals by taking them away from the drudgery of code development and programming and closer to business processes of their customers. In contrast, we had a stakeholder community of customers, sales executives, and project managers who were not willing to deviate from their current models and give SBP a chance.

Dilip, our CTO then, took on the role of an evangelist, and what followed was an intense period of engaging with all of them through training, awareness sessions, demonstrations of the power of the tool, and some prototypes for clients. He hit the road for about six to eight months meeting all our sales teams and key client teams, and it was only after the first SBP project win that we began to see the acceptability of the tool begin to come in slowly. It was not until almost a year later that we had big wins in all our key markets of Japan, the United States, and Europe through SBP. By the end of 2006, several project teams were using SBP-related tools for customers across retail, banking, health and property insurance, technology products, and service engineering. We now also had a growing population of developers with expertise to use SBP effectively in their projects.

SBP provided us distinct market advantage and technology differentiation, and we were leveraging this first-mover advantage that we had with SBP. Thus, it was both time and opportunity for us to commercialize SBP as it was clearly a disruptive technology, not just to Indian IT, but for the global IT industry. We decided to set up an independent business unit, called Innovative Technology Services (ITS), under Dilip's leadership to focus on commercializing SBP and solidifying our competitive advantage among other Indian tier II providers. We also wanted to build upon the success we were seeing in the markets in Asia, Africa, and Europe.

However, we realized that to build upon the early success of SBP and leverage its true potential, it was essential to isolate the ITS business unit from the rest of the organization and treat it very differently from the rest of the other business units. The investments in technology development, the caliber of the people, the team structures, as well as the measure of performance, all had to be very different. So by design, the ITS unit became an organization within an organization, quite inconsistent and incoherent with the rest of the organization.

In fact, Michael Tushman talks about this in detail in the Harvard Business Case Study on Zensar's innovation culture. Thus, the ITS unit continued to focus on leveraging SBP and associated innovative technology services. We also continued to invest in enhancing the power and capabilities of the SBP framework. We pioneered the Blue Print Foundry approach to templatized software development and introduced an innovative business model that linked development teams across near-shore and offshore facilities to create a distributed software production facility. We called the new SBP platform the Global Development Platform, which helped us in driving nonlinear growth for the next three years. The ITS business unit was dissolved subsequently when we moved to the vertical structure.

We have sustained our investment in the SBP platform, which continues to be our flagship innovation (IP) that incorporates software engineering practices by leveraging industry standards, as well as platform agnostic and component-based design models, for accelerated software delivery in a distributed global delivery model. Today, SBP is clearly a differentiator for our AMS services as it is driving reusability and hence higher productivity.

On the basis of our sustained investments in the development of innovative tools such as SBP, we have been formally accredited by DSIR for our R&D efforts.

Cluster Solution for the Automotive Sector: AutoZenics

We had been following the business and technology transformation that the Indian industry was going through in the first decade of the new century, where competitiveness and efficiency became more important now than at any time for the automotive industry. Automotive manufacturers were pressed to keep prices low while coming out with multiple new models to excite the marketplace. This led to enormous pressures on automotive suppliers.

To survive in the markets and be successful, suppliers to major automotive companies had to transform their businesses to adopt lean operations that are driven by demand and were focused on lowering the overall costs of their products. They were also expected to create operational transparency to support the supply chain operations and meet the OEM needs. They were also focusing on supporting the aftermarket channel efficiently by delivering products to dealers and retail outlets.

To meet these challenges, suppliers had to continually improve product quality while lowering product costs. They were looking at technology solutions to support them in all their key functions of design, manufacturing, financial, and CRM and improve operations as well as enhance visibility of the supply chain and increase their competitiveness. These challenges were even more acute for the small and medium suppliers who could not afford the high investments need in technology solutions such as the ERPs.

Sensing these challenges of the SME cluster of automotive suppliers, we invested in developing a cloud-based hosted ERP solution for the automotive cluster, called AutoZenics. It was designed based on our strong manufacturing domain knowledge base and deep insight of lean manufacturing techniques. We collaborated with Microsoft India and two of India's largest OEMs in the auto sector for helping us in designing the solution and also validating it with their suppliers from the auto cluster.

This was the first comprehensive cluster solution built for the auto cluster customized and for the needs of the Indian SMEs. It was built on an MS Dynamics Navision ERP platform as a hosted cloud solution. It was championed by two leading auto OEMs in India for their supplier community.

With a hosted ERP, the auto cluster SME suppliers could enjoy the benefits of a full-fledged ERP solution at a significantly lower cost, as they had to pay only a subscription cost of the services that they consumed, instead of investing in a complete ERP solution along with licenses and the necessary servers to deploy the solution on.

This was received very well by the cluster SME firms as it now gave them a level-playing ground with the other larger suppliers of the OEMs, in term of benefits from technology. They also did not have to worry about the maintenance and upgradation of the ERP as Zensar took the responsibility of keeping the solution updated with new functionalities and also took care of all technical support required for maintaining the solution.

Enabling B2B Conversations: nXchange

Strong business collaboration and process integration with partner and supplier networks are fundamental to any business enterprise, to ensure quick turnaround times, short business cycles, and hence better profitability.

Given our extensive experience with customers who run enterprises that manage very complex partner, dealer, and supplier networks, we identified the need for a solution to make these transactions for the enterprise with its partner/supplier ecosystem faster, cheaper, and better. This need exists for organizations whether they are large global enterprises with decentralized operations spread across geographies or SME enterprises operating locally with fewer business operations or even organizations dealing with integrating disparate entities post M&As.

nXchange is the solution we developed to address this business need. It provides a faster, economical, and a much simple way for enterprises to exchange documents and data with their business entities and facilitates seamless exchange of electronic data and information between networks or clusters of networks. Although there were a few solutions in the market at that time that catered to the needs for document exchange and transformation, they were focused only on exchange of data and information.

Our solution not only addressed the need for basic information exchange but also provided a framework for intelligent routing, which is not just about load balancing but also about prioritizing services for premium partners and suppliers. The inbuilt innovative and extremely flexible subscription framework serves as a one-stop shop to support a multitude of services for a wide range of partners with varied transformation and exchange needs. Moreover, the solution has been designed to allow external pluggables to reduce time to market (TTM) and enhance substantially without compromising the performance and core functionality.

The solution is built using the agile and lean technology principles, ensuring business visibility anywhere, anytime, and ease of business operations. We offer this as a hosted B2B-as-a-service, relieving clients of the hassles of high investments and allowing them to leverage the investments already made in existing IT infrastructure. nXchange helps customers in enhancing the overall effectiveness and efficiencies of the supply chain. It also enhances the transparency, diligence, and visibility of the business operations, thereby reducing costs and transaction turnaround times.

While nXchange is a complete independent solution by itself, we have now also integrated it with our other business solutions for manufacturers such as shop floor automation, dealer portals, and other OmniChannel solutions.

Retail Point-of-Sales Solution: SmartShop

As the Indian retail business was undergoing a transformation globally in the early 2000s, with rapid proliferation of multinational retail chains across geographies, local retailers in India also expanded their business within their domains, with smaller neighborhood shops also sprucing up their operations and strategies to retain their customers. Adding to this market shift, the power of the Internet had also opened up a whole new dimension for the retail industry. The result of this retail boom, quite rightly, was that customers were now not only better informed but also spoilt for choice for both products and prices. This meant that success for the retailers in the crowded and fiercely competitive marketplace now hinged critically on controlling and managing operations effectively.

This was the market need that we decided to address through SmartShop, the end-to-end point-of-sale and retail management solution, that we built to meet the unique and constantly changing requirements of retailers in India. Usable as an off-the-shelf solution, SmartShop is the perfect solution for the entire retail spectrum—right from the small neighborhood store to the large multilocation retail chain. It also works equally well for a very wide range of retail store formats, including, supermarket, general merchandise, grocery, hypermarket, department store, pharmacy, bakery, book shop, clothing and apparel, electronics and consumer durables, among others.

Besides boosting efficiencies at points of sale, SmartShop also provided fast and accurate information, analysis, and reporting. The solution is very simple to use and easy to learn, making it easy for even very small neighborhood retail stores to handle all aspects of their store operations more efficiently. SmartShop helped us in enabling our retail clients to survive and succeed in a very competitive retail environment. We have over 15 retailers in India and elsewhere who have benefited from SmartShop.

Technology Enabling Business: Technology Innovation Group

TIG, our Technology Innovation Group, was set up as early as 2001 when Dilip Ittyera joined us as our first CTO, and since then it has been engaged in continuous investment in new technology solutions in various areas to innovate, differentiate, and deliver value to Zensar and its customers.

The TIG team continues to drive all new technology initiatives and works in collaboration with our vertical and practice teams for the development of IP, accelerators, and tools to drive process automation and productivity improvement and domain solutions. The team has over the last five years, developed several solutions and accelerators, including some internationally patented methodologies in the areas of software engineering.

Ajit Pethkar, our CIO and CTO, is a strong believer that innovation can give Zensar a strong market differentiation. This is how he sees his role as the owner of technology innovation at Zensar:

> At Zensar, my team continuously focuses on building the differentiators for our services in the form of IP and solutions. The software engineering process has evolved over last 15 years and Zensar was the first of its kind to build the patented Solution Blueprint Platform for Global Solution delivery. The SBP platform has been key in implementing model driven designs for our customers.
>
> The trend of services oriented architecture has been well formulated in the form of ready-to-use toolkits for our technical teams. The

toolkits are also being used for reverse engineering of legacy code and enhanced operations management. Our solutions marketplace offers many such toolkits to improve the quality of service.

We are now focused on building new capabilities for Zensar in the space of Automation and Software Robotics as we clearly see the future of the IT Industry being disrupted by these new trends in software engineering practices. My team has a huge responsibility in partnering the practices organization for the adoption, adaption and assimilation of new technology trends like digital, agile, DevOps and autonomics. We are working to integrate the technology platforms with new delivery models like Cloud and Mobile to drive stronger business-IT alignment for our customers. Here is a snapshot of some of the solutions that our TIG has recently developed.

Scaling Incremental Innovations for Large-Scale Adoption

Many technology innovations in Zensar have started as small incremental innovations in the project teams, which were then scaled up with the support of the TIG to become enterprise tools and platforms that we have been able to take to our customers.

Service EDGE is one such innovation. In its current scaled-up form, it is our integrated managed services platform that we are using to deliver best-in-class service experience to our customers. It is built on the four key pillars of operational excellence for software support—service operations, knowledge management, project management, and analytics and reporting. It accelerates the customer's transformation journey by giving them a competitive edge through improved quality and faster time to market, leading to cost optimization.

Today, Service EDGE is the default platform for Zensar for delivering managed services to our clients across technologies. The current form of this integrated platform can be traced back to innovative work done by a project team in one of our largest customer accounts. The team, in its perennial quest for excellence by optimizing the service experience of its customer,

Technology Innovation Group

Technology Innovation Group (TIG)
CTO Office
DSIR Accredited R&D Center

Innovation Engine
Intellectual Property Mgmt
Technology Evangelism

Technology R&D
Emerging technology R&D
Proof-of-concepts

Differentiators
Technology-centric &
aligned to chosen services

Value Creation
Co-creation & technology
services to multiple
Stakeholders

Solution BluePrint
SOA Service-oriented Architecture
Software Engineering/SDLC
Cloud Computing
Big Data & Analytics

SOLUTIONS MARKETPLACE ServiceEdge Zensocial

conceived this platform. They tried to bring together the industry's best practices and Zensar's own extensive experience of service delivery in the form of a framework that provided a single integrated view of the health and efficiency of operations. This framework was then further worked upon by the technology practice teams to enhance its functionality and build it into a cutting-edge platform.

As Aniruddha Mhasitkar, the delivery manager, and Praveen Madhvapathi, the technical mind behind this original framework, remark:

> Continuous innovation is a culture that we have strongly imbibed in our teams and we are constantly looking for ways to work smarter and support our customers better. We are delighted to see that the framework that we have developed has now been scaled to become an Enterprise level platform for Zensar to deliver services to our global customers.

There are several such examples of small innovations being scaled up to become breakthrough innovations by catching these ideas early on and giving the teams the necessary support, guidance, and investment to scale their ideas.

Digital Solutions

ZenSocial is our platform that enables enterprises in their digital transformation journey, leveraging the disruptive changes brought in by social media, cloud computing, big data, and mobility. ZenSocial provides a platform for enterprises to actively listen to social conversations about them and derive actionable insights to address positive and trending behaviors that impact their business in today's globally connected world of consumers and partners.

Solutions MarketPlace is our internal Zensar app store that is available as a self-service platform to host all our mobile app solutions developed for Zensarians globally in a seamless subscription-based mode.

BUILDING THE CULTURE OF EXCELLENCE: ORGANIZATION EXCELLENCE PROGRAM

By 2010, following an aggressive growth and expansion phase, the details of which have been shared in the other chapters of the book, we had reached a point where we were among the top leaders in our peer group of tier II Indian IT players as far as growth was concerned. And this also saw us moving up the NASSCOM ranking from top 25 to top 15.

It was an exciting phase in our journey where we had begun to leverage the strong and enduring client relationships that we built through consistent performance coupled by a strong culture of customer centricity. We were enjoying the trust and confidence of all our strategic clients, and this saw us rapidly expanding our footprint in most of our client organizations and also successfully emerge as the vendor of choice from several vendor consolidation exercises.

By this time, we had created a niche slot for ourselves in all our global client organizations who were working with multiple IT vendors in line with their vendor management strategy of leveraging the tier I players for scale and tier II players for their agility and nimbleness.

Zensar was clearly their preferred tier II vendor as they greatly appreciated the flexibility in our approach and our willingness to adapt our engagement models and processes to their internal IT priorities and business needs. This put us in a good position where we were now competing only with tier I players in all our client accounts, and we were very successful not just in matching them on all performance parameters but also in truly raising the bar for customer centricity.

With the growth trajectory well on track, strongly fueled by mining of our client relationships, we decided that we were now ready for the next sigmoid of growth to take us into the $1 billion club.

So in 2012, we went back to the drawing board to create the blue print and roadmap for the $1 billion march with the aspiration of getting there by 2020.

By now, Zensar was performing consistently, growing the topline at 19 percent with a PAT growth of 20.4 percent by 2012. We had seen eight quarters of successive revenue growth, and our market position was also strengthened with the acquisition of "Akibia," which added $100 million to our topline.

The key imperatives of our $1 billion roadmap were to (a) build top of the class capabilities and (b) achieve operational excellence through efficient practices, processes, and systems.

Even as we started working on this roadmap, we realized that while we had moved into the top band of our peer group on the growth parameter, we were clearly not there as far as profits and operational excellence were concerned. We were aware that in trying to support and fuel the aggressive growth of the past four to five years, we had been focusing on making the necessary investments in building a strong resource pool and creating buffer delivery bandwidth to ensure scalability and also overinvesting in creating new capabilities in both technology services and industry solutions.

While these investments were deliberate, we realized that if we were to realize our bold ambition of the $1 billion target, there was an urgent need for us to identify and drive all levers for cost leadership to ensure we are back on track on operational excellence.

So in March 2012, after extensive research of industry best practices and an internal diagnostic exercise, we decided to embark upon an enterprise-wide organizational excellence program to bring in excellence, efficiency, and effectiveness in all our processes and practices, and thereby drive cost leadership.

Having decided that we will embark upon this journey of excellence, the dilemma that we were faced with was about driving this internally or engaging an external consulting firm to help us with the same. This was a serious dilemma, and the management team was divided on this one. While a part of the management team was of the opinion that we had the collective experience, capability, and discipline to lead an exercise of this nature, many others, including both the authors, believed that there was merit in engaging an external firm to help us with benchmarking our practices with the best-in-class in the industry and thereby benefit from their experience and learning.

Given that we were divided on the approach, we agreed that we will engage McKinsey and Company to do a comprehensive diagnostic study to help us with the benchmarking as well as identification of the key levers for cost leadership. Their excellence framework called P360 and their benchmarking models seemed very appropriate for what we had in mind for our exercise.

The Launch of the Organization Excellence Program

The Diagnostic was formally launched in May 2012, and what followed was six weeks of one of the most comprehensive benchmarking exercises that we ever did in Zensar. The scope of the exercise included all the functions of the organization, excluding only the strategy and sales and marketing functions.

Since the objective of the Diagnostic was to drive cost leadership, the exercise was focused on the following:

1. Cost optimization levers (direct cost, infrastructure costs, and general and administrative costs)
2. Delivery excellence (productivity and efficiency)
3. Contracting excellence
4. Organizational effectiveness (delivery team pyramids, resource management, systems)

The exercise also included direct interactions as well as surveys with all our stakeholders, including key customers, partners, senior management, and associates. The objective was to capture the perception of the stakeholders through these interactions and surveys and validate the same with the metrics and hard data.

We chose to benchmark ourselves with both the tier I and tier II Indian IT players who were in similar business of IT services as we wanted to work toward moving to the industry best-in-class on all key metrics.

The findings from the Diagnostic highlighted the following eight broad opportunity areas for cost optimization and market competitiveness with a savings potential of ₹1 billion over a period of three years.

OE Program 8 Areas of Opportunity

8 areas of opportunity identified with 60% that can be captured internally

Extent of customer touch
- ■ Minimum
- ▨ Moderate
- ■ High

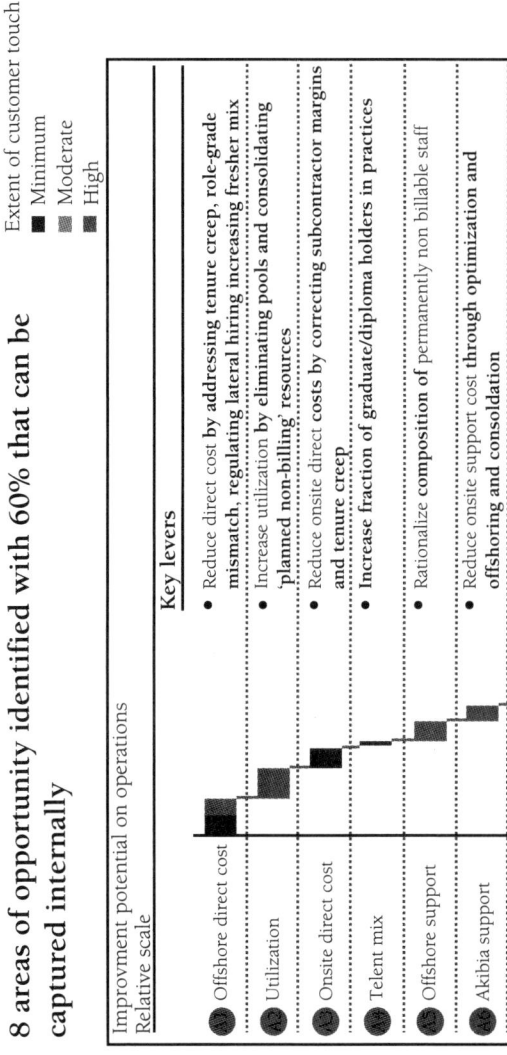

Improvement potential on operations
Relative scale

Key levers

- A1 Offshore direct cost
  - Reduce direct cost by addressing tenure creep, role-grade mismatch, regulating lateral hiring increasing fresher mix
- A2 Utilization
  - Increase utilization by eliminating pools and consolidating 'planned non-billing' resources
- A3 Onsite direct cost
  - Reduce onsite direct costs by correcting subcontractor margins and tenure creep
- A4 Talent mix
  - **Increase fraction of graduate/diploma holders in practices**
- A5 Offshore support
  - Rationalize composition of permanently non billable staff
- A6 Akibia support
  - Reduce onsite support cost through optimization and offshoring and consoldation
- B Productivity
  - Improve productivity by implementing lean levers
- C Contract excellence
  - Renegotiate or restructure contracts to cover key sources of under-recovery or risk to Zensar

Total 59% 16% 25%

We clearly had two choices ahead of us on phase 2 post the diagnostics—drive it internally through a dedicated and competent internal team or engage McKinsey to continue with the next phase of design and implementation of the necessary process and system changes to realize the identified potential cost savings.

We were divided in the management team over this choice. While the dominant view, having seen the McKinsey team in action during the diagnostics phase, was to let them continue with phases, a part of the management team felt that we could drive this internally, as this was no rocket science, as one of the management committee members remarked.

Since we believed that a complete buy in from the entire management team would be extremely crucial for the success of the program, the management team went to vote on this and except for two members voting for an internal team, the rest opted for the McKinsey team.

Looking back now, it was a very wise decision, as the period of seven months that followed saw the organization go through a journey of transformation, reengineering, and redefinition. At the end of the program, not only did we realize more than the projected cost savings, but we were a much stronger, scalable, and resilient organization that was now much more confident of staying on course for the $1 billion target and beyond.

Making It All Happen

It was made abundantly clear to us that the key to making this program successful would be to have two things in place:
1. Complete sponsorship of the CEO and the management team
2. A fully empowered and dedicated internal team led by a strong program leader with very high internal credibility

In fact, McKinsey insisted that we identify and announce the internal team before the formal launch of the program. Considerable thought went into the identification of the internal team as we were well aware that this program would be a transformation program and will demand strong frontline leadership and change management capabilities in addition to excellent execution skills.

Thus, after due internal deliberation, a team was put together by drawing people from across the organization, with diverse yet complementing skills, experience, and capabilities. And one of the authors of this book was given the leadership baton to drive this program. This team was given complete empowerment and access to the CEO and strategy council. And on hindsight, one of the key reasons for the outstanding success that we saw in this program was this empowerment.

There was a lot of deliberation about the positioning of this program internally because we were aware that this transformation program would involve some cost optimization actions that may not be very popular and may create apprehension and concerns in the organization. We were also aware that this was going to be a long-term sustained program. Therefore, we decided to formally brand the program and after considering several options, we agreed on calling it Organization Excellence (OE) program, given that the objective was to raise the bar for excellence in all our functions.

The Formal Launch

We formally launched the OE program with a road show for all our managers led by our leadership team where we shared the objectives, scope, and road map for the program. We also used this road show to address all concerns, queries, and apprehensions. This road show was followed up with a series of smaller group sessions to discuss when and how they would be participating in the program and, more importantly, how the program would benefit each of them both in the short and long term, thereby addressing the "What's-in-it-for-me" query that was on the minds of most of them.

This inclusive approach has greatly helped in setting the right context for the program and driving good adoption.

Delivering Value

The formal engagement with McKinsey ended in January 2013, and at the end of the nine-month assignment, they had helped us in brining transformative changes in the way we planned, designed, and executed our operations. In fact, by the end of the program, we had transformed the operational blueprint of the organization and laid down a strong foundation for profitably, delivering $1 billion business.

Measuring the tangible value from the OE program was straightforward as we had moved the needle on all operational metrics. On key metrics of delivery utilization and time-to-billability of lateral hires, we had moved into the industry best-in-class band for tier I group of firms. On the other metrics of the percentage of fresher intake and average direct cost, we moved up to industry averages, and both these again were important profit maximization levers. Optimization of the non-billable delivery resource cost and streamlining of the subcontractor hiring process also gave us tangible cost reductions. All these levers had a direct impact on our profitability and added three percentage points to our offshore gross margins.

Some of the significant initiatives that we implemented as a part of the program were as follows.

Setting of a Global Resource Management Group

While Zensar had a resource management group as part of the HR function, this was more of an operational function focusing on handling resource allocations and movements between projects and practices. As an outcome of the OE program, we set up a highly empowered resource management group (RMG) function that was accountable for sustaining optimized utilization levels of the delivery organization as well as resource forecasting, planning, and fulfillment to ensure effective resource scalability. We also introduced demand forecasting models, resource rotation guidelines, customized dashboards for effective resource pool management, and a comprehensive skills library.

This function continues to play a very critical role in sustaining optimum results.

Direct Cost Optimization

Standardizing of hiring and project staffing guidelines helped in optimizing direct costs. These included

1. increased intake of freshers and leveraging alternate talent pool by hiring non-engineers for services that did not need engineering skills
2. introduction of guidelines for managerial span to expand portfolios of managers and at the same time ensure healthy pyramid structures
3. revised promotion guidelines to ensure healthy spans and link individual career progression to organizational growth
4. implementation of tenure-based resource rotation across client accounts as well as shores to give associates the opportunity for diversifying their experience and also unlocking talent for staffing new projects

Lean Program for Delivery Excellence

This was one of the most tangible and sustainable outcomes of the OE program. We institutionalized lean delivery practices and processes across the delivery organization through a very robust and comprehensive lean program that involved

1. skilling our project managers in the principles of lean software engineering practices by setting up a lean academy that introduced internal lean certifications and began a lean council for sharing and institutionalizing best practices
2. creating a pool of lean navigators skilled by the McKinsey team in handholding the project teams and taking them through the lean journey

3. creating of lean cook books for all our key service lines, which are guide books for our practicing project managers in planning and executing projects in a lean way

Today, lean is an organization-wide movement that has seen high levels of adoption across our delivery teams and has been an energizing experience for our project managers.

The exercise involved the identification and reduction of waste, idle time, rework, overprocessing, and overproduction. Through the program, we had executed over 10 lean pilot projects of different types and realized a productivity improvement of over 20 percent in these projects.

The more valuable and sustained outcome of the lean exercise was the identification of islands of excellence of best practices and institutionalization of the same to make them a part of our standard operating processes. This also helped us in influencing the mindsets and behaviors of our project managers to think lean, plan lean, and execute lean.

We have now extended the lean approach beyond customer projects, to our business support functions of recruitment, finance, and internal IT and infrastructure systems. Thus, lean has become a part of how we now operate.

Contracting Excellence

This track has been a great learning experience for us. Customer contract management, which hitherto was something that we left entirely to our legal team to manage, has now become an important activity in managing our business. The program has given us some very critical insights into what goes into drawing up strong and sound contracts that was fair to both Zensar and our customers.

This track, which was initially not very popular with our sales teams for obvious reasons, was a tough one for us to implement and took the longest time for successful adoption. But today, the contracting excellence team that was set up as part of the OE program is very popular with our sales teams and has won their respect and is perceived as a strong business enabler. This has happened through a collaborative approach, active handholding,

Who's the Customer? Bonding at the Global Partnership Weekend

Everyone Has a Voice in Strategy Creation: One of Zensar's Path-Breaking Vision Communities

Work Hard, Play Hard: Top Team Leads the Way

You Can Check Out Anytime You Want, But You May Never Leave! An Engaged Zensar Alumni

The Race has Begun: Director Ajit Vaswani Sets the Pace at a Team Offsite in 2000

Many Bricks in the Wall: A Management Team Picture

The Gong Says it All: Celebrating 50 Years at the Bombay Stock Exchange

Cultural Immersion through Indian Kite Flying Festival at an Annual Customer Partnership Weekend

The Team that Makes it All Happen: Zensar's Strategy Council, 2015

The Home We Love: Zensar Campus at Pune

The Ultimate Accolade: CSR Recognition by Dr Abdul Kalam

Flying the Zensar Flag High

Zensar Volunteers Lending a Helping Hand toward a Clean Pune

and frontline leadership by our sales leaders. The sales teams today are much more comfortable and confident in actively participating in discussions with customer teams on coming up with contracts that was win–win for Zensar and its clients.

As part of this track, we also held awareness workshops to educate our project teams on the significance of customer contracts as well as interpretation of the contractual clauses. This has helped greatly in equipping them much better in setting and managing customer expectations on project deliverables. As part of this track, we also set up a pricing cell to streamline the process of pricing our proposals.

Systems and Data

One of the things that the Diagnostic revealed was the need for much stronger integration between our disparate systems of records to enable us to optimize our decisionmaking processes and practices. While we had built a host of internal IT systems over the past decade to automate and streamline our internal business and operational processes, we realized that the systems were not talking to each other in a seamless way, thereby impacting the efficiency and effectiveness of our operational management.

On top of this, with all the new changes that we implemented as part of the OE program, we now had the urgent need to fix this challenge of seamless integration between the systems if we had to sustain the process changes introduced by the program and equip our project managers with the necessary decision-making tools and reports. It was important to make sure that all our operational managers had access to relevant data and information in real time.

Thus, building the necessary systems and dashboards was an important track, and we started focusing on the same from the start of the program, so that we were ready with them by the time we moved from the design to implementation phase of the OE program. This required an overhaul of existing systems being used for project management, costing, and accounting systems. Systems for real-time data and metrics tracking and reporting and online dashboards were designed, built, and rolled out and made available for informed decision making and senior management insights. All this was done in a record time of six months.

Beyond Tangible Benefits

While the tangible business value from the program was significant and we exceeded the goals set for the program, the real value from the program was the change in mindset and culture that the program brought it. The initial apprehension and speculation in the organization about the need for this program were transformed largely into a positive and energizing experience for the stakeholders. Although some of the changes in the policies and guidelines put more emphasis on business value alignment and called for some fundamental changes in our way of working, there was no debate that these changes were needed for our to gear up for growth. The inclusive approach greatly helped in involving the stakeholders in finding, implementing, and adopting the new ways of working.

This was also a transformative experience for the Zensar core team that drove the exercise. They gained invaluable experience and skills in driving sustainable change in culture and mindsets, apart from solutioning and program management. We saw each of the core team members emerge as strong change agents.

Here is what Pushpal Kapadia, the current program leader for the OE program, says about her experience of leading this program:

> When I was offered the opportunity to lead the OE program, I was not sure how it would play out for me but I took it as a new challenge. Looking back now after 2 years in the role, that was a milestone decision for me professionally. The role gave me an opportunity to directly work on areas that were top of the priority list for the organisation at that time, driving cost leadership initiatives through the entire cycle of conceptualisation to execution and sustenance, driving significant bottom line benefits for Zensar.

This role being of a conscious-keeper of the Organisation health parameters demanded active engagement with all key stakeholders, collaboration with all business leaders and execution rigor—all of which helped me in honing my collaborative leadership skills and significantly broadened my horizons wrt [with respect to] understanding how the enterprise works. This has also made me a strong change leader. The exposure that this role gave me, working with the Executive leadership team and the Senior management team, helped me connect the dots and truly align the OE program objectives with the Organization strategy and business goals.

Personally this has been a great leadership journey for me and the value it has added to me personally and professionally is beyond measure.

What started as an India-centric effort was extended to all our overseas locations, including the acquired business of Akibia. This enterprise-level approach facilitated seamless integration of operations, policies, and systems across the organization and also helped in accelerated integration of the Akibia business with Zensar.

In the closing road show of the McKinsey engagement in January 2013, we had the individual track owners from Zensar present the summary of what they achieved in their respective tracks and their plans to sustain the same going forward. This was great for ensuring sustained ownership and focus long after the formal engagement with McKinsey ended.

Driving Adoption

A few things that helped in high adoption levels for the program were as follows:

1. Introduction of OE KRAs for the entire leadership and management team helped in topdown alignment of goals, starting with the CEO also carrying an KRA. The KRAs were customized based on the role of the individual in the OE program.

2. Establishment of a single primary owner from the leadership team for every OE. For example, the Contracting Excellence was owned by the CFO himself.
3. Strong governance and review framework: We instituted a monthly OE review meeting with the entire leadership team chaired by the CEO and weekly track-wise reviews with the track owners. This rigor in reviews was ruthlessly followed throughout the duration of the program and continues even today.
4. Inclusive solution design workshops involving all stakeholders ensured buy in and ownership of all stakeholders for the final solutions. This also greatly helped in presyndication and validation of solution options that has helped in coming up with practical and effective solutions. Through this program, the McKinsey team has helped in equipping our teams with some very effective tools for collaborative and inclusive solutioning. The Gallery Walks to showcase early wins and institutionalize new solutions and the collective solutioning using voting aids were two such tools that have been great enablers to make this an inclusive experience for all stakeholders. They have now become an integral part of all our large change management initiatives and are used widely by all functions.
5. Executive sponsorship from the CEO: A transformative program of this nature needed complete support, enablement, and empowerment from the CEO and the leadership. The CEO's direct involvement and participation was one of the biggest enablers.
6. Transparency and clarity of goals and objectives: The regular reviews and status updates to all the stakeholders at every stage of the program have helped in driving shared ownership and accountability of all stakeholders.

Sustaining the Culture of Excellence

While the program delivered on all its promises of moving Zensar into the best-in-class category on all key operational metrics and also helped in strengthening organizational effectiveness to gear up for the next growth cycle, what it has done for the organizational culture has been both much more valuable and intangible.

It has reenforced the culture of excellence and helped us raise the bar for ourselves on performance measures. The fact that the OE continues to run even now three years after the McKinsey engagement, with the same rigor, discipline, and business alignment, is a true manifestation of the impact that the program has had on the organization.

We continue to invest in a dedicated OE team that works directly with the strategy council on sustaining the high bar for operational excellence by focusing on all cost leadership and delivery excellence levers. Each year, the OE team engages with the strategy council and the business leaders in building the charter for the OE program for the year to ensure that the program is aligned with the business priorities of the organization.

Today, well into the fourth year of its inception, the OE program has established credibility for itself as Business Excellence function and is seen as a function for driving excellence through initiatives that support business growth and enable individuals to become better professionals, managers and leaders while continuously raising the bar for excellence.

It has transformed into a "way of life" and has got embedded into the organization's culture. It has become the custodian of all excellence initiatives in the organization and spearheads any new initiative that needs organization level change and ruthless execution.

CHAPTER 7

Motivating People

The Secret Sauce

The Zensar that was born on Valentine's Day in 2000 brought with it a great promise of change and an end to the long period of confusion and listlessness. The new name triggered both intrigue and curiosity and, as many of us who were witness to this rechristening of the organization would say, there was a newfound hope that finally there would be stability, sense of purpose, and a new direction.

The name Zensar was born from an elaborate rebranding exercise that was led by the then CEO, L.C. Singh, when he came onboard, putting an end to a period of fleeting leaders. The team went to vote on the new name, and "Zensar" scored easily over other options. We do believe that the birth of Zensar on Valentine's Day was no mere coincidence but carried a larger purpose that we now see being lived out by all of us.

Here is how Raj Dhillon, an ex-Zensarian who retired from the company after over two decades, recollects the renaming of the company:

Renaming of the Company as Zensar Technologies was a significant event in our history. Apart from the marketing benefits of presenting a common face to our customers across the world, "Zensar" brought together diverse entities with different work cultures and ethos under a single flag. Our people, dispersed in many countries, for once felt they belonged to a company "back home." It also helped us to break free from a past shaped by a declining hardware business and move forward with hope as a part of the successful software revolution that was shaping the future.

Zensar was built at a time and place that was unique in the Indian IT industry in the early 2000s, and we believe that we have made the most of the opportunity that was provided by history.

The values the team chose to steer the new organization under a new leadership through the reconstruction and transformation phases following the period of confusion were well thought through and have played an important role in shaping the culture of the organization in the years to come—a culture of curiosity, care, and openness.

Customers, people, and community continue to be our core values, while transparency, innovation, and passion for excellence in everything we do are the other values that have helped in shaping our organizational culture, which we proudly share as our 5F culture framework.

QUOTES FROM SHWETABH AND ISHITA

Fast, the first of the five Fs of our culture framework, is about speed in everything we do—from being fast in responding to the stated and unstated expectations of all our stakeholders and the dynamic external business environment. This has helped us in building the capability to successfully steer the organization through multiple restructuring and transformation exercises, be it in moving from being horizontal business units aligned to technology service lines to becoming truly verticalized business units or from transforming our sales organization that was region focused to becoming industry vertical focused.

Focus, the second F in our framework, is what keeps us hooked onto our chosen business strategies and goals and brings us back on track even as we meander into new business lines, territories, and domains. The constant revalidation of our strategic direction and plans and the midcourse corrections and amendments to cater for unanticipated internal and external developments come from this culture of focus.

Flexible, the third F in the framework, gives us the agility and flexibility to stay nimble enough to continuously reinvent and reorient ourselves to make the most of the opportunities that come our way and also stay relevant and ahead of the game. This is also something we very strongly encourage and reward in our people—willingness to take bold risks, experiment, and explore unchartered trails.

Friendly is the fourth pillar in our framework and truly embodies the essence of Zensar—the philosophy of love on which this organization has been built and continues to thrive is what this culture pillar is all about. This is very intrinsic to our culture and is very distinctly experienced by all our stakeholders, especially our customers. This is often the first word that our clients and partners use to describe their experience of working with Zensar, and this underlies the way we treat all our stakeholders.

The last pillar of the framework is the intrinsic part of our culture—fun. We have always believed that all work and no fun is what kills organizations and its people. For us, fun is about celebrating every aspect of being a Zensarian, it is the spirit that keeps us charged and going all the time. Fun for us is way beyond fun events and activities and is about enjoying the experience of being a part of this organization. Seeking out fun in everything we do is second nature to us now.

These 5Fs collectively make Zensar what it is—a very proud and responsible company that is large enough to deliver but small enough to care.

This 5F culture framework is what makes all of us proud Zensarian!

Even as we have grown manifold in numbers and our global presence over the past 15 years, we have sustained this strong culture, and we are truly proud of the foundation that we have built on which can stand many future generations of Zensar.

THE PHILOSOPHY OF LOVE FOR ASSOCIATES

We are often asked by our clients and partners about the philosophy of Zensar and its culture. They find it rather amusing when we say that Zensar is built on the philosophy of love. We truly believe in this, and this belief has been key to building a unique culture at Zensar that is a great blend of respect for both people and performance. Our conviction has always been and continues to be that a caring organization nurtures happy people who are most motivated to give their best to the organization. This and this alone will be the enduring competitive edge that organizations can and should aspire to build if they want to future-proof their business and growth strategies.

This philosophy of love has been the underlying theme in all our people practices at Zensar. People are at the center of everything we plan and do here at Zensar. We are immensely proud that we have been able to sustain this culture even as we have grown over the last 15 years to become a global organization across 15 nationalities and 22 countries, including five global acquisitions.

In the rest of the sections in this chapter, we have attempted to share some of our strong people engagement practices at Zensar. These are practices that have helped us not only in enjoying talent retention levels much higher than our peers but in also building strong, stable, and winning teams that are self-driven and motivated to drive the organization to success.

THE ATTRACT–ENABLE–RETAIN CONTINUUM AT ZENSAR

Our talent management framework has three dimensions of attract, enable, and retain, bringing innovation to the way we spot external talent, develop internal talent, as well as engage with them. This framework has enabled us in building an organization that we are truly proud of.

Attract–Enable–Retain Framework

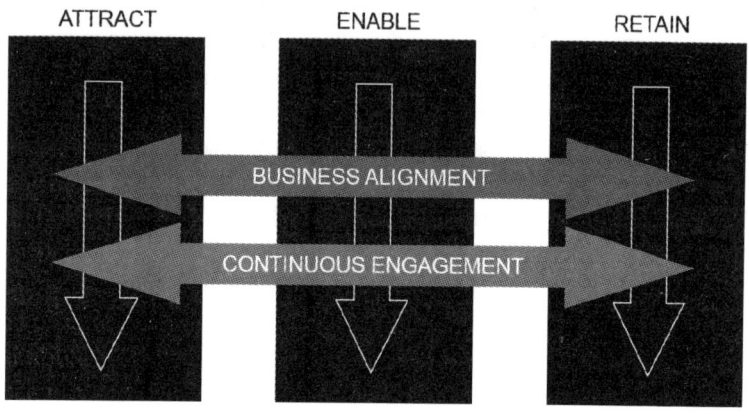

We are delighted to share some of these innovative people practices with our readers.

Bringing Talent Onboard

Boomerang Hiring

We have always stayed connected with ex-Zensarians through our very strong alumni network, rehiring many of them at all levels. We call this boomerang hiring, and this has now become an important hiring channel for us. With the connectedness powered by social media now, we include them in all our celebrations and keep them updated on the story of Zensar. Many of our senior alumni join us in our key annual events.

There is a very strong alumni network of ICIM, the entity that existed before we became Zensar. Even today, the ICIMers meet regularly almost 15 years after the renaming.

Many of our leaders in Zensar today have been Boomerang hires.

Zenrich, our employee referral program, is our dominant hiring channel, with over 35 percent of hiring happening through this referral program, and this includes senior hires too.

At Zensar, any candidate who accepts our offer immediately becomes a part of the family, way before he or she comes onboard. We have a dedicated team that engages with all the potential hires all through the offer-to-joining period, helping them with all the support they may need in moving to Zensar. This has helped us not only in sustaining very high offer conversion rates but also in keeping the engagement levels high.

Talent Enablement

Enabling talent at Zensar has not been just about skills and competency development. The focus has always been on building good professionals and a strong internal talent pool through on-the-job training and development. And for that, we have chosen to go beyond just formal training and development frameworks and provided platforms and forums for our associates to develop both technical and soft skills through applied learning. Forums such as Vision Communities (VCs), iZen, and JUGNU, which we discuss later in this section, have been excellent grooming grounds for talent development, and many of our successful leaders of today have been active in these forums.

The following is our integrated talent development framework:

We have a term for Zensarians who have joined us as young management trainees and have scaled and grown to become leaders and managers in the organization—"Made in Zensar." We are very proud that this tribe of "Made in Zensar" leaders is growing very fast in both numbers and diversity of roles. Shwetabh, one of our associates from this tribe, states as follows:

Integrated Talent Management Framework

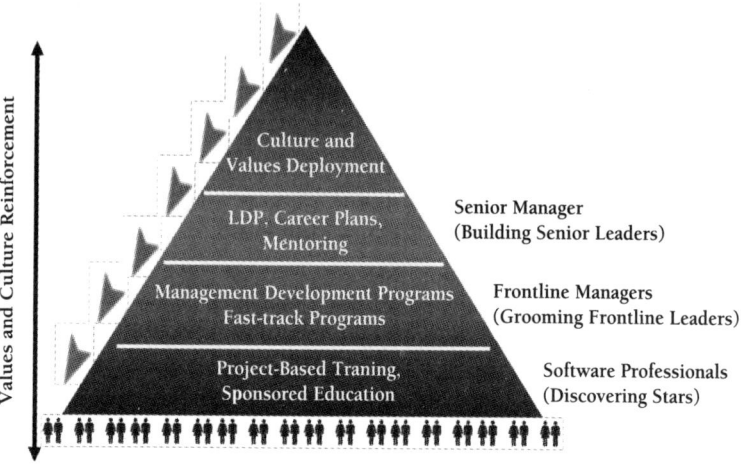

I joined Zensar more than 16 years back as a management trainee and I must say that this journey has been very exciting and fulfilling. I was entrusted with multiple challenging assignments during these years, which I have been able to manage successfully with the support and mentoring from "TEAM Zensar." I still remember the day way back in 2009 when I was given the responsibility of taking over the engagement management of our largest multi-million dollar Retail customer account even though I was relatively junior in years of experience for a responsibility of that size and strategic significance. This is a great testimony of Zensar's 5F culture of investing in the development of its people by presenting them with opportunities and challenges to grow. In Zensar, associates are valued for their capability and potential, both of which are not measured merely by the number of years of experience. There are several other examples like mine, where the organization has invested in developing associates by presenting them with opportunities to play to their strengths and has whole heartedly supported career movements across portfolios and functions. This is one of the key things about Zensar that makes me very proud of being a Zensarian.

Leadership development has always been a very serious and rigorous process at Zensar where we also leverage the strong people development practices of the RPG group. The framework we use for leadership development is called the Organization Management Review (OMR) and is a very robust and comprehensive framework for succession planning and leadership pipeline development. The framework allows us to create succession plans for all critical and key positions in the organizations as well as all high-potential associates in the middle and senior management bands. These succession plans are supported by comprehensive development plans that are owned by our learning and development (L&D) team. The OMR plans are reviewed twice every year by the strategy council as well as the management board members of the RPG group.

Another key HR practice in the talent development framework is the practice of having career dialogues with our critical talent and high-potential employees, to understand their career aspirations, discuss their strengths and areas of development, and jointly identify their development action plans as well as discuss career growth options and opportunities. These conversations also help our managers to realistically set and manage expectations of their teams on possible career growth opportunities.

These career dialogues are very sensitive conversations that need to be handled with great sensitivity and maturity, as they have a significant impact on the motivation and morale of the associates. Thus, we invest in training and skilling all of our managers to equip them for these conversations. All managers go through the training programs on "Crucial Conversations" and "Appreciative Enquiry."

While the OMR framework drives our Organization Development (OD) processes, we use the formal in-house development programs such as the Leadership Development Program (LDP) and Management Development Program (MDP) for development of our junior and middle managers. These programs are designed in-house and delivered entirely by our senior management.

Sushama Kulkarni, who heads our OD function as part of the HR organization, has been the custodian of our in-house LDP and

MDP programs. In her words:

> We started our in house LDP and MDP Programs in 2013 to enhance the capabilities of the senior and middle management associates and also build a strong internal talent pipeline for supporting organization growth and development. These programs were customized to equip our managers and leaders in effectively resolving business and managerial challenges that deal with in their roles.
>
> The Learning team that worked on the design had Focus group discussions with prospective participants, meetings with the CEO and other leaders, and also captured inputs from the HR leaders of the RPG group to design the courses and create the content. The pedagogy involved the use of classroom sessions, role plays, case studies and action learning.

While the focus of the LDP sessions was to offer participants a broader strategic perspective and industry trends in the global economy, the focus of the MDP sessions was project economics and team management.

Every year, we have over 100 managers going through these programs. For the senior management team, we leverage the advanced Leadership development programs at global institutes such as HBS, Wharton, INSEAD, IIMs, and ISB.

This mix of formal development programs and on-the-job learning programs supported by the very comprehensive OD framework of the OMR is what we use to develop a strong internal talent pool for the company.

Ishita Roy, who has joined us as a young software engineer 16 years back and is now one of the senior delivery leaders, reflects on her journey in Zensar:

> It was in late 1999 that I joined Zensar in their UK team, as a young professional coming from a short stint with one of our leading Indian tier I IT companies and was not sure of what to expect from a company much smaller in size and lesser known in the Industry. On the very first day, I received a call from our UK Country head, welcoming me onboard. This sweet and

unexpected gesture overwhelmed me and continues to stay imprinted permanently in my memory. That was an important value that I picked up about treating each individual in the team as an asset and I continue to practise this legacy of making people in my teams feel special.

It is several years now that I have moved my base from UK to India and even today my manager makes it a point to walk to my cabin to wish me on my birthday and hand me my birthday voucher. And this does make me feel like an excited and energetic sixteen year old even after 16 long years in the organization!

These are simple gestures but leave an enduring impact on people and this is where an employee transforms from being an individual to becoming a Zensarian and an integral part of the organization. I continue to be a proud Zensarian!

TECHNICAL COMPETENCY CENTER

The center addresses the ongoing skill development needs of the technical workforce throughout the hire-to-retire cycle of the associates. We have a strong internal faculty of practicing technical experts and professionals drawn from our global project teams. This team delivers a majority of our technical training programs, which are augmented by a robust eLearning program for our on-site teams.

Our internal certification programs like Project Management, Lean Delivery, as well as Agile Development practices are designed, developed, and delivered internally. By linking them to Career Progression of our technical workforce, we have been able to create a strong pull for continuous L&D.

Our Domain Academy supports our aggressive verticalization journey. It offers Domain skills ranging from foundation courses to advanced industry certifications to our technical workforce. This is helping us in linking our services and solutions to relevant business outcomes for our customers and thereby supporting them in their business transformation.

BUILDING BALANCED LEADERSHIP TEAMS

From a very poor gender diversity metric of 8 percent women in the workforce and Zero representation in the senior Leadership team, to 50 percent women at the entry level and 30 percent women in the management team, including an independent woman director on our board, the journey for us has been very exciting and also very challenging.

We are extremely proud that women leaders are now leading critical portfolios in Zensar, such as global marketing, contracting, quality, delivery excellence, and strategic services apart from HR and software delivery.

The second author herself started her Zensar story as a young project manager and is now the senior-most woman executive in the RPG group. We share with pride that 80 percent of the women leaders in the group are home grown from Zensar.

Women for Excellence (WE) was started by the two authors in 2004 as an initiative to identify, nurture, and groom women leaders internally. The WE initiative has significantly grown in relevance to growth and business and is today transformed into a very vibrant Women Executive Board (WEB) that in addition to continuing the focus on building strong women leaders is now also working with the management council on driving important organization-wide initiatives.

Shubha is one of our women leaders who have confidently taken on the challenge to head our quality function when the incumbent function head retired and the position opened up. We wanted to give the opportunity to our internal talent rather than look for an external replacement. Shubha was a young quality manager at that time and has confidently scaled to lead the organization through two major CMMI assessments in the last two years apart from driving key business-enabling initiatives. Shubha truly believes that if you have the ambition, then there is no dearth of opportunities in Zensar.

> At Zensar, there are no limitations on who you want to be- as long as you have the potential and conviction to make it happen.

My personal experience is that I have had the opportunity to traverse across diverse domains and territories and roles, always with tremendous support and mentoring from management.

In my current role as Head of Quality for Zensar, there is absolute empowerment to drive continuous improvement and excellence across the organization. There are no boundaries to the difference that we can make, the changes we can fashion towards holistic growth of the organization.

There are several young leaders like Shubha who have come forward to take on new responsibilities and grab opportunities that opened up as we have grown and expanded.

Zensar is also actively driving the diversity CoE for the RPG group and playing a leadership role in helping the other group companies in implementing the WE best practices of Zensar. In addition, our WEB team is also actively engaged in all the key industry initiatives focused on women leadership, and these include NASSCOM, CII, and WILL, among others.

The WEB is discussed in more detail in a later section in this chapter where we share how we are using the WEB forum to identify and nurture women leaders.

TALENT RETENTION

We have always enjoyed talent-retention level much higher than the industry peers. The secret sauce for this has been our entire approach toward retention. Our philosophy that happy people give their best to the organization is the cornerstone of our people-retention framework.

We famously call this the "Different Strokes for different folks" framework because we believe the needs, wants, and expectations of our associates at each level in the organization are very different, and hence our engagement framework needs to be also aligned to their needs and wants.

The framework is shown below.

Different Strokes for Different Folks

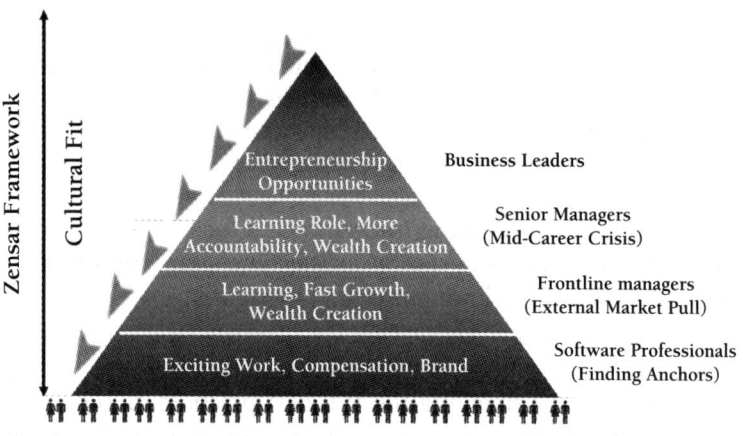

In an industry with double-digit attrition and single-digit average employee tenures, we do not believe in zero attrition. Some amount of talent churn is healthy for the organization as long as it does not hurt our business and we do not lose our high-potential talent. It allows us to bring in fresh talent with new perspectives, experiences, and approaches.

CRITICAL TALENT MANAGEMENT

While some amount of churn is good for bringing in new talent, we take our critical talent engagement and retention very seriously. Every year, we identify about 10 to 12 percent of our workforce as our critical talent through a very comprehensive talent identification process that allows us to look at both the performance and potential of our associates. Critical talent engagement is a very focused process that is driven by our managers and enabled by our HR team. We look at their engagement from a holistic view to ensure that we understand their career aspirations, give them ample opportunities to play to their strengths, and also ensure that they are compensated fairly and receive the necessary developmental inputs and mentoring to succeed in their roles.

We are proud that our critical talent retention across levels and functions in the organization has consistently been over 98 percent for the past many years. This, we believe, is a benchmark in an industry like ours.

One key enabler for such high retention levels is our philosophy that talent management is everybody's business in Zensar and is not outsourced to the HR function. Our leadership team, including the CEO, the line managers, and HR team, carries talent-retention goals as their KRAs, and this alignment has been a great enabler for us to ensure we take retention seriously and work as a team to ensure we retain our talent.

Deepanjan Banerjee, business head of our largest business unit, remarks on the business-enabling role that HR plays in talent retention:

> Sometimes you need a customer to recognize and appreciate the business value being provided by HR and other support functions. In case of the Mfg VBU and especially for Cisco, the HR function absolutely stands out as a prime example of this when a visiting Cisco customer delegation highlighted this as a major enabler for industry best retention metrics. The Business HR team is part of the Delivery teams in every sense of the term. From being physically seated in the midst of the delivery teams, from not just being an immediate point of contact but also being able to sense unstated demands, aspirations and grievances, the HR function is an extremely valuable business ally of my group.

THE ASSOCIATE RELATIONS FUNCTION

We were the first in the industry to set up the associate relations (AR) function, which today is largely responsible for the high employee engagement levels as well as the talent-retention levels in Zensar. This team takes the HR function to the employees by embedding AR executives in the project teams. They are the listening posts who directly engage with associates to ensure that the associates have a go-to person in the AR for any issues/concerns/queries. They cut across the reporting hierarchies and functional boundaries and work collaboratively with all other business-enabling functions to ensure that all the issues and concerns of associates are addressed and effectively resolved.

They are also a big part of our change champions group that drives all organization-wide change initiatives given their access to every associate in the organization and their ability to get the pulse of the organization culture and associate sentiment. They are a part of all key initiatives that involve associate participation and are the custodians of our 5F cultural framework.

Our process for hiring executives for the AR function is very robust, rigorous, and detailed. We take significant time and effort in finding candidates for this function, as it takes the right mix of head and heart to be able to play this role, and it is important that an AR is very responsible, highly motivated, and self-driven apart from being a good listener and strong in issue resolution. It has been our experience that it is easier to find this heady mix in a young HR executive than in a highly experienced HR professional. Thus, our AR function is staffed with very bright young HR professionals who have been chosen with great care. This team is constantly innovating to find ways to further strengthen the associate engagement and has direct access to the leadership team to put forth new ideas, suggestions, and thoughts.

The AR team has developed some very innovative engagement practices and tools taking employee engagement beyond the conventional and time-tested industry practices. The early warning system (EWS) is one such AR dashboard that each AR maintains for the group of associates that he or she is responsible for. The EWS helps the AR in proactively identifying disengaged associates and triggering timely interventions and actions in collaboration with the line managers to address the cause of disengagement. This has helped us in turning around potential attrition cases and is one of the potent ingredients in our secret sauce for very high talent-retention levels.

Another key enabler for talent retention has been the strong top-down alignment of retention goals across the leadership and management teams. We do not know of too many organizations where starting with the CEO, all leaders, and managers across all functions carries a hard KRA (performance measure) for talent retention and engagement. This alignment drives strong collaboration between the line and HR functions for all people management practices.

TALENT ON DEMAND

Zensar has been one of the first few IT organizations to anticipate the challenge of finding talent that is both skilled and relevant to support the anticipated business growth opportunity that the industry could foresee way back in the early 2000s. So we began to invest in building a "talent-on-demand" model in partnership with academic institutions and training partners for training and skilling fresh talent while they were still in the final year of their professional education. We also collaborated with the institutions in improvising their academic curriculum in making it more relevant for the industry needs and orienting the faculty in practical application-driven teaching practices. We work with our training partners to develop customer training programs that are a rich blend of fundamentals of software engineering practices, soft skills for working in a global environment, and practical application of the skills.

We have been continuously improvising on this model for the last decade, and based on our very positive experience with this Source and Train model, we have now successfully developed a very comprehensive employment skills development (ESD) program as part of Zensar Foundation, which is our CSR charter.

In this program, we are partnering with over 50 professional colleges in tier II and tier III cities of India, because we believe that there is a large raw talent pool available in these cities that is still waiting to be skilled and trained to meet the growing IT industry demands for good talent. Thus, we focus on students with below-average academic scores and soft skills and work with them in their final year of college to address the gap in both the technical and soft skills. In addition, through this program, we also invest in reskilling and reorientation of the faculty in the current IT practices and technologies as we strongly believe that it is equally, if not more, important to invest in the faculty. We run foundation courses for the faculty on our campus where they get to interact with our senior practitioners to get exposure to the new trends in software engineering, such as agile development, software automation, and digital technologies such as cloud and mobility.

Here is what Dr Anand Bhalerao, principal and dean of one of the engineering colleges in our ESD program, states about the program:

> It has been a privilege and honour to have signed an MOU with ZENSAR where in our students got an opportunity to be part of Employee Skill Development (ESD) program of Zensar Technologies. Zensar therefore occupies a very special space in the list of companies who conduct campus hiring in our College. ESD program by ZENSAR has been extremely fruitful and beneficial to the Students. It has definitely provided a platform which has made them Industry ready and made them realize the importance of Soft Skills and Technical Training pertinent to the Industry. Students have experienced a positive change in their personality and improvement in their soft skills as well as the importance of interpersonal skills.
>
> The program has helped students to shape their careers as IT professionals, right from learning programming languages to polishing their interpersonal skills. The ESD program is giving them an edge over others. The trainers were extremely helpful and their technical acumen has been above par and commendable.
>
> BVUCOEP and ZENSAR have forged a long lasting relationship mutually beneficial which has now been taken to another level by virtue of the ESD Program.

The ESD program is in its second year now, and over 2,000 students have been trained through this program so far, with over 70 percent of them being able to be employed in the industry in some of our tier I and tier II IT firms.

We hope to scale this program to over 100 colleges and 5,000 students in the year ahead and taking the program to all states in India.

SUSTAINING THE DIVERSE AND INCLUSIVE CULTURE AT ZENSAR

The inclusive and open culture that we have built in Zensar is the very core of our organization strategy and is something that we are truly proud of. It is important for us to sustain and continue to strengthen this even as we continue to scale and grow on all business dimensions.

Julie Machnik was heading the marketing function for Akibia, the business that Zensar acquired in 2010. She has now expanded her portfolio beyond Akibia and heads our entire Zensar US Marketing function. She states this about how she experienced the global culture of Zensar:

> I joined the Zensar family five years ago as part of the US Akibia acquisition. I've had the pleasure of traveling to our Europe and India headquarters allowing the opportunity to learn and embrace new cultures and work with cross functional teams across the globe. Along the way I've met and collaborated with so many amazing associates, something that has been fostered by the people-centric culture that Zensar provides. Working for a truly global organization has been an amazing journey so far and I'm looking forward to our shared adventures ahead!

Our strong diversity and inclusion (D&I) focus comes from our belief that diversity fosters creativity and innovation while inclusion drives alignment and collaborative leadership. Two D&I boards that are core to our strategy implementation are our Shadow Execution Board (SEB) and WEB.

VISION COMMUNITIES

Vision Community (VC) is a very powerful forum in Zensar for driving ideation, innovation, and experimentation What started as a forum for inclusive people engagement way back in 2001 has evolved over the years to become an integral part of our strategy formulation and implementation framework. The forum, which is run as an annual process, has given Zensar several innovative ideas, many of which have shaped the strategy and growth trajectory of the company in the last 15 years.

The VC cycle involves a very inclusive ideation process that runs both online and offline and is open to Zensarians across all levels, locations, and functions. This is followed by the formation of cross-functional teams that evaluate the ideas and shortlist those with significant relevance to Zensar's strategy and goals. The teams work on taking the shortlisted ideas from the drawing board to actual deliverables under the mentorship of the senior leaders. The power of the forum is in the inclusivity and opportunity for every Zensarian to stand up and be counted as well as contribute to the company's strategy and growth. The VC forums have also been excellent hunting grounds for spotting and grooming young talent into future leaders. Many of Zensar's current leaders have been active VC champions in the past. It is not surprising at all that the retention and engagement levels of our VC champions have always been relatively much higher than the rest of the organization.

The VC forum has been running for the last 15 years consistently driving innovation, intrapreneurship, and inclusivity. The success of the VC initiative at Zensar lies in the way new ideas are being transformed into tangible value addition for the organization through robust execution and collaboration, in addition to reinforcing Zensar's culture of inclusivity, openness, freedom, and innovation.

Ruchi Mathur, who led the VC program at Zensar last year, states:

> The Vision Community is an excellent equalizer, bringing everyone to the level of their ideas and offering personal growth

in terms of visibility and the experience of "marketing" one's idea. It also affords great business value. I was personally involved in implementing ZenPoints ... an idea that emerged from Vision Community and has been one of HR's most successful reward and recognition initiatives. ZenPoints has been around for 3 years now and is fully institutionalized, which is really the power of Vision Community ... the fact that the selected ideas actually get implemented and integrated within the system.

Our VC model caught the eye of Professor David Garvin of the Harvard Business School who captured our VC story in the form of an HBS case study in 2010. The case is now taught every year as part of the strategy course for the students of the MBA program at HBS.

What is even more remarkable is that an innovative idea from one of the early VC forums led to the investment in the development of a disruptive technology framework called SBP that redefined software development and delivery for Zensar. This gave Zensar an unfair advantage for several years before the industry caught onto the concept of automation and distributed global delivery models. This also gave us our second HBS case study on Technology Innovation by Professor Michael Tushman. This case is also taught regularly at HBS.

THE SHADOW EXECUTIVE BOARD

The SEB is run by a cross-functional and diverse group of young high-energy and high-potential Zensarians drawn from across the functions and chaired by a mentor from the management council. This team works very closely with the strategy council and contributes to our strategy formulation, validation, and implementation processes. Given their diversity, they bring in a different perspective and an alternate point of view to our strategic thinking and visioning and help us in validating our plans and approaches.

Participation in the SEB has also been a great opportunity for associates to develop strong understanding of our strategies and business imperatives apart from learning to work with a diverse set of stakeholders and driving strategic priorities and plans.

Sanjana Vaidya, one of our young HR leaders and an active SEB member, shares her SEB experience:

> I believe Leadership development takes place under conditions of real stress and SEB really gives you an opportunity to experience this stress and this helps in your development in a challenging environment.
>
> I was happy to have been a part of SEB for two consecutive years and also fortunate to get executive guidance and mentoring from the SEB mentors. For both the years, the challenges thrown at us were different and involved cross-functional, cross-geography interactions which have also helped in developing perseverance and tenacity needed to work with a diverse team, towards a common goal.
>
> Honest, objective and timely feedback received through interactions with the executive leadership gave us great insights to how top management looks at strategy and how they make strategic decisions by thinking and applying Business first! I am sure the SEB experience has made me a far more confident professional with a much better understanding of the organization and has helped me develop a very powerful internal network of stakeholders.
>
> This platform continues to be an aspiration for every associate!

THE WEB

The WEB is another very empowered D&I board that is run by a cross-functional team of women leaders from across the functions of the organization. This team is mentored by and works directly with the strategy council on strategic organizational initiatives that involve change management, consensus building, and perseverance. One of the key charters of the WEB team is also to identify and foster women leaders in the organization by ensuring that we provide an environment that is not only gender neutral, but allows our women to aspire and achieve leadership positions in Zensar. The WEB team is also constantly benchmarking our people practices with the best in class in the industry and brining in new practices. Thanks to the excellent effort of our WEB team, we were the first in the IT industry to have an on-campus day care center to support our young parents. This has helped us take the retention of women Zensarians proceeding on maternity leave to 100 percent, with all of them returning back to work.

Purnima Menon was the first convener of the WEB team and continues to play a very active role in the WEB initiatives. She has played a leadership role in making the creche-on the-campus plan happen. In her words:

> I have been a part of WEB ever since 2010 and my association with the WEB has been one of immense pride and pleasure. It has helped me expand my professional reach by taking personal responsibility for making things happen even beyond my role and work boundaries, within and outside Zensar as well.
>
> While WEB has helped deploy several best practices to foster work–life balance for all Zensar associates, establishing the crèche-on-campus was an initiative led by me and has been a personal achievement. It gives me immense joy to see the young parents dropping off their little ones at the Zensar crèche and getting to work without any worry.
>
> In the last few years, the WEB has evolved into an organization wide platform for inducting and grooming women leaders, providing them opportunities to hone their leadership skills and also pursue their career aspirations.

Our WEB team is also behind rolling out some very effective people engagement practices. Two such practices that are helping us in both talent acquisition and retention are the "work-from home" and the "time-off-scheme (TOS)" practices that give our associates flexibility in better managing their work–life balance.

Several Zensarians, both men and women, have been able to avail of these associate-friendly practices, and this has helped us not only in sustaining very high talent-retention levels but also in rehiring several ex-associates.

Preetha has been with Zensar for 19 long years, in multiple roles spanning across administration, CEO's office management, HR, and now CSR. She has found the TOS option very helpful in effectively managing her home and work priorities:

> In a career span of 19 years at Zensar, HR has pleasantly surprised me time and again with its associate friendly practices. Flexibility of the work-from-home option and the day-care centre on campus are great initiatives. My delight with the HR practices was enhanced further when I had a delicate situation at home and needed to attend to my family's immediate concern for an indefinite period. The unique facility of Time- Off-Scheme (TOS) came to my rescue. I was offered a 3 month break followed by a half day working option for a year to enable me to balance personal and professional priorities while keeping the income flowing. This has been a great enabler for me as it came at a time when I was forced to make a choice between my career and personal responsibilities.
>
> Kudos to Zensar for giving me this flexibility to stabilise my life! This is what makes me such a proud Zensarian.

While both the SEB and WEB teams are helping us in effectively driving some of our key strategies and business goals, these have also become great developmental tools for us to identify, groom, and coach our young Zensarians in taking ownership, driving change, and building successful teams. Some of our very successful leaders today have all been active members of our SEB and WEB teams.

WIRING A GLOBAL ORGANIZATION

A big part of our diversity and inclusion program has been about building strong and inclusive global teams with global mindsets. The last three acquisitions have all accelerated this process of building a global organization that is inclusive in its people practices, organizational culture, values, and ethos.

With each acquisition, we had new teams from diverse cultural backgrounds becoming a part of Zensar, and this helped us in learning to be sensitive and inclusive in all our practices and processes, including our engagement practices, internal communications, as well as policies and guidelines.

Scott Fiore, who became a part of Zensar as part of the Akibia acquisition and now heads a big part of our global IM business, has played a key role in integrating the two cultures:

> One of the first things that came through to me following the acquisition (Akibia) back in 2010 was the strong similarities in culture and customer focus of the two organizations. It is the strong people centric culture which has been a key contributor to Zensars success over the years. As a services organization, our people are our product, and the strong focus on the development of our associates has allowed us to be able to create and deliver a great product. Having lived and worked in Europe, cultural differences were there, however now with associates across the US, Europe, India, and China, it is amazing how we have bridged those differences and perform and a fully integrated organization in IBU.

GROWTH AND SUCCESS BY PARTICIPATIVE MANAGEMENT

Zensar has been built on a strong culture of "growth by participative management." This culture is very evident from the multiple forums that we have created to involve Zensarians in driving all key organizational initiatives. While the VCs that we talked about earlier in the chapter are one such forum, there are several such other initiatives for driving incremental and continuous innovation and improvement ideation and executions at all levels in the organization.

Two such initiatives are iZen and JUGNU.

iZen

We realized early on in our growth journey that we need excellent teams and not just excellent individuals to rewrite the future of Zensar and also that to create nonlinear impact through high-performing team, we need highly engaged frontline managers who, through consistent people management practices, can ensure that junior-level associates experience high engagement levels.

These priorities were ratified and fine-tuned by the outcomes of our annual Voice of Associates survey where over 500 associates that we reached out to through focus group discussions came together to help us put together the iZen program.

iZen: I Make Change Happen

The term "iZen" marries the concepts of freedom and accountability—the two being sides of the same coin. It provides a platform for each and every Zensarian to contribute in his/her own special way to Zensar's growth. It says that I am Zensar, and am accountable just like anyone else for making Zensar a great place for all of us. At the same time, it implies a freedom to make change happen.

Cross-functional iZen action teams and iZen engagement workshops for building exceptional teams across the organization created immense excitement in the organization. iZen action team members took on and drove several initiatives, big and small, strategic, and operational as well as short and medium term. A great example of an iZen idea that is today one of the most effective employee engagement drivers is that of ZenPoints.

In parallel, the iZen engagement workshops also led to concerted action on the part of managers to drive connectedness, feedback-effective delegation, and people development, which led to both self-motivation and team motivation.

The iZen initiative drove significant increase in the retention and engagement levels of the middle management group.

JUGNU

While the iZen movement helped us to empower, engage, and enthuse the junior and middle managers across Zensar, we wanted to take the initiative to the next level by unleashing the inherent passion in each individual Zensarian through the "JUGNU" initiative, thereby taking participative management to the next level.

"*Jugnu*" is the Hindi (India's national language) word for firefly and alludes to the inner glow in each of us. Our belief is that each of us is special in our own way and there is a *JUGNU* in us. This inner *Jugnu*, if evoked, gives us our greatest moments of passion and joy, which lead to excellence.

Our JUGNU movement is about rediscovering the JUGNU within and unleashing your passion for excellence." It takes the concept of iZen further by tapping the passion within individuals.

The JUGNU movement was led by excellence workshops across business units globally. They equipped employees with tools such as Appreciative Inquiry (leveraging positivity for a common goal) and "generative conversations" (through Open Space Technology) that helped the participants go through the process of discovery, dream, design, and destiny, which led to the implementation of a set of excellence ideas relevant for their business units.

The JUGNU initiative has helped us in creating like-minded communities across the organization and has seen the full involvement of leadership.

Both iZen and JUGNU are inherently linked to excellence. While iZen was about "Building Exceptional Teams," JUGNU was about igniting "Passion for Excellence." The belief is that breakthrough excellence cannot flourish consistently without engagement and nor can engagement deepen meaningfully without pushing the boundaries of excellence. We believe that our dream of building a great organization and sustaining it can only be achieved with Zensar being one large team, pulling together in excellence and harmony.

iZen and JUGNU are a formal articulation of a philosophy that Zensar has believed in for years—that the best ideas, solutions, and inputs come from Zensar's associates. Whether it be through VCs, the Voice of Associates survey, or more personalized platforms, such as the Pizza and Coke interaction sessions, there have always been platforms for expressing oneself and contributing ideas. The iZen and JUGNU initiatives carry forward and strengthen this philosophy, at the same time grounding it in Excellence, thus leading to the organizational aspiration of building a great company that is future proof.

While iZen and JUGNU were instrumental in driving the passion for excellence and unleashing the creativity of Zensarians as we were building the roadmap for the One Billion Dollar Journey, we continue to continuously conceive and implement such initiatives to fuel the organizational strategy.

One such campaign was the "Crazy Times call for Crazy Ideas" campaign that we rolled out in 2008–2009 when the entire industry was going through a trying period and reeling under the pressure of the US economic downturn that saw customer IT budgets being slashed and large IT programs being put on hold or rolled back. While we saw most other peer companies in the industry adopt large-scale employee layoffs, salary cuts, and forced leave, and so on, to manage the situation, we decided to stay true to our values of transparency and integrity and involve our people in finding a solution to the problem at hand.

Thus, we called for a meeting of the management team and the HR team and shared the management dilemma of optimizing costs to manage the slowdown of business. The team collectively discussed and debated on the options available with the management to address the situation and at the same time minimizing the impact to the employees. The team came up with some very out-of-box thinking on how we can all collectively see the organization through the difficult phase. These ideas were then further evaluated for impact on both business and people and were socialized with the people managers before we adopted a set of ideas that we proudly called the Crazy Ideas for Crazy Times.

The HR team took a leadership role in driving these ideas across the organization and driving effective adoption. They held multiple sessions across the organization to socialize these ideas with the associates and explain the context and take them along in the implementation. It was very inspiring to see our HR team truly partner the management team during this difficult phase and take charge of successfully driving the organization through the phase. We are very proud that Zensar did not have to resort to any of the industry practices at that time of letting employees go. This is a great example of how the values of transparency and integrity were upheld even in such trying circumstances.

BEING PROUDLY ZENSARIAN: OUR EMPLOYEE VALUE PROPOSITION

The Zensar that we have all collectively and fondly built over the years is a result of our strong belief in the philosophy of care and respect.

Underlying this philosophy are our strong value statements that best describe our employee value proposition:

1. Sensitivity toward diversity—of gender, age, nationality, and tenure
2. Culture of inclusiveness, transparency, and integrity in all our practices
3. Fairness, respect, and dignity for all stakeholders
4. Leadership from within driven by strong personal leadership
5. Opportunity for continuous learning and growing
6. Freedom to explore and experiment without the fear of consequences

We bring these value statements to life through our strong people practices and continuously strive to uphold these values under all circumstances.

Eric Brounstein, a senior sales leader in our US sales team, has been with us for several years now and grown to become a truly global Zensarian. In his own words, Eric talks about being a Zensarian:

> In my nine years at Zensar, I am amazed at the hard work, dedication, and drive of the individuals within the company that combined, have helped us grow to where we are today. Zensar has created and maintains a culture focused on the most valuable assets – the people. This shows by the loyalty and longevity of the talented staff which also has inspired me to make this my career home.

We have been steadfast in our intolerance for violation of any kind of our value system and have held the bar very high for all Zensarians with no one, including the senior-most leadership team, being above it.

We have consistently walked the talk even in the most trying circumstances and have not hesitated in invoking the harshest of actions in cases where we found our values being violated.

This is an organization built with immense passion and pride, and this explains why you experience the Zen in the interaction with every Zensarian.

Shahina Islam, who joined us as a young and bright HR manager 10 years back, is a great example of how the enabling organization culture and environment at Zensar has helped in nurturing and building strong leaders. She now heads our US HR function after having played several roles in the India HR organization. She shares her journey at Zensar here:

> My journey with Zensar began about 11 years ago when I was looking for my fifth employer in eight years of work experience post acquiring professional degree! If someone were to ask me to describe my experience with Zensar over the years in one word, I would say "Transformative." It has transformed me from a young, eager HR professional to a confident, passionate, risk taking HR leader in the past 11 years. In my 11 years at Zensar, I have moved between four roles—in Corporate and Business HR functions and I wouldn't hesitate in crediting these experiential learning opportunities for my professional growth over the years. At every point in my career at Zensar, I have had the freedom to challenge the status quo, to take risks, make mistakes, fail early, learn quickly and to keep pushing the envelope for new experiences and learning.

Motivating People: The Secret Sauce 173

Zensar generates a sense of pride in me not just for the scale it has achieved over past 15 years but for the strong ethos and culture it upholds—be it in practice of organization's Values at all levels, practices to promote Diversity and Inclusivity and very strong commitment to People and Community!

Even as we continue to chart am ambitious journey toward a billion-dollar enterprise, by bringing together all the forces, connecting the dots, and aligning our goals, our quest continues for sustaining the culture that we have fondly built over the past many years.

In our big dream for the future, we see many of our young stars and leaders taking charge of the future organization and continuing to add many more interesting chapters to this story of Zensar.

This dream is best described by Azfar Hussain, our new HR head, who has recently joined our Zensar family and is now the custodian of our people practices:

> After working with North American MNCs all my career, I was pleasantly surprised to find a high level of professionalism with which Zensar is managed when I joined here last year. The organizational values at the center of the One Zensar initiative, especially their focus on integrity and the support for transparency in all people related practices and processes, have resonated greatly with my own, and this congruence has helped me transition easily into the organization and my role as its Chief People Officer.
>
> Associate connect has historically been an area of strength in Zensar. Going forward we plan to build on this strong HR foundation and provide HR partnership to business by strengthening our Talent Advisory capability based on HR Analytics and Functional expertise, while simultaneously providing our associates with more structured opportunities for professional growth.

CHAPTER 8

The Story of Smiles

Corporate Social Responsibility at Zensar

This chapter is written in the form of a story, because CSR is about doing our bit to make the world a better place, a place that people are happy living in! And when it comes to people, it is all about stories. We see the world through our own prism and are constantly and continuously interpreting what we experience, in the form of stories. This story has a sequence, some ideas that should touch minds and hearts and of course a lot of little lessons on successful CSR.

ONCE UPON A TIME ...

It all started when, way back in 2004, Ganesh said that he would like Zensar to "put a smile on the face of every child from Koregaon Park to Kharadi." It is strange how the story of Zensar Foundation has unconsciously flowed toward this destination, through various twists and turns and interpretations of this line. And it continues to evolve.

THE EARLY YEARS (2004–2011)

With a budget of barely ₹5 lakhs, Zensar set out to change the world. The first step, taken on November 4, 2004, was to set up an independent trust called Zensar Foundation, with a Trustee Board comprising both external and internal trustees. This was a step far ahead if its time and speaks of Zensar's vision and commitment, as setting up a trust implies accountability to the external world as well as compliance to established governance practices.

The early years were about setting the overall approach and guiding principles in place, principles that were farseeing and are equally valid today. This flowed from the people behind it all: stalwarts who set a strong foundation in place, enabling Zensar Foundation to reach greater heights in the years to come. The initial trustees of Zensar Foundation were Anu Aga (external trustee: 2004 until today) and Rati Forbes (external trustee: 2004–2011).

Anu Aga continues to be an active trustee of the Foundation and is also a great mentor and guide for the CSR team. She has played a key role in ensuring that the culture and rigor of strong corporate governance was set in the DNA of Zensar Foundation. Hers is the voice of practicality, consistently questioning decisions to move into new spaces and ensuring that Zensar Foundation desists from what is "nice to do" and instead focuses on its core mandate:

> What makes the Zensar CSR initiative distinctive is that the CEO, Ganesh Natarajan takes very keen interest. Even before the Companies Act came into existence, Zensar had started a social Foundation and it invited outsiders like me to guide their CSR spending and help them evaluate it. The Foundation has taken up many interesting projects, such as developing an Environment Park in Pune, open to the general public.

Rati, a leader in CSR and associated social spaces, has demonstrated the efficacy of holistic community development through the work being done by Forbes Marshall and now by Zensar Foundation. Rati brought in the emphasis on sustainable, holistic interventions, which lies at the core of the program design and is the reason for urban slum community development being Zensar Foundation's key focus area. Both have been strong advocates of public–private partnerships (PPPs), which has influenced Zensar's social initiatives until today.

The Zensar team never let lack of substantive budgets come in the way of developing an integrated, scalable, and effective CSR program. They decided on direct intervention and volunteering as the means to supplement budgetary scope. Thus, the geographical area of interventions has always been in the neighborhood of Zensar offices, initially in Pune and now in Bengaluru, Hyderabad, and even Sandton near Johannesburg in South Africa. Ganesh has also consistently advocated the integration of technology in our CSR programs, thus enabling an inherent linkage with the core business of Zensar.

Bakul's Story

This story would not be complete without mentioning the pioneering work done by Bakul Deshpande, the earliest employee of Zensar Foundation. Armed with nothing but a heart full of caring and a bunch of volunteers, Bakul operated with courage and the trust that people would accept help and support from other quarters as long as it came with sincere intent. The initial projects were designed for children, but it was Bakul who recognized that in order to have a real impact, one must involve their families, school, and the rest of the community in which they spent most of their time. It is only through the creation of this complementing ecosystem that real change can occur. The greatest challenge Bakul faced was that of gaining acceptance from the people of the community, and she spent many an evening making home visits. She recalls singing with the women to be one with them and gain their trust. She played with the children, interacted with their teachers, supported the youth groups and started health projects for women and children. Her genuineness, openness, innate wisdom, and simplicity became the face of Zensar for years to come.

CSR Interventions: 2004–2011

This period was one of rapport and trust building with slum communities and schools, exploration of possible interventions, and setting the ground for considered selection of long-term focus areas and replicable models.

Adoption of Ambedkar Vasti Slum Community Within Chandan Nagar, Pune, and Anjaiah Nagar Slum Community, Hyderabad

With the intention of developing communities in the neighborhood of Zensar offices, the first two were selected as Ambedkar Vasti and Anjaiah Nagar, and holistic interventions initiated. The population of each community is approximately 2,000, with a sizable section being casual laborers and a third of the population below the poverty line. The interventions below refer to those undertaken in the Ambedkar Vasti community:

1. *Khelghar*: The initial interventions were focused directly on children. A play room was created for the children within the community itself. Children who were not going to school for various reasons came together under one roof to learn and play. It was a safe environment for children to explore their love of learning, and parents to experience it for their children. The objective was to build trust and rapport such that Zensar Foundation came to a position of being able to facilitate more sustainable interventions, such as sending the children to school. Accordingly, the center was closed in a few years.

   In the same spirit, Pragati Centre for non-formal education ran for a span of two years, catering to children in the six-to-nine-year age group. The teacher hailed from the same community and was trained and equipped to teach the children, thus providing livelihood and also ensuring ownership.

2. *Akanksha*: English and mathematics emerged as key priorities for the community and hence Zensar and Akanksha initiated a long-standing partnership to hold classes in both subjects. The children were taught using stimulating teaching aids and in a way that was fun, enabling personality development along with subject knowledge.
3. *IT education*: From its inception, Zensar has believed in the power of the digital world, which is also in keeping with Zensar's core business. Computer-literacy training was initiated in the government schools aligned to the community, starting from setting up the computer laboratory to hiring a teacher and ensuring incorporation of the classes within the school timetable.
4. *Healthcare*: Just like Khelghar, health too was an entry point into the community, being of immediate importance to all. Apart from general illnesses, the need for maternal and child care came to the fore when a nine-month pregnant woman delivered a baby then and there when she jumped a short wall to reach the space for open defecation. Health camps and weekly doctor visits were started, and continue to this day.
5. Livelihood programs for community women.

Employability Program

Recognizing the growing skills gap across India, Zensar Foundation made forays into the employability space through a partnership with Dr Reddy's Foundation. The learnings from this experience set the base for later employability programs.

Environment Sustenance

The IT industry is a young one, with the average age of employees being 27 years or so. Sustainable living is close to their hearts and Zensar Foundation started various programs led by Zensarians, including the development of a carbon-footprint measuring application for individuals. This was also the period in which the development of a two-acre piece of barren land was initiated, for the purpose of setting up a biodiversity park. The park has subsequently been developed in partnership with the Pune Municipal Corporation (PMC) and is maintained by Zensar Foundation, boasting 141 plant species from 63 botanical families and attracting over 300 visitors daily.

During the first seven years, the progress was slow but measured, with the Zensar team, including hundreds of volunteers, making a perceptible difference to every life they touched. The leadership of CSR passed from the HR group to marketing and then back to HR when Ruchi Mathur, an IIM Ahmedabad alumnus with substantial experience in both the corporate and social sectors, took on the role of OD and CSR at Zensar in March 2011. While continuity through the years has been provided by Ganesh and Anu, the strengthening of the team and the presence of two senior leaders, CFO Bala and Executive Vice President Prameela, on the trustee group has ensured strong organization commitment to the triple bottom line through the years.

The addition of Pervin Varma (external trustee: 2011 until today) has also provided a new thrust to the depth of interventions undertaken by Zensar Foundation. Pervin has a unique blend of skills, including experience in the advertising sector, NGO leadership (having been CEO of CRY from 1998 to 2004), academic knowledge through extensive work with TISS and an OD approach by dint of her engagement with Behavioural Labs. She has helped bind the best of Zensar Foundation together, building on the strong foundation of the early years and enabling flight through a cohesive strategy geared for city-wide transformation through fostering the "agency" of individuals.

WIDTH AND DEPTH OF CSR AT ZENSAR TODAY

Core Belief

The story of Jonathan Livingston Seagull is a strong motivator of the Zensar Foundation vision, mission, strategy, and interventions—belief in each individual's innate desire to reach new heights and the power of the individual once "in flight." Social studies show that if 15 to 20 percent of the population changes, an inflexion point is reached, which can tilt the entire population toward that change. In order to "put a smile on the face of every child between Kharadi and Koregaon Park," at least 15 to 20 percent of the children must have smiles! Those children, and the ecosystem that has enabled them to smile, will create change for the rest of the population. *That* is the power of the individual. "Children" here stands for not just children, but the people as a whole—be it men, women, youth, or children. The belief is that social transformation (smiles on every face) will come about through *individual* transformation. It is not specific interventions such as employability programs, or educational offerings, or access to health that will cause social transformation. These are all merely part of a nurturing ecosystem, but actual transformation will happen when individuals discover their *agency*.

What Is "Agency?"

We are all familiar with the concept of going to an "agency" for achieving certain outcomes. For example, we may hire a travel "agency" for booking a tour. Or, we may hire an "agent" to get our passport issued. The concept of having *agency* refers to the capacity of an individual to be their own agent. That is, for an individual to be able to achieve for herself or himself, the outcome that she or he desires.

This belief in the agency of individuals is at the core of what we do and emanates from the experience of the first few years. Therefore, Zensar Foundation's work is focused on facilitating an ecosystem that fosters agency in individuals.

Measure of Agency

Agency is a "feeling," not an action; however, in order to provide an indicative measure of agency, we can measure the number of instances in which agency is manifested, such as

1. independent decision making
2. taking initiative toward one's goals

3. ability to find information/knowledge as per requirements
4. working toward or obtaining livelihood/entrepreneurship
5. leadership for change in external environment
6. advocating for own rights and those of others
7. enabling "agency" in others

> The Power of Agency…
>
> *When you know who you are;*
> *when your mission is clear and you*
> *burn with the inner fire of unbreakable will;*
> *no cold can touch your heart;*
> *no deluge can dampen your purpose. You know that you are alive.*
>
> Chief Seattle, of the Suquamish Indians of Washington State. The city of Seattle was named for him, a man who dealt peaceably with whites.

INTERVENTION STRATEGY

While the directional strategy is to bring about social transformation through the facilitation of individual agency, the following diagram illustrates the intervention strategy followed by Zensar Foundation, in each city of operation. The approach is four-pronged:

1. Holistic community development—could be urban slum communities or villages
2. Development of specific verticals for which work would be done across the city and not just in specific communities
3. Development of replicable models in order to facilitate scaling of operations by entities other than Zensar Foundation
4. Involvement of volunteers, which could range from supportive to leading roles

For example, Zensar Foundation's interventions in the city of Pune are as follows:

ZF Interventions in City of Pune

Thrust areas (verticals):

Replicable models in Pune:
1. Udaan English Center
2. School Development model
3. Slum Community Development model
4. NDLM* Centers
5. Udaan Biodiversity Park

Digital Literacy
- NDLM* Centers in ZF core area of operation: CN slum community; YN slum community and associated schools
- Elsewhere in Pune through Digital Literacy Bus, other NDLM centers

Employability
- Unnati Employability Center
- IT-enabled skilling
- Employability program in colleges
- Tailoring, cooking, beautician programs

Environment
- Udaan Biodiversity Park
- Swacch Toilets
- Associate-driven initiatives

Ambedkar Vasti community in Chandan Nagar

Leadership | Education | Health | Employability | Social Issues | Life Skills

Kruti Dals, Home-to-home visits, Peer Counsellors, Digital Empowerment

Yamuna Nagar community | Sudumbre Village

Involvement of volunteers (Zensar associates)

*National Digital Literacy Mission

OVERVIEW OF ZENSAR'S CSR INTERVENTIONS

At Zensar, we believe in the triple bottom-line approach as the way to ensure sustainable success. The credibility of an organization lies in the way it generates profits, the concerns it shows for people, and its contribution to the planet. The focus areas of Zensar Foundation are community development as a "horizontal," with digital literacy, employability enhancement and environment sustenance as "vertical" thrust areas (see the section Intervention Strategy).

Under community development, the education-related interventions are in the areas of English and IT. In line with Zensar's core business, the idea is to facilitate a digitally ready citizen and one who can hold their own in IT-related jobs. This implies English proficiency and digital literacy as key focus areas, which in turn have led to the Udaan English Learning Centre, English programs in schools, computer training in schools, and digital literacy training in communities. Health interventions involve regular visits by a general practitioner for checkups and free medicines, along with health camps in the communities that Zensar works with. Zensar Foundation is working in partnership with *Anganwadis* (a government sponsored child-care and mother-care centre) for reduction of malnutrition in the community. A program to train and sensitize young boys in relation to gender equality in partnership with Equal Community Foundation has been highly successful in sensitizing adolescent boys to gender equity and even becoming advocates for it. Children from the community are mentored by Zensar volunteers in partnership with Mentor Together. A strong community mobilization program is led by the volunteers in partnership with Connecting NGO to enable people in Ambedkar Vasti to realize their strengths and potential in order to lead change for themselves.

> **Case Story: Unleashing Agency: The Boy Who Won a National Level Competition**
> Marzodi Narsimha is a student of Anjaiah Nagar Mandal Parishad Primary School in Hyderabad. His father is a daily-wage laborer and his mother is a homemaker. Narsimha was trained in English at Zensar's class. He was sincere and showed enormous dedication. He was extremely self-disciplined. He used his own creativity and enabled for himself a schedule of at least three hours of English learning a day. His trainer Seshu says, "he learnt at the rate of 300 words a month!" He went on to participate in the "Learnasium Open Vocabulary Contest" organized by "The Atlanta Foundation" in 2013. He stood first among 2,000 students from 25 schools and won the competition, bagging a cash prize of ₹50,000. On asking what is his dream, is he says, "I want to be a software engineer!"

There are several employability enhancement programs, one of which runs in partnership with Thermax Social Initiatives Foundation and Unnati and enables youth to be job-ready. The unique aspect of the program is that it offers 100 percent placement guarantee. In Hyderabad, tailoring, cooking, and other livelihood programs for women have been undertaken to create social entrepreneurs and make the women financially independent. The Employability Skills Development Program caters to industry needs by providing practical exposure and training to college students to be employed in the IT industry, whereas our Learnership Development Program is a global training program addressing the growing needs of young black South Africans to be trained in contemporary technologies with the objective of finding gainful employment. Zensar has graduated more than 150 to full-time employment.

The Story of Smiles: Corporate Social Responsibility at Zensar

Diagrammatic Representation of Zensar's CSR

People

Community Transformation

EDUCATION

English proficiency		Computer literacy	Digital literacy
Udaan English Centre; Zensar Campus, Pune **107 students**	Udaan English program; Chandan Nagar, Kharadi, and Yamuna Nagar schools, Pune **700 students**	IT school program (Pune and Hyderabad) **1,500 students**	Community centers for National Digital Literacy Mission, Pune and Hyderabad slum communities **1,100 households**

HEALTHCARE

Treatment of illnesses
- Physicians attending in Pune and Hyderabad communities for free checkup and medicines
- Monthly general healthcare camps at Pune and Hyderabad
- **2,000 people per annum**

Reduction of malnutrition
... through partnering with the Integrated Child Development Scheme (ICDS) program and supporting its effective implementation. **Children in Ambedkar Vasti community**

COMMUNITY MOBILIZATION

House-to-house visits and facilitating people to build their dreams and advocating for their rights
Addressing 2,000 people across Ambedkar Vasti community

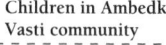
MENTORING

Mentoring program for community children
30 children and 30 mentors

GENDER EQUITY

Gender sensitization program by Equal Community Foundation
50 youth

Employability Programs

EMPLOYABILITY

Unnati Skill Development Centre **133 youth**	Tailoring program **90 women**	Employability Skills Development Programme **850 students**	Global Leadership Development Programme **150 youth**

Planet

UDAAN BIODIVERSITY PARK

A two-acre park, situated in Viman Nagar in Pune, comprising diverse flora and walking trails with informative signages
Over 300 visitors per day; 141 plant species, 63 botanical families; 44 bird/butterfly/dragonfly species

IN-HOUSE RESOURCE MANAGEMENT

Energy management	Waste management	Water consumption	Fuel management	Miscellaneous initiatives

As part of environment sustenance, Zensar has created a two-acre biodiversity park in Viman Nagar, Pune. The park is unique with informative signages in three languages, viz., English, Marathi, and Braille. It is an educative park and has both residents and school students visiting regularly.

Spreading Our Wings

Today, Zensar's CSR initiatives are strong not just in Pune but also in Hyderabad, where a number of the key initiatives have been replicated, including the setting up of a digital literacy center in the Anjaiah Nagar Community School and a large volunteering movement within the city. The creation of agency has also been adopted by Zensar South Africa in the setting up of a learnership center that successfully trains hundreds of young members of the black communities near Johannesburg and enables them to join the workforce.

DEEP DIVE INTO A FEW REPLICABLE MODELS: UDAAN ENGLISH CENTRE, UDAAN BIODIVERSITY PARK, AND AMBEDKAR VASTI COMMUNITY

Exemplar 1: Udaan English Centre

Zensar is committed to transforming children's lives, especially by enabling them to be "citizens of the world." Two ways to make that possible is through proficiency in the English language and an understanding of the digital medium of the virtual world.

The Udaan English Centre with a unique blend of both was established on February 1, 2012. English education is imparted using classroom teaching blended with e-learning. Children from Ambedkar Vasti community are selected for the program based on their interest, commitment, and the seriousness of the parents.

A baseline assessment of every child is conducted at the time of admission. There are regular assessments during the course and an end-line assessment at the end of each module.

Methodology

The program has been developed in consultation with Sonali Ojha, who brings with her 26 years of rich experience and expertise in the field of child development. There are three modular programs used at Udaan with increasing levels of difficulty. The children spend two hours daily learning English. Since they learn through computers, they not only learn English but also learn how to operate a computer. In order to solve queries, help slow learners, and facilitate the process, teachers are present at all times. The teachers use unique methods of play and physical cues to learn English and create individual progress plans for students requiring special attention. However, more than the English per se, it is the *environment* in which English is taught, which has resulted in the development of "agency" in the children. It starts with the principles underlying the Udaan intervention, which are those of acceptance, inclusion, appreciation, and positive reinforcement. This safe environment is otherwise not available to children coming from underprivileged communities. By consistent experience of respect, the children develop an expanded sense of self. In order to heighten self-awareness, each teaching session starts with 15 minutes of meditation. Besides, the students are taught to self-learn (for example, through use of dictionaries/Google), learn from peers and teach them, set goals, and track achievement of the same and other such life skills, which have broadened their horizon.

At Udaan, multiple stakeholders are involved to create an ecosystem that enables holistic changes to occur. Parents are involved right from the time of admissions to the time of the final assessment. They are invited to see the classroom, and children guide their parents around the center explaining what their classes involve. As a parent said, "I feel proud that my daughter can speak English. Now I feel *"Hum bhi kisi se kam nahi"* (I am no less than anyone else). Volunteers from Zensar are also actively involved in the activities at Udaan. They bring their unique strengths and talents, which they pass on to the children through recreational sessions, such as movie screenings and discussions, story-telling sessions, dance, music, and so on. Moreover, the teachers at Udaan are siblings/spouses of Zensar associates, in keeping with the spirit of volunteering and involvement of the whole Zensar family. The teachers have reported a change in their own lives. They learn from their students on a daily basis. The teachers are able to think beyond the conventional ways of teaching and address challenges with confidence.

Demonstration of Replicability

Besides impacting these 100 children and their families and the community at large, the Udaan English program has been scaled into six municipal schools. Zensar Foundation has always viewed the Udaan center as a pilot, with the objective of working within and along with government schools, in order to create sustainable change. An elaborate teaching kit has been developed with comprehensive lesson plans covering e-learning modules, online resources, videos, classroom activities, and daily assessments. This kit is being used as the basis for teaching in a standardized way, in the schools. In the year 2015–2016, an additional version of the program, "Speedy Spoken English," is being created as per the request of the schools.

> **Case Study: The Power of Empathy (Core Value of Zensar Foundation)**
> Dipti, a teacher at Udaan, when asked to share a few success stories, said, "Every student at Udaan is a success story in her/ his own right." The story of Akshay, as shared in the words of his teacher, Shweta Madhur, demonstrates the experience of respect and emotional connect, provided to each child....

Akshay was arrogant and attention seeking. He had come to the point of dropping out. He would sit on the chair and not on the floor with the rest of the kids. He would give rude responses, the kind that were illogical and irritating. The class was focusing only on him and his behaviour. It took time to discipline the class and bring them back to pay attention to the lesson being taught. Akshay's mother was very supportive. I made a couple of home visits. But then I was told that it had resulted in his mother informing his father and his father hitting him, as punishment. I went to his home again and explained that he is a teenager who will not change through violence. I asked his mother to go along with his way of doing things and bring him round to her ways eventually. I learnt this from my parents when they incentivized badminton for me to complete my engineering degree. Akshay loved to dance. His mother made a deal that she would let him dance and perform if he attended Udaan regularly. There was verbal negotiation instead of violence. He started opening up. He learnt dance from me and I learnt his likes and dislikes. Now he is learning by himself through the dictionary activity. He is well behaved.

> *"You don't love hatred and evil, of course. You have to practice and see the real gull, the good in every one of them, and to help them see it in themselves. That's what I mean by love."*
>
> Richard Bach, Jonathan Livingston Seagull

The children's English language skills have improved by leaps and bounds. They can understand and comprehend, read and write, and speak fluent English. The greatest outcome has been that the children have started *thinking* in English, which is evident from the speed from their verbal response.

Besides improvement in English, Udaan has had an impact on the children that is beyond the tangible. The children have transformed into confident and assertive human beings. They are aware of their rights and have the courage to voice their opinion. They have unearthed the agency within themselves, which puts them in a uniquely empowered position within the community. It is evident through this statement made by a 14-year-old girl at Udaan:

> The age of 15–18 years is the prime age for a girl's career. We all feel that girls should be allowed to go for higher studies. There are many organizations that are present and willing to help. It is our request to the parents to see girls through high school and college and change our lives.

These children have become change agents in their own right. When volunteers from Zensar make household visits in the community, it is the Udaan children who lead the volunteers and work as ambassadors of change. Parents in the community have experienced this transformation of the children in many ways—the way in which they hold themselves, their sense of dignity, their helpful nature, and their positivity. This in turn has created a demand from all families to enroll their children in the Udaan program, and in July 2015, Udaan opened its doors to all, resulting in an immediate enrollment of almost 100 children.

> **Case Story: Enabling Freedom of Choice (Freedom Is a Core Value of Zensar Foundation)**
> Pragati was one of the earliest enrollments at Zensar's Udaan English Centre. A shy child who never expressed her opinion, she was quiet, and kept to herself. Over three years of grooming by the teachers at Udaan, she has transformed into a beautiful bird and has developed the wings to fly as well. Initially underconfident and without communication skills, today she stands tall among all the children at Udaan. She has completed her 10th standard examinations with flying colors. She expresses her opinions openly and is confident while speaking to others.

What is amazing is that she has developed the agency to make her own decisions. She is aware of her rights and is clear about her future. After her 10th standard results, she insisted that she wants to continue higher education. Her parents agreed on the terms that she take up Arts, which is considered a "soft" stream. However, she confronted her parents and over weeks of persuasive discussions convinced them to let her take admission in the Science stream. She says, "My teacher at Udaan always told me that what you do now matters, because it is what will make or break your future. It is a lesson I will never forget."

Impact: Udaan English Program

This diagram illustrates how the underlying principles changed the entire "how" of the program, leading to the program becoming

Udaan English Program

| Impact: | Udaan | English | Program |

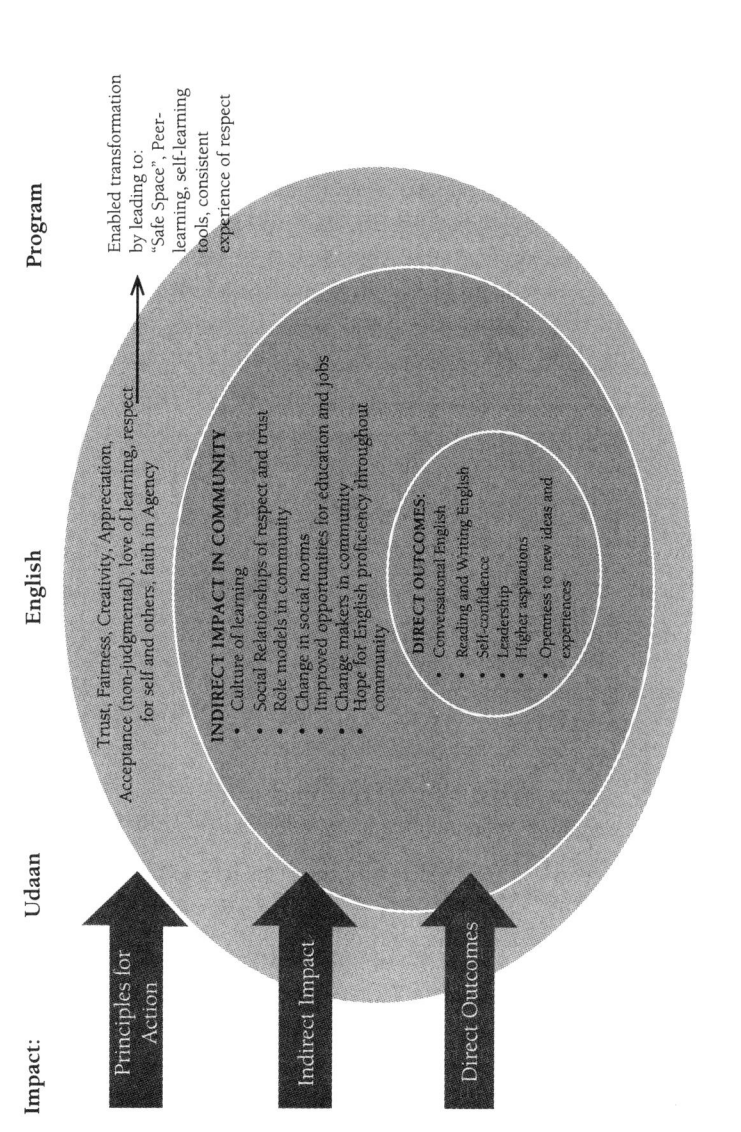

a "leadership program" for children, instead of restricting itself to an English-teaching program. This is the reason why Zensar Foundation sets immense store by its values and principles. Using them to define the "how" converts otherwise operational programs to transformational ones.

The model also exemplifies how the right ecosystem facilitates the development of agency in individuals. The Udaan ecosystem acts at a deeply personal level, changing the way children see themselves. This, in turn, has led to transformation in the community as a whole—be it the renewed hope with which the community is looking toward the future, the sudden surge across the community of the desire to learn, or the children challenging social norms, such as child marriage. This is a demonstration of the strategy of "social transformation through individual agency."

Exemplar 2: Udaan Biodiversity Park

In the months leading to September 2012, Zensar Foundation undertook the responsibility of creating a green zone in Pune's Vimaan Nagar, in partnership with the PMC. This PPP model has been structured such that while the land belongs to the PMC, it has been leased to Zensar Foundation for development and maintenance. The Foundation was keen on creating something new, something that would not be just of greenification value but also of educational and conservational value. With this intent, the park was created with utmost care and love as one would nurture a child.

The two-acre Udaan Biodiversity Park has been crafted in a creative manner. It is designed in the shape of a butterfly, as can be seen aerially. There are a number of plant ecologists and experts who have been involved in conceptualizing and creating it. The park attempts to create a self-sustaining ecological system and hence has diverse flora, be it aromatic plants for the bees, colorful flowers for the butterflies, trees that flower in varied seasons, medicinal plants, endemic plants, rare and endangered species, vegetables, or water-loving plants. As of early 2015, the park supports 141 plant species, which represent 63 botanical families and comprise 31 tree species, 50 shrubs, 46 herbaceous plants, and 14 climbers. The rocks that were found naturally on the land have been retained within the park; some are used in creating a waterfall and others left just as they are as natural sitting areas. Natural elements have been used wherever possible, for example in the Gazebo, which has a thatched roof. Water bodies are provided in the form of the waterfall and a pond.

As a result of this diversity, there is diverse fauna that inhabits the park. Nineteen bird species, 16 species of butterfly, 9 dragonfly species, 12 insect arachnid species, and 1 reptilian species have been observed to flourish in the park.

The park fulfills the role that any conventional park is expected to, such as being an oxygen zone in the midst of a concrete urban jungle, a recreational place for individuals and families to unwind, and a restful space for senior citizens. However, what makes this park unique is its attempt to create a world of plants that can be explored and experienced in the true sense. To this end, there is a useful plants trail comprising sections such as "Fun with plants," "Extinct/endangered plants," "Joint and bone remedies," "Aromatic plants," and so on. There are signages giving details of each plant species along with instructions to touch, smell, or chew the plant. Thus, the park addresses all senses: the use of colorful plants proximate to the entrance welcomes visitors (sight), followed by a segment comprising medicinally therapeutic herbs (touch and taste), aromatic herbs (smell), the use of bird-friendly trees (sound), and a 500-square-feet water body (sight). What is more, there are braille signages for the visually impaired. In fact, the emphasis on experiencing the plants through sense other than sight is for the purpose of catering to visually impaired visitors.

The park attracts over 300 visitors daily and is much loved by visitors, as is evident from the touching remarks in the visitor feedback book. Recognizing its educational value, a number of schools bring their students to learn about nature and plants. The park is a wonderland for children, a delight for nature lovers, and a refreshing green space for all citizens. A visit leaves one with a deep sense of being one with nature and with thought-provoking ideas, such as that of the extinction of plants that we take for granted. The park nurtures several rare and endangered species within its confines, and in order to encourage conservation, citizens are welcome to carry away potted plans free of cost. These potted plants are kept in the park nursery. In this way, citizens get to take action and start their own urban balconies, creating their own love stories with nature!

> **Quotes by Park Visitors: Demonstrating the Use of Creativity (a Core Value of Zensar Foundation) in Development of the Park**
>
> *"Beautiful space! Love the tasting and smelling of all the wonderful Indian herbs and plants. Wish we had something like this in Australia. But we do have Eucalyptus + Koalas! I love India."*—Mesi
>
> *"Visited so many countries and found this to be such a pleasure to come to. You should be extremely proud of this piece of art, passion and nature that you have created and maintained. Cheers & Jai Ho!"*—Mrinalini
>
> *"One of the most amazing parks I have seen. All the diversity is stunning. Good luck and keep it going."*—Agnel
>
> *"It's an excellent initiative to familiarise our young generation about the useful values/property of plants in our day-to-day life. Let there be more such plants and good maintenance of the same."*—R.C. Pri
>
> *"Udaan Biodiversity Park is fantastic. The park is providing ecological service to a number of insects, birds and invertebrates. I wish Zensar Foundation could replicate such activities in other parts of the city which will certainly nurture and enhance the dwindling biodiversity of urban Pune. All the very best."*—Sachin Punekar

Exemplar 3: Community Development Model for Ambedkar Vasti

Community development is Zensar Foundation's most significant focus area. During the early years, it was about programmatic development within the community. This approach has gradually and steadily changed to a more holistic one over the years. Zensar has always had faith in the agency of individuals, thus involving the members of the community at all times. The interventions in the community have been conducted through participatory action, which has contributed to making change occur in a sustainable manner.

The vision and mission for Ambedkar Vasti, as put together by the community and Zensar Foundation together, are as follows:

> *Vision:* Empower Ambedkar Vasti community to meet its basic needs of social and economic security and set a virtuous circle in place for improved quality of life.
> Note: Quality of life includes employment, built environment, physical and mental health, education, recreation and leisure time, and social belonging.
> *Mission:* To enrich lives of the inhabitants of the Ambedkar Vasti community by providing access to digital experience, enabling effective partnership with local government and bringing forward the best of the human resource of Zensar to unleash agency in individuals.

The diagram provides an overview of the community development model.

Layer 1: Volunteer-Led Home Visits

Volunteers of Zensar have played, and continue to play, a critical role in the ecosystem of community development, which is why they are an integral part of the mission statement above. They laid a strong foundation for community work through home-to-home visits conducted over two Saturdays each month, for two years, starting August 2013. The home visits, carried out under the guidance of Bobby Zachariah and team from Connecting NGO, are

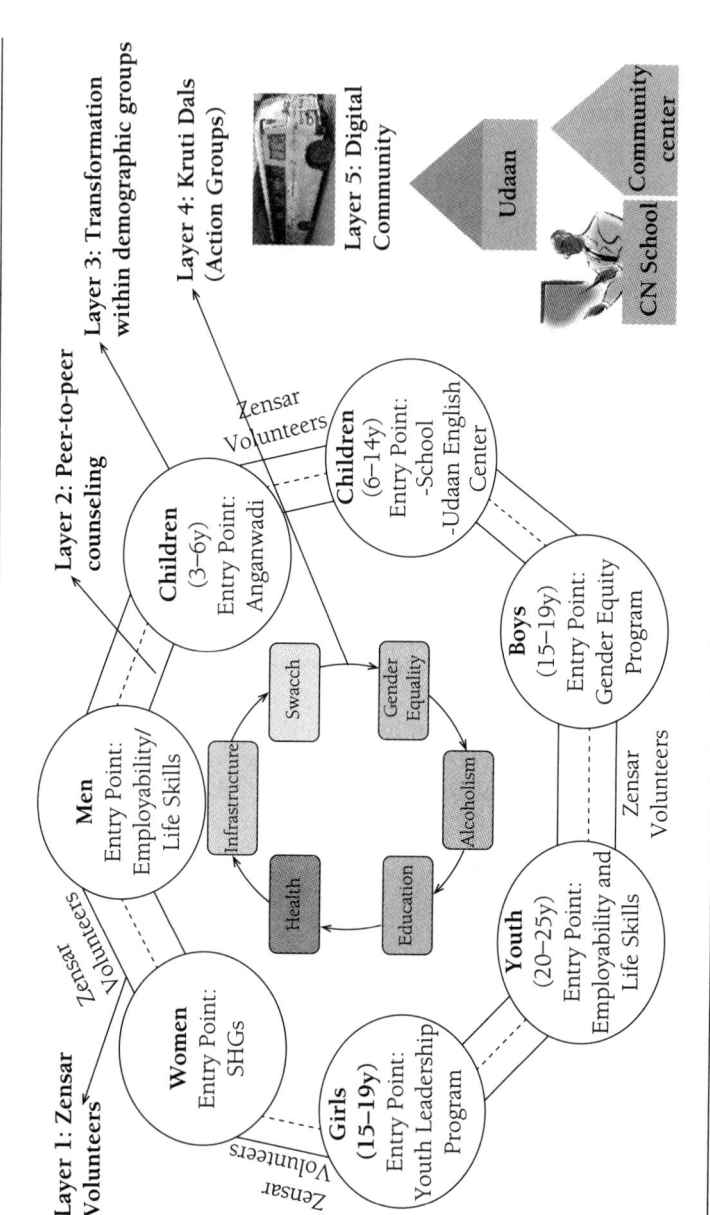

essentially to listen and understand the stories of the people and play a facilitative role in the formation of neighborhood groups, demographic groups such as Bal Panchayat, and issue-focused groups such as for sanitation. Owing to the home visits, Zensar has become a household name (literally) in Ambedkar Vasti. Partners of Zensar Foundation, volunteers, and others associated with Zensar are willingly welcomed in the homes and hearts of the people. These home visits established deep familiarity, trust, and rapport with the community while enabling an understanding of the real issues as articulated by the people. In parallel, the formation of the groups resulted in a natural emergence of community leaders/change agents. In the model illustrated above, volunteers continue to do home-to-home visits in order to play a connecting role between all the intervention layers and between the people in the community.

Layer 2: Peer Counselors

In order to set a virtuous circle in place for improved quality of life, it is essential to have a support system of mentors/facilitators, within the community itself. This would enable a self-sustaining system for emotional and facilitative support. Hence, Zensar Foundation is embarking on a capacity-building program for members of the community from across demographic groups, who will then become a support network for the rest of the community. This program is being undertaken in partnership with Connecting NGO, which has successfully integrated peer counseling programs in several schools in Pune.

Layer 3: Transformational Interventions in Each Demographic Group

Going by the strategy of social transformation through individual agency, and the principle that the transformation of 15 to 20 percent of the population enables a tipping point for transformation of the entire population, Zensar Foundation works with each of the seven demographic groups in the community (as in the diagram above) for transformation of minimum 15 to 20 percent individuals within the group. This is an attempt to cater to all groups and work toward inclusive growth. Thus, the 15 to 20 percent set of beneficiaries will cause a ripple effect through the community.

For the transformation of individuals in each demographic group, the learnings from the Udaan English Centre will be used (see Exemplar 1). An *entry point* will be leveraged, for example English in the case of school children, to bring about overall transformation and agency in the individual. The choice of entry point has to emerge from the community itself, as it is based on what they perceive as an immediate need. For example, women have clearly stated that they would like to form self-help groups (SHGs). Hence, an SHG program is being undertaken; however, the implementation of the program will be such that it facilitates the emergence of agency in the participating women. The SHG will be a "by the way"—the important impact will be transformation of the women into assertive, confident, and self-dependent individuals.

Layer 4: Kruti Dals (Action Groups)

In July 2015, there was a large group intervention with the community people (approximately 80 men, women, youth, and children) where the community articulated its dreams, strengths, challenges, and goals. They also self-organized themselves into "Kruti Dals," which would work on different issues being faced by the community. These are infrastructure inadequacy, alcoholism, gender inequity, lack of quality education, need for good health, and unhealthy sanitation. The Kruti Dals will work along with volunteers and the Zensar Foundation team to find resolutions to these concerns. Interestingly, the Kruti Dals are triangulated, that is, each Dal consists of representatives of different demographic groups. For example, the Sanitation Kruti Dal has women, children, and men. This makes the task force much stronger, as each demographic has something unique to offer, whether it is hope, planning capability, wisdom, energy, and so on. The work done by these groups will bring about larger systemic changes that will be beneficial across the community. Zensar Foundation has also facilitated PPPs where possible; for example, the Infrastructure Kruti Dal is working with the PMC in demanding civic amenities. As a result, construction of a concrete road has started in the community, after years!

Layer 5: Digital Community

Digital citizenship forms a significant part of the model, in accordance with the principle of "alignment to market reality." We are entering a digital era, and for a community to hold its own, there must be digital literacy, access to digital devices, as well as access to the Internet. There is tremendous demand for this from the community, as they too are aware that the digital divide can be extremely harmful. On the other hand, where the digital divide is bridged, it accelerates the bridging of the divide between the rich and the poor. Apart from enabling digital literacy and access to devices and the Internet, the other interventions too will integrate digital technology, for example, simple instances such as connecting the SHG women through WhatsApp for easier communication.

The five intervention layers, implemented simultaneously, offer a powerful platform to induce community-wide unleashing of agency. The Kruti Dals, the transformation interventions, and the digital community will enable a sense of social belonging and not just economic opportunities. The peer counseling will set an inherent support system in place within the community, and the home visits by volunteers will be the connecting glue to all the interventions. There is also an extensive school program being undertaken in parallel, in five municipal schools nearby, in order to extend the same ecosystem to as many points of the community's life as possible.

> **Case Story: Growing with the Zensar Family: Facilitating Appreciation of Dignity and Equality (Core Values of Zensar Foundation)—Example of a Transformational Intervention**
> Deepak, a young boy from the community, was part of the English program supported by Zensar Foundation around eight years back, and has been part of the Zensar Foundation family since then. Recently, he enrolled into the Gender Equity program being run in partnership with Equal Community

Foundation. A bright child, he has developed very good communication skills through the English program. He talks of how gender was something he did not even consider or think about before joining the program. He found the lessons on the ancient history of patriarchy to be an eye opener for him. He then started observing the play of gender roles and inequality in the neighborhood and in his own home. He says, "I suddenly realized how tough the lives of women must be. There are so many ways in which they suffer."

He has been transformed over the course of the program and takes responsibility for household chores, initially undertaken only by his mother. He learnt dignity of labor through practice. He is also constantly motivating his sisters to study and fight for their rights, which is evident in the change that his sister Komal has undergone. What stands out in Deepak's story is that through the gender sensitization program, he felt empowered enough to speak up against his alcoholic father, who engaged in domestic violence, when the community met to discuss alcoholism—courage that he never thought he possessed.

DIGITAL LITERACY AS A THRUST AREA FOR CITY TRANSFORMATION

Mission 100 Percent Digital Literacy

The National Digital Literacy Mission (NDLM) mandates training at least one member per household in India by the year 2020.

Once trained, beneficiaries are able to send emails, connect on social media, buy from ecommerce web sites, make better informed decisions for their livelihood/health/finance and so on and use the Internet to avail various government services, including the newly announced Digital India services.

Bridging the digital divide greatly accelerates the bridging of the divide between the rich and the poor, and Zensar's vision is nothing less than to see a 100 percent digitally literate Pune.

With this mission in focus, Zensar's areas of work include setting up of NDLM centers, as well as facilitating a cohesive plan for corporates, citizens, and the PMC to work together in enabling 100 percent digital literacy in Pune, through an organization called Pune City Connect.

In less than a year, the first two NDLM centers set up by Zensar Foundation have trained over 60 percent of total households in the communities and enhanced their job prospects by enabling them with digital skills. Zensar Foundation's third center, Digital Literacy Bus, launched in August 2015, is a novel one. This bus is a joint initiative of Zensar Foundation and the PMC and runs in partnership with NASSCOM Foundation. The bus is outfitted with 16 computers and preloaded with the digital literacy curriculum, thus enabling the bus to move from community to community in order to train participants from across Pune. The bus provides impetus to the plan for a 100 percent digital literacy.

Zensar Foundation is committed to the Mission 100 percent Digital Literacy and will be following it through, in terms of both individual contribution and fostering collaborative networks.

> **Case Stories: Enabling Agency and Creativity**
> Mudramoni Laxmi is an *Anganwadi* teacher from the Siddique Nagar slum community in Hyderabad. She used to maintain handwritten records in a book, which consumed much of her time and made it difficult for her to work. Says Laxmi, "I heard of the NDLM center that Zensar Foundation has started. I had never seen or touched a computer before. Gradually, I learnt what a computer is and how to use it." She now maintains her office records in an Excel sheet, which saves her an enormous amount of time. Not only this, she also has an email account and Facebook account. Through Internet searches, she helps women with knowledge regarding healthy eating habits, procedure to procure birth certificates, and so on.
>
> Nilesh Eknath Garud is a 22-year-old, class 10 pass out and a street-food vendor from Viman Nagar in Pune. After the NDLM course, he records his business expenses in an Excel sheet, searches for new recipes, and calculates the day's earnings with ease, resulting in a healthy growth for the business!

Volunteering

As a corporate, Zensar is uniquely positioned to have access to the "privileged class" through its employee base. This affords a golden opportunity to create a social transformation model that involves citizens from all walks of life—that is, both privileged and underprivileged working together.

Volunteering has historically been a core tenet of the CSR interventions at Zensar. In the early years, most of the CSR interventions were either volunteer led or had a significant component of volunteering. Zensar's employee base is a young one, with an average age of approximately 27 years, and it is a sign of the times that many of them are looking for a cause that they can align themselves to. CSR provides a choice of possible causes, and associates have been more than willing to come forward, with a whopping 20 percent of associates (in Pune and Hyderabad) participating in at least one instance of volunteering, outside of their working hours. Sixty-seven percent of associates contribute monetarily through monthly payroll donations. Volunteers do not consider their age, language, or any other aspect as an obstacle in volunteering. There is a spirit of giving and learning among volunteers, along with a sense of commitment, which is greatly fostered by Zensar's leadership, driving this ethos from the front. There is many an occasion and intervention with direct involvement of Zensar's top management team, who are personally committed to the spirit of volunteering.

Zensar Foundation offers well-defined volunteering tracks in order to give clarity of opportunities to the volunteers. These tracks are defined at the beginning of each year, based on the CSR focus areas for that year. For instance, the tracks chosen for the year 2015–2016 in Pune are the following.

Volunteering Tracks

- Teaching in government schools: English and Computers
- Digital literacy: Each One Teach Two campaign (see the section Digital Literacy as a Thrust Area for City Transformation)

- Recreational activities for community children
- Development of urban slum communities (see the section Exemplar 3: Community Development Model)
- ZenViro Team: Environment sustenance
- Citizenship center
- Volunteering by family members

While some of the volunteers participate as and when possible, others take end-to-end responsibility for their work and are involved in the planning as well as execution. For example, at the time when Zensar Foundation needed associates to pitch in for creation of the school computer literacy curriculum, a group of 40 volunteers took it upon themselves to work over a period of nine months and create what was required.

Core Group of Change Agents

We found that over a period of time, a "core group" of volunteers has emerged, where the contribution to CSR is far beyond 10 or 20 hours in a year and, more importantly, they take ownership for what they are driving. They champion their cause to enroll more volunteers, decide on outcomes, drive the same, and so on. This group constitutes approximately 80 associates between Pune and Hyderabad and is an invaluable extension to the CSR team. They can be called upon to be available in case of any specific need that arises.

What's in It for Them?

Recently, Pervin Varma, one of the external trustees, and the Zensar Foundation team had a meeting with some of the core volunteers to understand what drives them. This was a group of volunteers that has been spending every alternate Saturday at the community, fairly consistently. In fact, the volunteering work in Ambedkar Vasti has set the base for the entire community development model (see the section Exemplar 3: Community Development Model; Layer 1).

The surprising thing was that when we spoke with this group, none of them attributed their interest to "making someone else happy." They shared their experiences, which were heart-warming and overwhelming. They referred to self-fulfillment rather than altruism, demonstrating that volunteering leads to an expansion of self. People "find themselves" and self-actualize in unexpected ways through the CSR platform. In a way, participating in CSR leads to the volunteers discovering the agency in their personal competency areas. Where there is expansion of self, there is a far higher sense of belonging. When people bring their personal selves to work, their engagement levels are far higher because they feel better "rooted." As a consequence, all sorts of agency unleashes, both in the CSR space and the work space. The CSR platform, in fact, is nothing but a leadership development program.

Ankit Parashar is one of our active volunteers who finds great motivation and draws inspiration from his CSR work. Here is what he has to say about why the opportunity to meaningfully contribute to the community means so much to him:

> I'm enough of a realist to understand that I can't help the whole nation, but I am more of an optimist to get up every morning and try.
>
> I have always been a focused person but am also a lazy one. Life was going on uneventfully until one day I was introduced to CSR. It helped me realize, how much I had in my life to be grateful for. And that was when I decided to contribute in whatever way I could. I began to experience the power and joy of giving. This motivated me in all aspects of my life. I was now suddenly more energetic and dedicated at work and also more content at home. CSR completely transformed my life and now I feel more responsible for the country as well as Zensar. And there has been no looking back since then. Being a proud Zensarian, I am now fully committed to give my best to the organization.

Volunteering as a Leadership Development Program

Words of volunteers such as Ankit Parashar provide a clear glimpse of how qualities of leadership emerge through the volunteering process. There is enormous skill building involved in areas of communication, negotiation, persuasion, and so on. Volunteers have reported self-transformation, leading to changes in their personal and professional lives. Some express having gained listening skills, tolerance, and patience, some report increased hope during difficult circumstances, some develop innovative problem-solving methods, and yet others discover a sense of leadership.

Going Forward: Fostering Citizenship

The experience so far has been very encouraging, and there seems to be a readiness in volunteers to lead change not just within Zensar but outside of Zensar as well. Going forward, the idea is to enable movement up the "ladder of citizenship."

The idea behind moving volunteers up the ladder is that they will have an opportunity to explore social change in a manner that is guided and steady and that eventually brings out one's agency to become a change maker in his or her own right.

ROLE OF LEADERSHIP

Directional Leadership

Ruchi Mathur, head Zensar Foundation (March 2011–to date) says, "CSR is not part of anybody's KRAs but it is everyone's job." This sentiment is strongly exemplified by Zensar's leadership team. Zensar truly is a company with a heart, and this has contributed greatly to the progress made by Zensar Foundation.

Zensar Foundation has been incredibly fortunate in the external support received. In addition to the guidance and advice of the trustees, as per the trusteeship established in November 2004, there is also a CSR Board Committee. This committee, established in April 2014, includes board members of Zensar Technologies who come in with a wealth of experience. Members of the Board Committee, such as Arvind Agarwal and Pradipto Mohapatra, have provided outstanding guidance, while other members of the Zensar Board, such as A.T. Vaswani, John Levack, and V. Kasturirangan, have informally given generously of their time in order to acquaint

Ladder of Citizenship

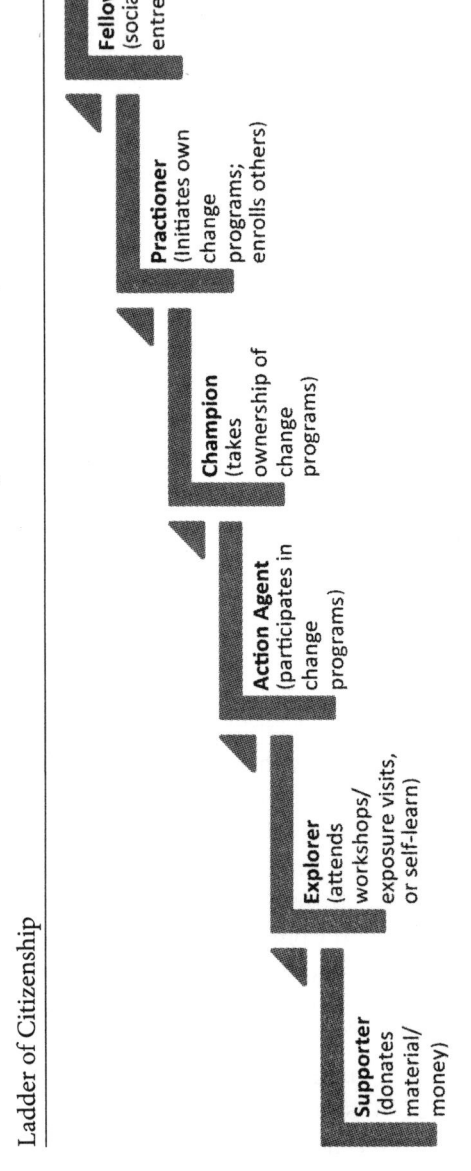

themselves with the work being done within CSR and provide valuable insights. It is these insightful discussions that input into the thought bank of innovations at Zensar Foundation.

In fact, the role of leadership in driving CSR cannot be overemphasized, as it would have been impossible for Zensar Foundation to reach where it has reached without the personal support, involvement, and visible commitment of the leadership team. This support has made CSR a mainstream activity and a way of life at Zensar.

Thought Leadership

While Zensar's leadership team, the trustees, and the Board Committee have provided exemplary support and guidance, Zensar Foundation has been fortunate to have the benefit of outstanding thought leadership from its Partner Ecosystem. The Foundation's partners have challenged conventional ways of thinking or else innovated on their own to demonstrate transformational results. These conversations and reflection sessions with partners have led to the very formation of Zensar Foundation's strategy and its emphasis on the transformational approach rooted in values.

Action Leadership

It is the Zensar volunteers, the children participating in Zensar Foundation's programs, and in fact the beneficiaries across our programs who have shown the way in terms of the power of agency. Zensar Foundation did not start with this concept in mind. However, the experience with our stakeholders compelled an acknowledgment of the power of agency and is now a core belief and underlies all the Foundation's programs. In this and many other ways, Zensar Foundation has been shown the way through the action leadership of various stakeholders.

Pervin Varma, one of the external trustees of Zensar Foundation, brings strong NGO leadership to the Foundation, having been a CEO of CRY for several years. She has been the cohesive force for building on the past and bringing together the guidance, thought leadership, and action leadership of stakeholders across the system in order to facilitate a deep-rooted change leading to achievement of full potential by individuals and finally to social transformation.

Being a part of the Zensar CSR journey has been a singular privilege. Particularly because Zensar's CSR program seeks to engage in a very substantive way, its employees, the community within which it is located and partners from the NGO sector who share our vision, all focussed on transforming lives through fostering and supporting peoples' agency and voice.

To read a powerful story written in English by a young girl who just three years ago could only read three-letter words, is a testimony to what is possible when teachers and children discover their immense potential for change and action. To then witness the same children become champions of education, activists against violence within their families and community, role models to the next generation of children is simply remarkable. To see poor and very often illiterate parents articulate their hopes for their children and take positive action reaffirms our belief that when empowered, children and communities will lead transformative change.

All this has been possible because of the inspirational volunteers of Zensar led by a deeply committed CSR team. We therefore have a tremendous opportunity to create and nurture substantive and replicable development models that can create lasting change.

GOING FORWARD

The emerging area for Zensar Foundation in terms of strategy is the development of city-wide transformation models. In 2014–2015, Zensar Foundation facilitated and supported the emergence of Pune City Connect, a platform for collaborative CSR by Pune's corporates, acting in synergy with the PMC. This may be a suitable platform for a beginning to be made with a ward-wide transformation model, which demonstrates social transformation of a higher order, that is, at the level of an entire ward rather than at the level of a slum community. Since a ward is a mix of privileged and underprivileged communities, its transformation calls for a different level of co-creation and collaboration among the haves, the have-nots, and governance structures. Once a ward-level model is in place, it can be extended to other wards and finally to the entire city.

In this context, the synergistic development of Ambedkar Vasti community, the five neighboring schools and the fostering of citizenship in volunteers, and the learnings thereof in terms of the facilitation of agency and the interlinkages/challenges/enablers of change could serve as a pilot and microcosm of the ward-wide transformation model. This will bring Zensar Foundation much closer to its vision being realized at city level.

In addition, Zensar is also looking at stretching its wings further, globally. The success of the Global Leadership Program running in South Africa encourages a wider horizon, and we hope to set up centers soon across Europe and America, the other key countries of operation for Zensar.

Zensar Foundation's Vision and Mission

Vision
To foster happiness and well-being of people and communities, enabling them to realize their full potential.

Mission
To build empowered communities and foster the agency of individuals to lead and enable social transformation.

Zensar Foundation has come a long way, from the "heart full of caring" and a "bunch of volunteers" to an organization with clarity of thought in terms of bringing about city-wide impact, whether through replicable models or through active participation in collaborative movements. All the same, these goals will come to fruition only with the continuation of the love, care, and authenticity that have stood Zensar Foundation in good stead from the beginning. With the strategy of social transformation through individual agency, the determination is more than ever to have a smile on the face of every child from Koregaon Park to Kharadi, and far beyond.

CHAPTER 9

Vision for a Digital World

Digital—a word that almost innocuously meant a series of zeroes and ones—has now acquired an almost all-pervasive connotation. Departments, organizations, communities, towns, and even nations are being transformed as they seek to embrace digital technologies. The challenge and the opportunity today go well beyond the traditional SMAC stack, because each of the letters—social, mobility, analytics, and cloud—has taken on much more significance and is growing in importance literally every week in every part of the world.

This chapter is inspired largely by some path-breaking work and predictions done by Mckinsey India and the Mckinsey Global Institute for industry association NASSCOM, which is now forming the basis for thinking and discussions at the industry's highest echelons of leadership. In developing a construct not only for key industry segments but also for providers from the industry in the next 10 years, the Mckinsey research supported by major work done by Gartner and other advisory firms provides a strong foundation on which not just Zensar but most of the ambitious and successful industry players are likely to build their new strategies and organization.

FUTURE ENTERPRISE BUYERS: KEY TRENDS

The Mckinsey analysis starts with a macro warning that 15 to 25 percent of current enterprise buying will disappear in the next five years, largely caused by the elimination of traditional on-premise software applications and the need to maintain them. The move to the cloud, the adoption of software, platforms, and infrastructure as a service, and the inexorable move to replace capital expenditure by pay per use IT consumption will drive this trend. Enterprises of the future will have no choice but to embed technology drivers deep into their business architecture, resulting in the transformation of their products and services, their approach to customers and supply chain partners, and their entire ecosystem of suppliers and employees who will be called upon to deliver a whole new range of responses and services to discerning and demanding customers.

From the IT user or CIO's point of view, there will be a demand for more standardization in computing architecture and a demand for higher levels of performance. New partnerships will ensure that every process can be reengineered and every role potentially made redundant. A case in point is India's own fast-growing e-commerce firms Snapdeal and Flipkart, each with business turnover in the range of three to five billion dollars, where aggressive deployment of technology and relentless outsourcing—of logistics, customer relationship management, and most business processes—are resulting in nimble organizations with the ability to take quick decisions and turn on a dime to meet the demands of newer and newer demographic segments who are rushing to join the e-commerce party. It is not only e-commerce firms but also traditional manufacturers, retailers, and financial services, and healthcare institutions who have to plan 20 to 30 percent of their technology spending to be on "digital" in the years to come to compete or sometimes just stay relevant in a fast-changing business environment. Digital cannot be ignored by any industry segment, and while it may be life or death for industries such retail and media, it could call for end-to-end digitization in industries such as retail banking and healthcare, whereas more traditional industries such as transportation and oil and gas could well get away with the implementation of a few "point" solutions.

The Mckinsey description of the enterprise of the future bears repetition in this chapter, just to demonstrate the extent of business impact that is being forecast. The creation of digital products with ability to provide solutions to each individual customer has been demonstrated by the "mobility-as-a-service" innovations of Uber and TaxiForSure, which has made it almost unnecessary for the average citizen of a city to own a car. AirBnB has enabled real estate utilization to be maximized, and soon every asset created in the world will be optimized by similar sharing models. The implications, Mckinsey points out, will be to make ownership a thing of the past, declining spend on physical products, and the rise of platforms that permit shared ownership. The trends are expected to be dramatic with a dozen or more owned cars being replaced by a single shared car and car sales in the United States declining by over a million a year because consumers will discover that for usage of less than 25 miles a day, it makes to no sense whatsoever to purchase a car in a big city.

The evolution of digital channels will also lead to the worldwide disintermediation of services such as banking. Mckinsey points out that in the 10 years from 2003 to 2012, 40 to 50 percent of bank branches have been shut down with little or no decline in market share of the banks. The implications for service providers clearly are that banks will have less need for massive core banking applications, and there will be a transition in spend from branch expansion to digital channels. In the sale of consumer products, which Apple Computer has so effectively demonstrated, retail outlets will become experience centers. In our own experience at Zensar, one of our key multibrand retailers, a market leader in the West expects that its high street stores could become locations for round-the-year fashion shows and cookery demonstrations, where the costumes or ingredients would be incidental to the experience and consumer buying would eventually happen from the comfort of an armchair at home through a computer or more likely a smartphone.

And this is not just futuristic thinking. Ganesh had the opportunity to spend the Thanksgiving weekend in New York with his daughter, who lives in midtown Manhattan, and the duo was wandering around Fifth Avenue on Black Friday, when traditionally all the stores sell deeply discounted merchandise. Amazed to find all his favorite brands available at 40 to 60 percent discounts, Ganesh was all set to make some big purchases when his daughter advised him to use the physical shop walk-through as just a visual experience. The commerce could be done at even deeper discounts on Cyber Monday, the Monday following the Thanksgiving holiday, she explained. And sure enough, he made his purchases after a three-day gap and became converted to the new modalities of retail buying.

No wonder then that the Mckinsey research points to the average number of showroom visits having declined from four in the past to just one today, and dealership as an information or commercial outlet having declined to five and 10 percent, respectively, with 85 percent of showroom visits only for the purpose of availing services. Accordingly, the prediction is that new showrooms and dealerships will completely transform, with complete driving-like experiences and feature comparisons and learning available on large plasma screens. Any sensory experience that can be availed at home will clearly not be a reason to come to a store any longer, it will have to deliver a substantially superior experience.

The third big transformational force will be the availability of big data and analytics to drive decisions with two or three times made by automated processes than human judgment. Predicting that the number of processes, customer facing, support, and internal that make heavy use of analytics will jump from 10 to 50 percent, the Mckinsey research points to a number of new use cases that will emerge, including triggers for cash replenishment in ATMs and multiple one-to-one retailing opportunities. This use of analytics will be dependent on, and create opportunities for, extensive process automation, with banks expected to move from 30 to 80 percent process automation and manufacturing firms using robotics for 75 percent of their activities on the shop floor.

Our experience with customers in all markets, including federal and provincial governments, bears out this inexorable push toward digital transformation. Manufacturing companies are embracing IoT with connected shop floors becoming the order of the day. Sensors feed date from machines in a continuous stream and analytics engines integrate these data with traditional enterprise resource planning systems to track and plan production schedules and communications between the corporate IT systems and machine-generated data and information. Many retailers are contemplating store-wide as well as city-wide beacons and other sensing devices to track the movement of large buyers and deliver targeted messages to attract them to their stores. And in a recent example of digital on the streets of a city, a technology being evaluated in one of India's cities is garbage collection management using sensors fitted in garbage cans that can sense when the can is 80 percent full and plan the routing of the garbage truck to ensure route plan optimization as well as minimum inconvenience to citizens. Mckinsey predicts that IoT-related use cases and technology will become significant and disrupt multiple elements in the manufacturing process chain. R&D and design can expect a 20 to 50 percent reduction in time to market through 3D printing, and better supply chain management can add two to three percent to the operating profits. Robotics on the shop floor can lead to 10 to 25 percent improvement in operating costs in production; distribution planning lead times can be shrunk by 50 to 70 percent; and 10 to 40 percent of maintenance costs can be reduced by well-targeted predictive maintenance.

The opportunities are clearly enormous, but the challenges are huge as well. Mckinsey recommends a five-stage model to strategize an enterprise's approach to digital transformation—development of a digital strategy and a clear migration plan with phased investments, target a new architecture for operations, applications, data, and infrastructure, plan required approaches to delivery and delivery discipline, build a plan for reskilling people for the new digital era, and build new partnerships to better leverage the digital ecosystem.

The creation of the digital ecosystem with new partnerships by CIOs of future-thinking organizations is where the opportunity as well as the threat for companies like Zensar and all our peers in the industry will lie. During the last year, Gartner has researched and presented extensively on the theme of bimodal IT, wherein traditional models of project life cycle management will continue to exist for building and managing legacy systems and some new mission-critical applications, but a bulk of new developments will adopt an agile and prototype-based approach. Gartner has also exhorted CIOs to consider adaptive sourcing, where traditional vendor selection and engagement will be restricted to the large mission-critical "run-the-bank" applications, whereas functional leaders will have the flexibility to choose their own partners to generate the best design and quick development cycles for market or supply chain facing applications. And the emergence of the chief digital officer will create a new area of idea crowdsourcing, which could threaten to make the traditional waterfall model of application building redundant.

There will be technology options galore for the discerning organization to choose from. Mckinsey predicts that by 2025, the total revenue of technology companies will rise from four trillion dollars in 2014 to a level as high as four to nine times the current level. This jump in revenues is largely attributable to automation, Internet technology, IoT, robotics, cloud, and mobility. In fact, the cumulative revenues of the top-six "digital attackers," including Facebook and PayPal, have already climbed to the top 20 in the banking league tables and can be expected to climb much further in a very short time frame.

UNDERSTANDING THE NEW TECHNOLOGY STACK

There was a time not so far away when IT was a happy coexistence of legacy systems and new fourth- and fifth-generation systems that enabled quick development and access to new functionality as desired by system users. In a typically on-premise deployment of technology solutions, the sophistication of technology used was as much a function on the capital investment appetite of the firm as the availability of technology itself, and companies could consciously stay away from embracing the latest and greatest technology simply because their organization was not complex enough or mature enough to need it.

All this has changed with the emergence of digital technologies—the cloud has made it possible for the poorest of firms to avail the best technologies—infrastructure, software, and platforms on a pay-per-use service basis, and the proliferation of mobile technologies have made the mobile Internet come alive and transform life and work. The IoT with its related automated transportation and logistics capabilities and the proliferation of sensors and beacons within and outside the enterprise have made large amounts of data accessible. This, coupled with the new generation of geographical information systems and mapping software, has made the use of big data and analytics a necessity just to make sense of all the proliferation of data in the home and business environment.

One technology that has so far been used in a very superficial level is social media. While Twitter and Facebook have become communication and collaboration platforms of choice for a vast majority of middle- and upper-income folks even in emerging countries, the true power of social media will be evident when corporations and governments move beyond using social for public propaganda and start active "social listening." Social command centers will enable companies to discern the real response of their customers to new product launches and service-related issues, and policymakers and government bureaucrats will be able to gauge the mood of their constituencies and predict flash points so that proactive steps can be taken to mitigate and address the issues.

The Mckinsey analysis of the widespread adoption of digital technologies throws up some mind-boggling possibilities just for India. By 2025, cloud technology users for business can jump from 2 to 20 million, including 50 percent of all SMEs, all government services to citizens can be provided on the cloud, smart grids could move from 1 percent of the grid to over 60 percent, and 3 to 10 billion devices could be connected using IoT technologies. This could provide $500 to $1,000 billion of economic impact and contribute 20 to 30 percent of the incremental GDP in the period 2012 to 2025. The Prime Minister's Jana Dhan Yojana and similar financial inclusion schemes, if they include 75 percent of the adult poor population, would enable up to $30 billion of micro credit for the new financially included and over $175 billion of nonfood government transfers, with over 80 percent made digitally. This will enable double-digit productivity gains for the financially included, multibillion financial gains for intermediaries, and substantial reduction in leakages through e-payments.

One of the most dramatic transformation areas pointed out by Mckinsey is healthcare, with over 30,000 new technology-enabled health centers facilitating over a billion high-quality new consultations, with nearly 35 percent improvement occurring because of time-to-access improvements and another 15 percent improvement due to the quality of consultation. Add to this, the advances in genomics-based personalized medicine and hundreds of thousands more cancer patients and a couple of million new cardiovascular patients could be treated every year, adding one or two years to overall life expectancy, and addressing an additional 15 to 50 percent patients. Add to this, the substantial improvements possible in the detection of counterfeit drugs that proliferate in the Indian market and the Mckinsey estimate of over $25 billion of annual economic impact seem very feasible.

Even more impressive is the prognosis for education, arguably India's weakest area of progress. Technology can enable schools and really create "countrywide classrooms," transform the average mediocrity in skills and college education, and even transform the output of the Industrial Training Institutes in the country. With the Ministry of Skill Development and Entrepreneurship now promoting the layers of livelihood colleges and multiskill institutes, in addition to schools and colleges, and it is with the National Skills Universities at the top of the pyramid that extensive deployment of technology can dramatically improve graduation rates and the gross enrolment ratios in higher education programs, enable 20 to 25 percent improvement in vocational training capacity every year, and add millions of well-trained citizens to the workforce. The consequent productivity impact is expected to yield a total economic benefit in excess of $60 billion annually.

The story goes on! Mckinsey estimates that $40 to $80 billion can be gained in agriculture through reduced land waste, hybrid and genetically modified crops, precision farming, and real-time market information. In addition, infrastructure could yield $30 to $45 billion of economic impact through electronic tolling, smart ports and national highways, and affordable housing, transforming efficiency, and ease and timeliness of availability.

The opportunity for technology and application innovators is huge if all these changes have to happen and all the benefits garnered in a timely manner. Verifiable digital identity and digital payments have to be enabled and a whole generation of people reskilled and retooled in their appreciation of and adoption of Internet technologies. The challenge and the opportunity for service providers will be immense.

THE MORPHING OF THE SERVICE PROVIDERS

The alarm bells are ringing for all IT service providers who, like the proverbial ostrich, keep their hands in the sand and expect that the traditional buying patterns for large customers will continue or only shift marginally toward digital. Gartner predicts that by 2018, 30 percent or more of the overall IT spend of banking, financial services, and insurance firms will be focused on digital technology and the integration of digital into legacy applications. Hence, 15 to 25 percent of spend on traditional areas such as applications development and maintenance, package applications, infrastructure, and BPM will just disappear as the trio of software, platforms, and infrastructure as a service eat away at traditional on premise investments.

For financial services institutions, the drivers are likely to be the prodigious increase in digital transactions with nearly half the spend happening through the Internet, the four trends in products, processes, channels, and decision making mentioned earlier, and the refreshing of legacy systems with digital technologies from partners.

The resultant impact on service providers will be broadly in three areas: a decline in spending on the traditional areas that have been the focus of all successful offshore consulting firms, almost half the future spending having a digital component to refresh legacy applications, and most important significant 20 to 30 percent of budgets focused on spending on new digital applications and related areas such as cyber security. The estimate is that from the current state at the end of 2014 to the new state in 2018, banking financial services and insurance firms alone will be spending upward of 17 percent more on technology, but nearly a third of that total spend will be on digital, in contrast with the three percent in 2014. Can we expect that the digital percentage for successful providers will also follow suit and drive those percentage levels?

There is no doubt that we are entering another stage of consolidation in the IT software and services industry. The one good thing going for incumbent vendors to global corporations is that the deep understanding of legacy technologies and business processes will enable them to be better partners for digital transformation than sexy new technology providers who have the new sizzle but not the steak that makes a transformation feasible. However, this is no reason to be complacent, and all service providers will need to recreate a vision for the future, which consists of key answers to three questions.

1. What customers will we serve in future and with what products or services?
2. What is the business and commercial model we will choose to serve the existing and new customers?
3. What are the new skills we will need to hire or train our people for if we are to stay relevant and grow our business in the digital landscape?

Answers to these questions are still evolving, and while some service providers can claim to further ahead on the transition journey as compared with others, there is no doubt that a paradigm shift is occurring where everybody has started again from zero, and the winners in the digital transformation space are far from clear.

The customer profile has changed sharply from the times less than a decade ago where the IT director or the CIO called all the shots. Today, there are at least three categories of buyers:

the CIO who still has his traditional comfort zone of large mission-critical "run-the-bank" kind of applications built with time-tested methodologies and thoroughly engineered to meet peak production loads. On the other hand, a rising amount of power and now budgets is residing in the hands of CMOs and COOs, who have an ear to the ground always in search of shifting consumer demand and accelerating information needs of supply chain partners within and beyond the boundaries of the organization. And finally, the CEO herself, whose external market and shareholder facing role makes her extremely susceptible to being lured by the latest trend or even fad in the marketplace. One could argue that the role of the chief digital officer, which has gained acceptance in recent times, has been created largely through the frustration of members of the board room with the slow pace of change in IT and the desire to induct new thinking into the process of digital transformation in the organization.

The bimodal IT approach advocated by Gartner is a suggested response to this paradox, where organizations still have to do the heavy lifting with systems and technologies that will not fail to deliver the information that the whole organization and its customers are traditionally comfortable with while preparing for new agile applications that can be created in a fraction of the time it takes to build robust mission-critical systems. In this process, organizations, if not their IT leaders, will have to prepare to plan and develop two speeds of designing and delivering IT and digital applications to meet the fast-changing needs of the firm.

The message for the service provider community comes from the adaptive sourcing model, also advocated by Gartner. Recognizing clearly that there will be various options available to the organization to buy and consume the technology solutions of the future, Gartner advocates the traditional buying approach for large systems, choosing from nimble providers of agile development and point solutions for the digital systems, the CMO and COO may choose to buy and a crowdsourcing approach to conceptualizing new digital solutions for the market place. A case in point is a large insurance and wellness solutions service provider in one of the emerging countries. Given the scope and scale of their operations, the core insurance applications still form the bedrock of their IT architecture, and they have worked in the last couple of years to add a large number of mobile and cloud applications to create light and useful extensions to the information availability for key customers around the country in which they operate. One breakthrough digital application they are planning is to install tens of thousands of beacons in one of the key cities of their operation that would use geo-positioning and geo-fencing to identify the movements of any customer or prospect and offer solutions based on previous medical history or recent exercise or buying preferences. This company believes that this innovation will add the cutting edge to their competitive positioning in the marketplace.

This leads to a number of new imperatives for service providers. They too will have to work in a bimodal fashion, where the large systems development teams continue to use robust system development life cycle and waterfall models to build industry strength core systems, whereas the digital and cloud teams use agile methodologies to offer quick and iterative systems and solutions for clients. Investing on a continuous basis in new technologies and methodologies will not only be an internal must, it will also be important to have sourcing teams that scour the start-up landscape for new products that may be introduced in any part of the world and make them part of the company's ecosystem and "go-to-market" solution suite. Supporting intrapreneurs, investing in entrepreneurs, buying small firms that add value to the digital-solutions portfolio are all options to be considered to expand the solutions offerings to the customer of the future.

New ways of working will also lead to new engagement models and commercial agreements with customers. The good old formats of "time and material" and "fixed price," where the difference was only the quantum of risk the service provider would take by betting on timely development and project completion and hence an accurate "function point"–based time and cost estimate for a project bid, are now yielding to a number of outcome-based pricing models. In these models, the service provider has skin in the game and might only get paid in part or full if the end outcomes for which the project, be it a legacy modernization effort or a digital transformation program, are commissioned by the client. This will call for intimate knowledge of the business dynamics and the risks and challenges in achieving outcomes that may have nothing to do with the technical competence shown by the project team.

The final hurdle to be crossed before service providers themselves can claim to be ready for the new digital world is the capabilities and skills of the entire organization. For a very long time, the IT and BPM industry has prided itself on the fact that its raw material is people and its processes are also people dependent. However, as the paradigm shifts, over three million industry professionals, schooled and trained in a previous era, might find their skills obsolete and their ability to cope with new challenges and expectations woefully inadequate. This transcends all functions in the services organization. Marketing will need to focus on the business rather than the technology needs, inside sales or telemarketing agents will need a brief that focuses on business benefits and have the overall understanding to converse in the business language of the prospect, sales and pre-sales folks will need complete vertical alignment and deep domain understanding, and people tasked with putting together large multisolution deals will need an intimate knowledge of "as-is" and "to-be" processes that will emanate from clarity about the changing expectations of the customer's customers.

Upon taking over the reins of one of the IT services firms in India, a new CEO with his background in the global products industry remarked, "we will have to retrain everybody." While this may sound too extreme, it is not far from the truth. The willingness to completely reorient mindsets will have to exist or be created in the organization and multiple waves of training will have to be undertaken to provide everybody, from the CEO suites to sales and delivery, the skills needed to compete and succeed in the new digital world.

ZENSAR'S APPROACH TO DIGITAL

We live in the era of exponential technologies, and change is the only constant today. We are basing our strategy, investments, and actions on four tenets that we believe are the foundational elements for being successful at leveraging the potential of the digital era.

How We Think about Digital

The four Cs that guide our approach to digital both internally and for services and solutions that we offer our customers are

1. converse
2. context
3. convenience, and
4. culture

The 4C Digital Framework

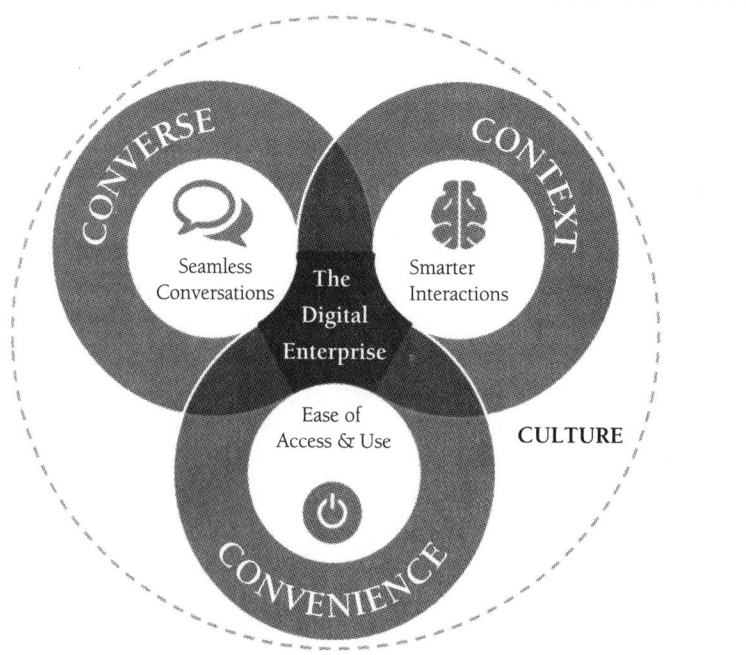

Although each element is an essential cog in the digital machine, the real magic happens when all four come together, we like to think of the formula to digital success as

Digital Success = (Converse + Context + Convenience) × Culture

Converse

People are engaging, forming perceptions, making decisions, and sharing their experiences on digital channels, such as social media networks and various enterprise collaboration systems—these channels give unprecedented power to consumers to vent, share, discuss, and promote. How you participate in and make sense of all these conversations that include customers, partners, employees, and even competitors can make a large difference in your approach to the market. Successful digital enterprises leverage the power of social and the wisdom of the crowd to cost effectively pull away from the pack. In today's age, you do not have to wait for market research to get feedback on your product or service, it is already out there.

We have seen very interesting use cases emerge from our discussions with customers across verticals about the insights from analytics on social media data. From being able to correlate sales with social buzz for an apparel retailer in the United States, to understanding how partners promote a franchised wellness brand in their respective territories for a South African health insurance company. The social command center in our Pune headquarters has ignited interest from a number of our customers, as they are able to now easily see the value of social media and analytics, going beyond the traditional listening and customer service applications for social.

Context

Context has always been essential for meaningful interactions. Today you can use what you know (data in your internal systems and systems of record), what they hear, feel, and see (external data sources such as social media and other published information), to create context from the multiple conversations, interactions that happen all around us. Today, sensors and other readily available data can help you automate the creation of context for any interaction. Context enables intelligent interactions; you have the ability to identify trends, predict outcomes, and enrich experiences. The real objective of all analytics and big data initiatives should be to create real-time context, which can be used to automate actions or enable us to make more informed decisions. With the IoT (everything) gathering momentum, the ability to create context from the data flood and act on it will be the difference between success and failure.

We are investing in partnerships with Aruba & Cisco to develop a solution for brick-and-mortar retailers to give them the same level of insight into how customers who walk the aisles in their stores behave, as e-commerce web sites do for what people click on, hover over, and visit next. Using Wi-Fi and mobile apps, we are working with a leading African retailer to provide real-time promotions and a personalized experience to shoppers who are in their stores. In addition, the retailer will be able to know what the flow of visitors is like in their stores, and what areas of the store attract the most people, so that they know how effective in-store displays and lay outs are.

Convenience

Attention spans and the need for instant gratification make convenience a critical consideration for all products and services. Everything has to be available everywhere, at any time, and on any device. Disintermediation is happening all around us; people prefer to do things themselves using interfaces that require no training. You can empower customers, employees, and partners to interact from anywhere, at any time, and using any device by making access to information and productivity tools, location as well as device agnostic. Natural user interfaces, such as touch, voice, and gestures, make it possible to create altogether new ways to create experiences that are easy and convenient. You can use emerging mobile technologies and the pervasive computing power of the cloud to help people do things for themselves and get instant responses from context-aware systems. Make it easier for people to interact, work, and play.

Recently, we have worked with one of our clients to develop a gamified onboarding and learning management program for new hires. This system, while being available for any device, also enables new hires to network with each other, find experts and mentors within the company, and complete onboarding activities like they are playing a game. Engagement is up by more than 60 percent, and the time taken to complete formalities is down significantly as self-service makes it possible for the employees to do the tasks from wherever they are and at their own pace.

Culture

Change is the only constant today; it is therefore imperative that your enterprise have the right attitude and culture to embrace new things. The right mindset to trying and experimenting with perhaps yet unproven technologies will set you in good stead for the digital era, because today enterprises that are succeeding are failing fast as well as scaling even faster. While the digital leaders may adopt different technologies to fuel their success, some common traits define their digital DNA, they not only experiment, their internal processes allow ideas and innovation to flourish, but they also have the organizational agility to scale experiments that have promise. Competitive advantage in the digital era is usually fleeting; therefore, the company culture that helps people thrive in a constantly changing environment will usually be the difference between mediocrity and a stellar performance.

OUR APPROACH TO DELIVERING SERVICES

Getting started on the digital journey can seem daunting, especially because this journey is not just about technology, it is about how business gets done with an amalgamation of platforms and across multiple applications having distinct features. It is, therefore, critical to have a partner who not only understands your business, but is also able to leverage its technical expertise to help you discover what opportunities and pitfalls that may lie on your path.

Zensar's modular approach can be suited to most requirements; we provide consulting services to help you identify what you could be doing as well as execution services to get initiatives off the ground and into production, so that you can start reaping benefits.

Our portfolio of services spans the entire continuum from aspiration (blue ocean thinking) to execution (the brass tacks of digitalization).

Aspire: Create a Burning Platform

Enterprises that are in this stage of the journey are more interested in knowing how they are affected and what others are doing in the digital space to create competitive advantage. This phase seeks to answer the question "what is happening around us and what can we do?"

We have conducted CXO-level workshops for many of our customers in collaboration with the Boston Consulting Group. The workshops helped these customers in various verticals understand how digital will impact them and what they could be doing to take advantage of this wave. For example, one of our customers, a Bio Pharma distribution company, has started a revamp of their B2B sales channel, allowing customers to place orders online, track inventory, as well as help the pharma company offer a managed inventory service through an RFID-enabled fridge that is connected to the inventory fulfillment system at the distributors headquarters, a harmonious union of IoT and e-commerce.

Zensar is a member sponsor of the MIT SLOAN Initiative on the Digital Economy, which is a global think tank that is studying the impact of digital on people, corporations, governments, and society as a whole. We use this research and access to leading thinkers in the digital space to shape our approach to client situations.

Our business consulting-led services for the aspiration phase of your journey help you align stakeholders, create awareness, and perhaps a sense of urgency as well as understand what the potential impact of digital is and how you should shape your response.

Design: Architecting the Future

Once you have an idea of how digital can be applied to your business, and are starting to think about how best to integrate digital in the way that you do business, you can embark upon the design phase. The main question this phase seeks to address is: "How do we do it?"

We clear the fog around what your target-to-be state looks like, what technologies and platforms to consider, and deploy some quick proofs-of-concept to gauge viability. Our team of experts and access to various technologies through our partnerships with leading vendors enable us to turn around designs, concepts, and prototypes rapidly, adding agility to our clients' IT operations teams and helping them cope with the demand from business.

Execution: Getting It Done!

This is the part that traditional IT service providers have excelled at, developing and supporting systems that support business. As is the case with most digital initiatives, the execution is an iterative process to build solutions or features, test them in use, and improve them based on feedback received almost in real time. This phase is focused on "getting it done and doing it right!"

In this phase, we bring our experience and expertise to help you evaluate and adopt technologies and platforms while monitoring outcomes in order to ensure that the envisioned benefits are realized.

WINNING IN THE DIGITAL SPACE

Zensar is betting big on digital transformation and electronic and mobile commerce as key focus areas for the future, which will ensure the company clocks growth rates that are better than those of its peers in the industry and widen the differentiation gap between the company and all competitors. In an environment where every company has jumped on to the digital bandwagon and both start-ups and large incumbents are showcasing competencies and solutions to demonstrate their ability to partner customers on their digital journey, there are five reasons why Zensar believes it will emerge a winner and stay in the lead for major wallet share in the world's digital spend.

The first stepping stone to success has already been taken by Zensar through its investment in collaborative workshops with the Boston Consulting Group, which has enabled deep research into the customer domains—manufacturing, retail, banking, and insurance—in which the company operates and the ability to provide well-articulated digital themes to the C suite of many of its customers through intensive "deep dive" workshops.

The choice of customers to which digital solutions will be offered has been carefully made by the strategy council of Zensar, based on an assessment of which industry segments are likely to see the biggest contest for digital domination. Retail, followed by manufacturing and insurance, emerges as a focus vertical and Zensar has decided to focus on its traditional customer segment of medium and large incumbent players rather than new-age digital commerce start-ups. The choice of products and services has also been made to fit the needs of this segment. For example, providing comprehensive web storefronts and "click-and-collect" options for large retailers is seen as a solution that will mitigate the risk of elimination by upstart e-commerce vendors, and Zensar's formidable technology depth and width is being strengthened to ensure that customers get leading-edge solutions to ease access and provide offerings width to their end customers. Partnering with digital design and interactive marketing agencies has commenced, and Zensar is building the comfort that its teams can engage with CMOs and supply chain heads with the same comfort that has been demonstrated with CIOs and IT directors in the past.

The business and commercial models for existing and new clients have also been widened substantially. From the traditional time and materials and fixed-price models of engagement, the company today offers a wide variety of choices from pay-per-use software and infrastructure as a service to the creation of comprehensive platforms that can be set up in partnership with large OEMs or even governments, and made available on a usage-fee basis to small and medium firms. A case in point is the proposal currently under discussion with one of the larger states in India where tens of thousands of small manufacturing firms will have access to a cloud-based production and materials management application that will be hosted on the state's data center and made available at an access fee that starts as low as ₹7,000 or just over $100 a month. The investment in a full-fledged social listening center that enables services to be offered to capture and analyze stakeholder voices and design appropriate responses has already become a "must-visit" location for every customer that arrives at the Zensar campus, and this and other similar investments in showcase technologies have demonstrated the seriousness of Zensar in the digital arena to its customer base.

Extensive skills building across the organization has also been undertaken. From consultants to delivery teams to the technology innovation group of the company, extensive familiarization with cloud and mobile technologies has been completed, and every customer touch point, from sales to telemarketing to inside sales and proposal builders, is being coached on the new narrative of the company and given the confidence and the ability to proactively address concerns and questions about digital that every customer has in this relatively new area of investment. The company's partnerships with major firms such as Mckinsey and interactions with leading-edge academicians and researchers at MIT Harvard,

Insead, and GIBS South Africa among others ensure that the thinking and discussions on digital are always leading edge at Zensar.

Finally, the company has started executing on an ambidextrous strategy to dominate the digital and commerce arena. Every horizontal strategic solutions unit, from infrastructure management to applications development and maintenance to package implementations and support, has assessed both the potential negative impact and the new opportunities created by the move to cloud and the emergence of smart nimble competitors nipping at the heels of incumbents. Each vertical business unit too has configured solutions that will facilitate the entry of their customers into the digital domain and built capabilities for re-architecting the processes and technology in its customer bases to enable to service their customers and supply chain partners better in an era of hyperpersonalization. And a very clear agenda has been drawn up for acquisitions and partnering/joint ventures to ensure that no time is lost in building a comprehensive capability set for end-to-end digital transformation. The acquisition of PA has enabled the retail vertical to develop a formidable capability in all aspects of digital commerce, and the company is looking at big data, analytics, IoT, and a range of niche areas and scanning the global environment for opportunities to strengthen the core and add niche capabilities.

We will summarize this chapter with the words of Krishna Ramaswami, head of our Digital Enterprise Services business and also a Zensarian for over 10 years:

> It's been a small yet a steady start for Zensar's Digital Business. The business grew to about 13% of Zensar's total revenue for the fiscal ended 2014–15. Let me rewind and take you twenty-four months back which is when I was given the charter to establish our Digital Enterprise services business. We too, like many other tier 2 providers, set about defining our Point of View and Go-to market strategies for Digital. As a service provider, we focused on being the interface between the customer (business) and the cutting edge of technology. We have applied our business understanding (in chosen verticals) to identify problems that can be addressed using digital technologies.

Zensar's Digital approach is a modular process that can be adapted for any organization at any level of maturity in their digital initiatives, right from those who don't know how to leverage Digital to those who simply want to find the best way to execute on initiatives that have already been decided upon. In this very exciting journey I've seen some very interesting use cases emerge from our discussions with customers across verticals be it about extracting actionable insights from analytics on Social Media Data or use of wifi analytics and proximity solutions (beacons) to enhance the in-store or in-venue customer experience. I personally believe that our solutions portfolio will evolve rapidly as we participate in many such business conversations with our customers.

As we set our sights to meet the lofty goal of being a USD 250 million digital business by 2020, one of our key initiatives is about creating a Digital platform which will extract data from multiple resources, wrangle it (ingest, clean and manage the data) and get it ready for analysis. The platform shall provide tools for visualization and exploration and visualization leads to hypothesis building and eventually to building predictive models. Last but not the least, it will allow integration and automation of the action systems wherein business rules can be automatically triggered based on derived insights. Our vision is to build a preconfigured end to end platform that can be provisioned in hours enabled in days and provide actionable insights within weeks, thus making an enterprise truly agile.

If Digital is the future of this industry, Zensar is already there!

CHAPTER 10

Toward a Billion Dollar Zensar

HOW DID WE REACH WHERE WE HAVE REACHED?

Zensar has indeed come a long way from that fateful day, February 28, 2001, when a new CEO, Ganesh, spoke to the assembled 500 employees at the old campus in Pune. He had exhorted them to forget the disasters of the previous 12 months and build a new vision for the future. A vision and mission that would make it a company with a different point of view and give it the right to hold its head high at the top table of IT champions from India.

As has been recounted in some detail in the chapters of this book, the journey to a defensible position of innovation and strength did not come easy. The three phases of growth have been simply categorized as the first five years of building a credible offshore story, the next four with the profit centers building credibility around the world, and finally the fully verticalized organization, supported by the three service pillars building the platform in the three chosen territories to prepare Zensar for its next assault on leadership in its chosen segments.

The reality of course is not as simple as this phasing, and the organization has gone through many twists and turns and encountered several setbacks. However, the team can take pride in the fact that revenues and profits have grown every year through this period. As important as this is the reputation the company has built for consistent value addition to shareholders, customers, employees, or associates, and the communities in which the company operates.

During the years, the endorsement of the Zensar story has come from many quarters. Rise in the market capitalization of the company, particularly in the last few years, recognition of the company's contribution by local governments from India to South Africa, and case studies and presentations on the company's unique approach in the Indian Institutes of Management in Bengaluru and Ahmedabad, the Gordon Institute of Business in South Africa, and the Harvard Business School, where the Vision Community case study has become a regular feature of the second-year MBA curriculum.

One of the crowning moments of the recent past has been the decision by Apax Partners to acquire a 23.2 percent stake in Zensar through Marina Holdco (FPI) Ltd., a company backed by funds advised by Apax. One of the leading private equity investors in the world, Apax has advised funds that have over $40 billion of investment in world-class companies.

As mentioned by Zensar Chairman Harsh Goenka in a press announcement:

> [T]he association is a welcome development and is expected to bring significant value to the company. With Apax's track record in the technology services space, Zensar is expected to benefit through access to a wider global customer base and best practices. Zensar looks forward to engaging with Apax with a renewed focus on core differentiated capabilities and key accounts to drive the next wave of growth and value creation.

Apax has highlighted that Zensar's status as a leading business in the technology services space with differentiated capabilities in retail, manufacturing, and Oracle technologies provides the platform to drive transformational growth. For the team that has taken Zensar to this level, it is an endorsement of success and a belief in a great future where the winning ways will continue.

There are three primary reasons that the management of Zensar assigns to its steady growth and success for over a decade—the strong support of its shareholders and board of directors, the commitment of its global teams to fly the Zensar flag high in all countries where it operates, and the common vision to transform and focus on customer sovereignty in everything the company has done through the years. In concert, these three have been a heady potion for every Zensarian to feel empowered and take the company to its present level of success.

THE NEED FOR A "ONE ZENSAR" AGENDA

A track record of double-digit growth (nearly 14 percent in constant currency terms) in the financial year 2014–2015, the organization steadying its 3 × 3 × 3 focus and morale at a high level throughout the organization—all this would seem to be adequate to give a sense of satisfaction to all Zensar's stakeholders, but internally the ambition to do more is as strong as it always has been. Hence the need for a new vision and a compelling "One Zensar" agenda, which has been launched in 2015 and is expected to drive the organization to new levels of success in the coming years.

The need to define a new agenda has been created through two different forces, a capability push and a customer pull. The push has come through some significant successes since 2011. A few data points will demonstrate this. In 2011–2012, the strong alignment of deliveries to vertical domains resulted in a 30 percent growth in all strategic customers within the chosen verticals. In 2012–2013, the focus on selling into the chosen verticals resulted in over 80 percent of new customer wins coming from the target verticals and a 45 percent growth in the manufacturing and insurance verticals. The growth in vertical customers continued in 2013–2014 with the development of end-to-end solution capabilities and the creation of arrowheads that were much focused on the vertical applications. All this had led to a stage in the beginning of the financial year 2014–2015 where all was set for a new thrust to be given to the transformation agenda. Keeping the customer at the center of the Zensar universe as always, the time had come to put every product, service, and process under the microscope and fine tune to meet emerging customer needs.

In Ajay Bhandari's words:

> We are now having transformative discussions with Customers on how their business can fundamentally change with Cloud and Digital and have also realized that we need to transform ourselves if we want to succeed in the Digital Era. This led to the "One Zensar" movement within Zensar. "One Zensar" not only redefined our Vision, Mission and Values but also an attempt to bring all 8,000 Zensarians on one platform—A platform where every associate has a clear understanding of what Zensar aspires to achieve and the role they can play in its success. Through this effort associates were educated on the rapid shifts Zensar is making to succeed in the Digital era. It is now a year since we acquired PA and I think we are on the right track with the right blend of Services and Solutions. We now have the ability to have business impacting outsourcing conversations with our customers, which integrate Application Management, Infrastructure Management and Digital technologies. I do believe that with this the best years of Zensar are not behind us but ahead of us.

The changing needs of the customers have been the pull that provides a new impetus to the "One Zensar" agenda. The previous chapter has demonstrated the bimodal IT approach and the adaptive sourcing predilection of global customers and Zensar, like all its peers in the industry could have ill-afforded to ignore the changing expectations of customers. Given Zensar's ear to the ground with all its customers and prospects, it was only to be expected that the company would "fix the model before it broke" and create a new empowering agenda—"One Zensar."

ONE ZENSAR: THE PROCESS

What started as an idea in a discussion at the strategy management council has, in typical Zensar style, become a movement that is all-pervasive in Zensar. Always a believer in the crowdsourcing of ideas, which the Vision Community is a living testimony to, the vision for One Zensar and the discussion sessions across all geographies, verticals, and service units has been a process of intense consultations, many points and counterpoints, and finally a consensus that has emerged at the end of the financial year 2014–2015.

As a process, One Zensar has been deliberated at length at a series of management council meetings and then socialized at multiple meetings addressed by members of the management council at all company locations. The emergence of a consensus on objectives, desired outcomes, and strategies needed to get there has happened in early 2015 and subsequent actions undertaken by the 2015 OD, L&D Internal Communications, and Vision Community teams have been initiated to make One Zensar a culture across the organization.

The willingness to revisit everything has led to a new articulation of the vision, mission, values, goals, and strategy for the company, which are explained in subsequent sections in this chapter. While the longer-term vision is for 2020, by which time Zensar fully expects to have entered the billion-dollar club, the specifics of goals and strategies have been defined for a three-year time frame.

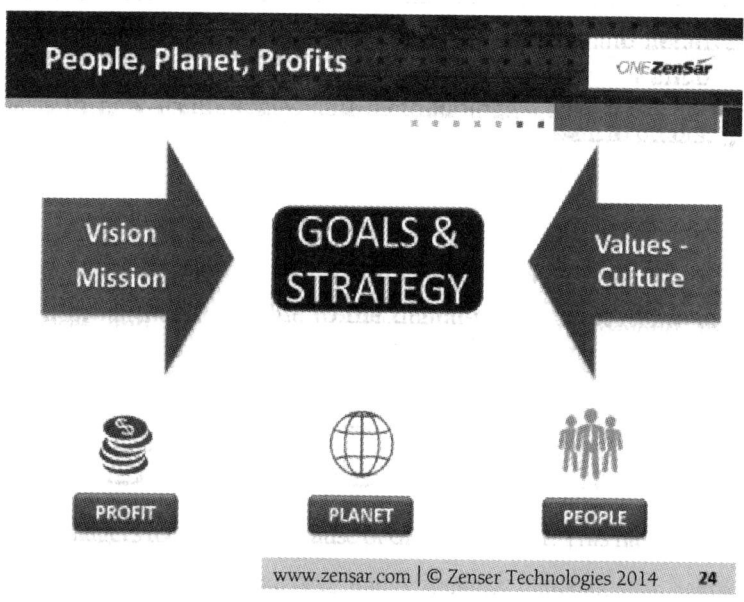

In keeping with the triple bottom-line focus of the company, which has kept us firmly grounded even when our eyes collectively look toward the stars, a model for One Zensar has emerged, as shown in the chart below.

The collective belief of all members of the Zensar organization is that we can craft three-year goals and strategies that emerge from an empowering vision and mission for 2020, which are embedded in the value and culture that have brought us this far and which will enable us to retain our focus on the triple bottom line. This would be a journey that every Zensarian would be proud to embark on and goals that would be lofty and worthy of attainment.

ONE ZENSAR: CREATING A LOFTY VISION

The vision for Zensar is a desired destination and articulates the big challenge that we are taking on for ourselves and what we expect to accomplish.

Leaders in Business Transformation

Definitions

- **Business transformation:** Solutions that provide business outcomes – Topline and/or bottomline

- **Leader:** To be amongst the top-3 IT solutions' business transformation companies in the world in everything that we do

Each word in the new vision has been put down after intense deliberation, and some key nuances are worth emphasizing. Business transformation has been a desired future for Zensar since 2001, and the company has often felt that most of the customers we serve should see us as a partner that provides value beyond the mere development of IT applications or the optimization of business processes. However, in this vision we are willing to commit ourselves to success being defined by measurable business outcomes. We no longer feel happy at being acknowledged in general terms for having improved productivity or improved customer satisfaction for our customers. We want to prove that we shaved off X percent from the cost of a supply chain operation through judicious process optimization or added Y dollars to the topline of a product line by our innovative new brick to click application.

Given this definition of business transformation, we have committed ourselves to being among the top three in the world by the year 2020 in making this happen for our customers around the world.

ONE ZENSAR: THE MISSION

The mission describes what we want to do, what unique contribution we wish to make toward our clients and other stakeholders, and the way in which we intend to serve our clients.

The mission expands on the destination described by the vision and sets a specific purpose for everything we will do in the future. Extending our successful focus on three key verticals, we would like to drive the industry focus in our solutions way beyond the generic high-quality services that we would offer in the past. Innovation is a deliberate commitment to ensure that every Zensarian strives to look for the "different way" and an "out-of-box" solution to business problems that our customers may be facing and would not settle for ordinary processes, solutions, or outcomes.

Mission

We will be the best in delivering innovative industry-focused solutions with measurable business outcomes. We will partner customers for their success

Definitions
- **Best-in-class:** Set benchmarks for the IT industry for high-quality, sustainable solutions which impact business outcomes.
- **Innovative:** Continuous and disruptive, including application of new technologies/ processes/commercial models/ industry solutions.
- **Industry-focused solutions:** Manifest best global business processes and practices for chosen verticals.
- **Measurable:** Direct and positive correlation established between solutions we provide and improvement in business outcomes, quantifies where possible.
- **Business Outcomes:** KPIs relevant to the specific customer in the specific domain. e.g. reduce inventory cost by 10%, improve receivables period to 30 days, etc.

ONE ZENSAR: THE VALUES

The values describe the ideals and ethics that define the way we work. Values for Zensar are more important than almost any other parameter that defines the way we work and the meaning we find in what we offer to all our stakeholders.

The value articulation at Zensar has emanated from a strong and deep-rooted set of beliefs, principles, and standards that starts from the individual, pervades teams, and finally defines the organization. They enable a collective view on what is desirable and truly important for every Zensarian. We believe that the values serve as guides to enable us to choose the correct actions and take the right decisions at critical phases in projects and all customer and other stakeholder touch points and moments of truth.

The authors' favorite metaphor about values comes from one of their favorite management videos of all time, "The Power of Vision" by Joel Barker. The video describes a situation where a team is going through an arduous trek through tough terrain and their path brings them to a fast flowing river they must cross. The currents are strong and there is a rope that reaches across to the group from the other side and they know that if they clutch on to this rope, they will have no problem in navigating the current and reaching the other side. This rope defines the true values of an organization and, for all of us at Zensar, this is the rope that we will always hold on to, whatever are the circumstances or business exigencies in which we operate.

In our articulation of the value set for Zensar, we decided to start with personal values and had multiple sessions with key stakeholders asking questions like "What is most important to you?" "What drives you?" and "What takes you toward your personal goals?" Words like curiosity, integrity, authenticity, loyalty, and passion have been discussed in great detail, and each individual is encouraged to explore and articulate what really touches their hearts. The transition toward organization values and words like collaboration, respect, service, and success is then more natural, because there is a natural connection that emerges between what the organization espouses and what each individual truly feels.

During this process, the erstwhile six value statements of Zensar have been shortened to three, what we now fondly call the "three Cs."

Since each value is extremely important, both to us as individuals and to the collective teams that will take the organization forward to achieve its goals, some of the key elements bear elaboration here.

Customer centricity or what we used to call customer sovereignty is a value that is extremely dear to all Zensar hearts and has undergone its share of change and strengthening over the years. Customer satisfaction has always been a key ethos at Zensar and the reason why our Fortune 500 and FTSE 100 clients reward us with their business and in most cases increase our wallet share of the work they handout is because of our commitment to ensure they are happy and stay happy. Anticipating their needs and working proactively toward positive technical and process outcomes is where we started.

Our Values: The 3Cs

- Customer Centricity

- Commitment to People and Community

- Continuous Innovation and Excellence

www.zensar.com | © Zensar Technologies 2014

Our focus on meeting and exceeding our customer expectations is well articulated by one of our long-time customers, Veresh Sita (CIO, Alaska Airlines).

I have had the pleasure of working with Zensar for more than a decade. I have watched the organization grow from small and distributed offices to a large world-class campus. Through all of this growth, the organization has continued to be humble, modest, and customer focused. Over the years, I have come to value the easy access to great talent and key leaders in the organization. Zensar is truly a relationship-based organization that is flexible, creative, and innovative—and above all, it has a customer first mindset.

In recent times, with our ability to deliver a full suite of solutions, we have been able to ensure that we are even more proactive and are able to create opportunities for our teams to sell and deliver and for the customer to benefit by anticipating new needs, particularly in the exciting arena of digital and e-commerce. From the days when an associate could joke, "when the customer says jump, we say how high?" we have come a long way in our ability to push back at times and in many cases obviate the need for either of us or our customer to feel the need to jump in the first place.

Russell Winder, CIO of C. Hoare & Co., UK, reiterates the same about our partnership of many years:

> The Bank looks to work with suppliers and partners that share its values and we believe Zensar is a partner that does. We set out 6 years ago to build a relationship where the Zensar team work as an extension of the Banks own team. Our working relationship has gone from strength to strength, we together have built and operate as one team and we have made many friends along the way.

Partnering our customers has been the key evolution over the years and the vision for the future, which includes delivering business, rather than technology and process outcomes, meeting stated and unstated business needs and, in all cases, setting the right customer expectations are ways we have defined to continually build and enhance the trust levels that we expect to see in a true partnership approach.

Ryan Bacher, the managing director of Net Florist, a leading South African online florist, shares his experience of working with Zensar:

> We have been working with Zensar now for over 5 years and they have been instrumental in helping us grow our business year on year by over 30%. They have helped with our development strategy as well as implementation in terms of our ecommerce, mobi, UI and back-office functionality. We utilise their onshore and offshore services and they have become an invaluable part of

our development arm. We are also often in discussions with their offshore team with regards the latest ecommerce global thinking and their knowledge base in this respect is a major advantage for our competitiveness.

This strong spirit of partnering our customers has been well appreciated by our long-term customers, who have time and again reiterated their confidence in us by trusting us with enabling them in their IT and business strategies. The relationship of over 17 years that we enjoy with Cisco Systems is a great example how we have partnered our customers to build enduring win–win relationships.

V.C. Gopalratnam, President, IT and CIO, APJ&GC and Chief of Strategy, Planning and Operations, Cisco India, resonates with the same:

> Zensar is a leader in delivering IT services that help customers gain greater efficiency and value. Through its deep focus on operational excellence, talent development, service capabilities and industry leading solutions, Zensar has been a strong partner in helping simplify IT and deliver business outcomes.

The commitment to people and community has also been emphasized through this book as one of the key differentiators at Zensar, and this is a core value that is very dear to our board, our management council, and every associate in the organization. We believe every stakeholder is entitled to be treated with the utmost respect, empathy and dignity, and the doors of everybody in senior management are open, literally and philosophically to listen to views, however contrarian they may be. The key value of providing an empowering environment is expected to be substantially enriched in the years to come through a much-expanded organization development and learning function, that will anticipate and satisfy our associates' needs to grow, personally and professionally, and make them the best in the business at all times. In this process, what makes the people aspect of the value truly come alive will be the belief in every individual's potential, the expansion of the 5F culture (fast, focused, flexible, friendly, and fun) and the climate of inclusiveness which will make every Zensarian feel a coveted member of the company's ever-expanding Vision Community. Sensitivity toward diversity, as has been enshrined in the company's latest annual report for the financial year 2014–2015, whether in the form of culture, age, or gender, propagation of an environment of transparency and integrity and building leadership from within will continue to be key value pillars on which the future Zensar will proudly stand.

Harish Gala, who leads all our Strategic Enterprise Practices globally, came to Zensar after an extensive stint with global multinational companies (MNCs) and found the culture at Zensar refreshingly different from the MNC culture that he was used to. Here he shares his experience:

> "To do, and not just be—this encapsulates my refreshingly differentiated Zensar experience. When a stable and resolute organization is led by an euphoric leadership team, magic runs amuck. Innovation is part of Zensar team's fabric, as we constantly challenge ourselves to redefine the impossible with the leadership team relentlessly disrupting the traditional technology paradigm. I am pleasantly surprised at my workplace every day, and I believe that it indicates our confidence in not backing down from daunting battles. Transformative projects for our clients involves introspection of our ability to deliver cutting-edge services; Zensar's ultimate objective to create a truly inspiring consultative experience for our clients is integrated with our own goals of achieving the zenith of technology advisory. As we go down the road of trying to create magic; nothing but satisfaction is left in its wake.

The communities we serve have always benefitted from our presence and this is expected to be substantially enhanced in the years to come. The Chandannagar and Yamunanagar communities in Pune, the Anjaiahnagar community in Hyderabad, and the learnership center in Rivonia near Johannesburg are living examples of the transformation we have been able to achieve in the communities and people in our vicinity and our ability to not only create employability in hitherto unserved or underserved students in these countries but also add them to the Zensar workforce has served as an exemplar to many in the industry who have emulated our model. In the years to come, we expect to expand the reach of these community- and employability-building activities to other key theaters in Kenya, the UK, the United States, and parts of Europe with the full commitment that it is this inclusiveness value alone that can create a lasting impact for Zensar in all the geographies in which we operate.

Continuous innovation and excellence as a value is not new or curious for any services company focused on serving discerning customers in an environment of hypercompetition. However, for a company like Zensar, having come from behind and caught up with the best of global competitors in just a dozen or so years, this value has been and will continue to be the key differentiator when competing for new clients or seeking to enhance market share within a large customer account.

Building a strong sense of achievement orientation has been seen as essential, not only in long-term Zensarians who have been with the company since its early chrysalis from a multipurpose IT caterpillar to a software butterfly, but also in new recruits anywhere in the world and the thousand and more associates who have become of part of Zensar through the acquisition of an OBT or Thought Digital or Akibia or PA. Not being content with the status quo and raising the bar in all functions and service areas of the company to set new industry benchmarks has been a key focus of the innovation and excellence movement in the company and will need expansion and enhancement in the years to come. The creation of a risk-free climate of experimentation, rewarding agility in processes, and infusing passion for excellence in all associates is the new rhythm for Zensar.

Bala S, our CFO for the past 10 years and a veteran of over 30 years with the RPG group, has heralded the growth of the organization over the last decade with the highest standards of corporate governance, wining us the respect and trust of our shareholders, the market, and of course our board. Winning the Golden Peacock award for corporate governance for three successive years is a testimony to our culture of transparency and integrity. Bala talks about the journey in the last decade:

> In 2005, we set ourselves a modest goal of Rs 500 crores in Turnover and Rs 50 crores in PBT. We crossed it in 2007–08. The next milestone was doubling that. We achieved it in 2011–12. Maintaining good control on our Finance, and building a strong Balance Sheet, enabled us to fund our multiple Acquisitions. I had to close the Thought Digital loan in 7 days, and the one for the Akibia in a matter of 15 days, both at enviable terms from our Bankers. Astute Cash Management, good forex risk practices and top class reporting standards have given us the much needed edge in the financial community, and the respect that comes with it.

The ambidextrous approach to innovation advocated by Professor Michael Tushman of the Harvard Business School was adopted by Zensar as its model for combining incremental innovation in all its processes with spurts of breakthrough innovation that would create new ideas for commercialization. The need for investing in new ideas and build intellectual property is now seen as a business imperative for all industry participants and Zensar fully intends to leave no stone unturned to establish itself as an innovation leader.

Michael Tushman talks of Zensar's approach to innovation and the role of leadership in building innovative organizations:

> Ganesh's case in the AMP was on how to execute a bold software innovation (SBP) within Zensar. We had many discussions on his execution options. How should he execute SBP while not disturbing his existing software business? There are many options for executives to consider. Ganesh and I stayed in touch after he left AMP. I learned about how he and his colleagues were executing this ambidextrous challenge. I found his approach to this problem to be very sophisticated. His ability to build a complex senior team, to get his firm to aspire to greatness, to host very different strategic aspirations, and to build what was initially a fragile exploratory unit was of great interest.

Better yet, once this SBP unit got going, Ganesh was able to create a social movement inside Zensar such that initial resisting factions became enthusiastic about the opportunity of SBP. This notion of strategic insight coupled with executional agility is now a very fine case I use in multiple executive education settings. From, the data and insights from this case are now referenced in my research on senior teams and ambidextrous organizations.

Acquisition of or strategic investments in IP as well as companies that fit into the larger blueprint of digital transformation and e-commerce that is Zensar's focus area will see investment dollars as well as management time in the coming years.

ONE ZENSAR: THE GOALS

The goals articulate the concrete and tangible targets we intend to achieve within prescribed time frames. It should be very obvious that a billion-dollar dream, while it is aspirational and worthy of an organization's full commitment, will remain a dream unless very specific targets for each of the constituent parts of the firm are defined and granular strategies and plans articulated to achieve every milestone on the journey to the big goal.

Zensar teams have been hard at work since mid-2014 to draw out these detailed plans. The creation of the 3 × 3 × 3 cube to define the organization's focus in terms of geographies (the United States, Europe, and Africa), verticals (manufacturing, retail, and BFSI), and service areas (applications, infrastructure, and digital) have provided 27 combination cells to work on. The most profitable and high-growth cell—applications services around manufacturing in the United States—has been a subject of admiration in the past and is now being put under a microscope to see what makes it so successful and what can be learnt and replicated in the other cells.

While it is obvious that, for competitive reasons, all the goals and strategies cannot be detailed in this book, a few examples will throw light on the process and the detailing. Leadership in end-to-end retail solutions in all three markets is a clear goal that is shared by all associates involved in any way with the retail vertical, and there are multiple agendas that the company will chase assiduously in the years to come.

1. Build out a comprehensive end-to-end capability to transform any retail operation, from infrastructure to supply chain and store management applications to the design and deployment of path-breaking digital and e-commerce applications.
2. Become the leading provider of Oracle ATG Endeca and Fusion Middleware solutions from India to the retail segment while building competence in all other technologies—SAP IBM and challenger platforms such as Magento all figure in the competence-building strategy list.
3. Create defensible design and retail consulting strengths to complement the technology acumen that already abounds in the firm for the billion-dollar plus client segment and at the same time build solutions to cater to the 200 million to billion-dollar retailer who may want to have comprehensive digital commerce capabilities without paying a multimillion-dollar price for the solutions. The January 2015 launch of PARACDE, a rapid deployment commerce platform built on Oracle technology, is a case in point.
4. Build and buy solutions that provide niche competencies in areas such as flexible supply chains, omnipresent commerce, and connected enterprise solutions for all retailers.
5. Build the competence to manage the reengineering of business processes, 24×7 availability, and customer service culture that will be the hallmark of the retailer of the future.

With the successful acquisition and integration of PA and the resultant deployment of solution marketing and end-to-end retail technology capabilities in the target markets and also countries in Latin America and South Asia, the success of Zensar in retail in the next couple of years will be one indicator of the likelihood of success of the billion-dollar plan.

There are goals that span all business areas and also look at strengthening of many of the functions and support processes that will be necessary as the organization grows in size and capability.

On the revenue maximization front, goals for working more closely with analyst firms and third-party advisors have been drawn out for all markets as well as specific means of maximizing the annual value of business from the existing customer logos on the one hand and adding new logos with large spending capability through targeted marketing and "big-deal" targeting and bagging. New segments including government and a more thoughtful and patient approach to winning in this area have been articulated.

The transition from being a customer-centric provider of world-class technology and processes to being a true transformation partner has also percolated down to many of the goals that our teams have set for themselves. Solution building is in progress in all verticals, from reinsurance and modernization platforms in insurance to customer experience management and connected shop floor solutions, embellished with sensor deployment and big data capabilities for customers seeking quick deployment of robust solutions akin to PARADE in retail.

On the digital and e-commerce front, being the key focus area with clear targets of doubling its contribution from the 13 percent (2014–2015) of Zensar revenues as the year 2020 approaches, there are granular plans and activities that have already been initiated in each vertical horizontal and technology stack. Here, a case in point is the area of "social"! Social media analytics spend globally is expected to grow at over 35 percent per annum for the next five years, reaching a level of three billion dollars plus by 2020. Zensar already has competence in a wide range of social media analytics platforms and has been one of the first firms to install a full-fledged social command center at its corporate campus in Pune.

The company recognizes that, to do justice to its potential to be a leader in this space, it needs to learn a new language and understand the thinking of global marketers and CMOs who can no longer have the luxury to wait for potential customers but will have to sense and, in many cases, create new customers from hitherto-unserved or underserved constituencies. Sentiment analysis, customer intent forecasting and management, brand perception study and management, and purchasing funnel management and insight integration across social, public, and enterprise information sources are just of the tricks that have to be mastered to become a full solution transformation partner. Zensar teams understand the imperative and the urgency and have robust plans to get there.

Continuing the story for just this one micro area of social, Zensar in the next two years will build capabilities in a multitude of areas. In the consulting domain, the company will be advising clients on enterprise collaboration, social media monitoring and management strategies, and choice of the right tools and platforms to implement their social media outreach and response strategies.

In the area of tools deployment and application building, Zensar will have the ability to configure, customize, and implement an array of third-party solutions such as Radian 6 from Oracle, play the systems integrator role either on premise or on the cloud and customize and implement social listening and data analysis solutions from remote locations or in situ at the client premises. And on an ongoing basis, transformation partnerships in this area will see Zensar providing "ZenSocial as a service," maintaining, managing, and enhancing the customers' reputation with their end customers both B2B and B2C, monitor, report, analyze, and optimize service across the customer footprint and provide governance in an area that tends to be very subjective. Building production standards in an area as complex as "social" will be an area of focus for Zensar and will play a key role in positioning the company as the partner of choice for the new world of customer identification and partnerships.

In addition, a few of the softer goals are worth understanding for readers of this book who are students of the complex art of sustainable capability building. In the area of people management, Zensar fully intends to continue to be a thought leader and we are setting goals for diversity and inclusion that will see us establishing resourcing bases in key global locations and using a blended learning approach to providing skills and capabilities across a spectrum of areas to all our associates. We will also continue to be a supportive partner for our community members. Zensar in Pune is a prime mover of the Pune Action Task Force, a collaborative initiative with other corporate leaders and the municipal government for improving education in the city's schools, imparting 100 percent digital literacy and building "smart city" initiatives in cleanliness and government–citizen interfaces. Bringing our considerable consulting and technology and process optimization capabilities to bear to solve local social problems will be as important to Zensar in all the locations we operate in as the maximization of customer and shareholder value. The triple bottom-line approach will always by the philosophy with which we build this institution in the years to come.

ONE ZENSAR: THE STRATEGY

The strategy is defined as the specific steps and also the critical pillars and approaches that will help us to realize our mission and achieve the goals. In an industry as fast changing as the IT sector, it is virtually impossible to set long-term goals and, in the same vein, it is difficult to cast strategies in stone, because some discontinuity in technology or market-induced change in customer preferences may need a new approach to offering solutions and services.

Given this context, Zensar has always relied on its inherent capability to innovate to take it to success, whatever the circumstances and irrespective of the curve balls that may be thrown at us, to use a baseball analogy. However, the management has a pretty good idea of what it intends to do in the next couple of years.

Again, without getting too granular and revealing any sources of competitive advantage, the strategy set of Zensar addresses each goal and subgoal and articulates our intent and the steps we intend to take, in each vertical, horizontal and territory. For instance, in the fast-growing area of digital, we have clear ideas on how to build capabilities in the fast-evolving big data and IoT space. We also know the kind of skills we will need and have a fair sense of where and when recruitment action will be initiated. And on a broader basis, we have very carefully thought through and articulated strategies for people management, through the entire attract–enable–retain continuum and how we will get every Zensarian aligned to the broader One Zensar theme of the organization.

If there is one cultural tenet that has stood the test of time at Zensar and continues to contribute to goal setting as well as strategic thrusts in all areas, it is the 5F framework that both of us authors are particularly fond of. The first F (fast) has been the driving force behind many of our initiatives, and if we are leading much of the pack in the exciting area of digital transformation, it has been by moving fast—to listen to the voice of our customers in this area, to partner with BCG to develop and deliver customized workshops for our key clients, to address the ongoing work in each sub-opportunity area in a granular fashion, to develop microstrategies for capacity and capability building, and to build plans for marketing and delivery of new service and solution offerings in each area.

Focus has been an area we neglected a little in the first phase of our growth, coming as we did from a virtual nonentity position and looking at opportunities in all directions to becoming meaningful vendors initially and thoughtful partners later for our clients. After having built out the services portfolio in the chosen verticals to the satisfaction of all our stakeholders, we have become very focused in the last year and more, shutting down underperforming territories, such as Japan and China, and being fairly ruthless in choosing what we should do and how we should do it. In all this we have successfully retained the third F (flexibility) that enables all our associates to retain and strengthen the spirit of innovation that has brought us to our current level of success and kept our key customers delighted during the many transitions we have seen in the company.

The final two Fs—friendly and fun—are fundamental to the way we are—as are Zensarians everywhere in the world. We do not believe that fun is a weekend activity and find every opportunity to bond as a team and have fun in the workplace. And the friendly culture we have built in every territory and every function will continue to make Zensar one of the aspirational places to work. Do we have a method in this madness? If we do, we are still trying to find it and we are happy just being who and what we are.

Ten years ago, somebody in the Zensar management team famously said, "Zensar is an idea whose time has come." Through the years, we have proved that the Zensar idea never stales and our time comes time and again—to prove our focus on the customer, to demonstrate our commitment to people, and to establish our place on the planet.

We have had a great time building this company, and the good news is that every stakeholder in the company has benefited enormously in the process. As the team tightens its ranks and girds up for the next half billion march toward the Billion Dollar Company vision, there is one commitment that every Zensarian will surely say about the journey to the future—it may be bumpy at times but we are sure everyone will enjoy the ride.

The Last Word

These are very dynamic times with respect to the way technology is consumed, leveraged, and used across economies and industries. Digitalization continues to hold center stage in the way companies recruit, sell, create, and profit. Social, cloud, analytics, and big data have grown in terms of their reach and sphere of influence, directly impacting the way we work with technology. Internet of Things has become omnipresent, affecting various aspects at an individual, corporate, city, and community level. It is important to leverage these all-pervasive trends as they act as barometers to success, helping one maintain relevance to changing needs of customers.

Zensar's vertical-centric approach continues to display rewarding visible results with double-digit growth. One of the highlights includes ramping up of our focus in the growth-oriented e-commerce and retail space with the successful acquisition of Professional Access. Our focus on strategic deals and new client acquisitions across the geographies we operate in has helped us in creating value for our shareholders consistently.

We continue to transform businesses of our worldwide customers by integrating capabilities along with expertise and ensuring visible business outcomes every time. The key areas of focus continue to remain across manufacturing, insurance, and retail, with new capabilities in the emerging world of digital enterprise. Our profitability comes from our multifaceted set of offerings, operations, and the pool of talent inherent across locations.

The future is going to be even more exciting, but I believe this company has very strong foundations, innovative vertical, and horizontal value propositions and a confident management team. I am sure Zensar will continue to blaze new trails and win.

Harsh V. Goenka
Chairman, Zensar Technologies

About the Authors

Ganesh Natarajan has been the CEO of Zensar since 2001. Prior to taking over the reins at Zensar, he was the CEO of Aptech where he scripted its growth to global leadership. He is the Chairman of NASSCOM Foundation and President of the HBS Club of India. He lectures at business schools worldwide and writes columns and books on management, digital transformation, and leadership.

Prameela Kalive is the Executive Vice President and Head of Zensar's largest delivery center in Pune. She has been with Zensar since 2000 and before that she was a Missile Scientist with the DRDO. She is a member of CII's National Committee on IT and ITeS, and also active in industry forums on digital, HR, and balanced leadership.